Rivers, Mountains, Sky and Sea

The Materiality of Spirit and Place

Edited by
Luci Attala

SOPHIA CENTRE PRESS
Ceredigion, Wales
2023

Rivers, Mountains, Sky and Sea: The Materiality of Spirit and Place
edited by Luci Attala

Sophia Centre Press
University of Wales Trinity Saint David
Ceredigion, Wales SA48 7ED, United Kingdom.
www.sophiacentrepress.com

Typeset by Daniela Puia
Cover design: Jenn Zahrt
Cover image: Aydin Hassan

ISBN: 978-1-907767-15-9

Names: Attala, Luci, editor.
Title: Rivers, mountains, sky and sea : the materiality of spirit and place / edited by Luci Attala.
Description: Ceredigion, Wales : Sophia Centre Press, 2023. | Series: Studies in cultural astronomy
          and astrology ; volume 12 | Includes bibliographical references and index.
Identifiers: ISBN: 978-1-907767-15-9 (paperback) | 978-1-907767-56-2 (ebook)
Subjects: LCSH: Human ecology. | Human beings--Effect of environment on. | Nature--Social
          aspects. | Sacred space. | Wilderness areas--Social aspects.
Classification: LCC: GF41 .R58 2023 | DDC: 304.2--dc23

Published with the support of the Harmony Institute

Prifysgol Cymru
Y Drindod Dewi Sant
University of Wales
Trinity Saint David

Y Sefydliad Cytgord
The Harmony Institute

Printed by Lightning Source.

RIVERS, MOUNTAINS, SKY AND SEA

CONTENTS

INTRODUCTION:
MATERIALITY, LIVELINESS AND PERSONHOOD
IN THE ANTHROPOCENE

Luci Attala and Nicholas Campion

*To grasp our unbreakable reliance and connectivity to everything else
is the beginning of reshaping how we imagine ourselves, our actions
and the vast material event of which we are a part.[1]*

This anthology draws together a range of papers originally delivered at the 16th Sophia Centre conference in 2018. The conference, titled *Rivers, Mountains, Sky and Sea: The Materiality of Spirit and Place*, was designed to inspire discussion around the complex and culturally significant intersections and influences experienced between humans and other entities or bodies in and of the environment or landscape. The conference emerged from a research culture at the University of Wales Trinity Saint David which has resulted in the creation of a series of volumes that deal with what is now known as the 'New Materialities'. This culture has resulted in the creation of a series of volumes at the University of Wales Press, driven by Luci Attala and Louise Steel.[2] From the Sophia Centre, Bernadette Brady and Darrelyn Gunzburg have produced a significant volume on space and place for the Bloomsbury Studies in Material Religion.[3]

The approach taken by the New Materialities focuses on attempts to suture – heal or resolve – the intellectual division between people and the living world that anthropocentric thinking has created. It does this by providing examples of how the landscape (and other 'scapes, including skyscapes, seascapes, taskscapes and inscapes), substances, and all living entities not only inspire thought and action, but also play a key role in physically shaping how humanity is able to be and to exist, always emphasising the fundamental connections that constitute life. Following Karen Barad and Donna Haraway, it remembers that all ways of being emerge from the physics or methods of matter-in-relationship and therefore attends to a reconsideration of agency, what an agent (a thing or substance which initiates change) is, and even how we understand individuality.[4] Where, we ask, does an individual end and the wider environment begin? Consequently, the term 'materiality', as it is used here, does not simply describe objects or things nor is it concerned with the vicissitudes of production *per se*, but rather is used to

> encourage thinking that realises being human is not a state divorced from a broader set of material conditions, but rather emerges-with and is (in)formed-by being-with the physics of wider interacting ecologies.[5]

The conference was organised by the Sophia Centre for the Study of Cosmology in Culture and the Harmony Initiative, now the Harmony Institute.[6] The Sophia Centre's remit is the study of the ways in which human beings make or identify meaning in, and engage with, the wider cosmos, while the Harmony Institute explores notions of the universe as a single integrated whole and their practical applications and consequences. Our guiding view of Harmony is taken from David Cadman, one of the university's Honorary Professors of Practice:

> Harmony is an expression of wholeness, a way of looking at ourselves and the world of which we are part. It's about connections and relationships. The emotional, intellectual and physical are all connected. We are connected to our environments, both built and natural; and all the parts of our communities and their environments are connected, too. Harmony asks questions about relationship, justice, fairness and respect in economic, social and political relationships. As an integrative discipline it can be expressed in ideas and practice.[7]

This all takes us to the question of shallow ecology and deep ecology, the two versions of the ecological movement as defined by Arne Naess in his seminar lecture in 1972.[8] In Naess's distinction, shallow ecology is functional and pragmatic and focuses on the fight against pollution and resource depletion. It is completely anthropocentric. By contrast, deep ecology assumes that there is no distinction between humanity and nature. The first principle of Deep Ecology, with capital letters, as defined by Arne Naess, is: 'Rejection of the man-in-environment image in favour of the relational, total-field image. Organisms as knots in the biospherical nest or field of intrinsic relations'.[9]

Consequently, the chapters in this volume pay keen attention – and offer a colourful ethnographic assortment of meanings and approaches – to how the materiality of being and of spaces and places as integrated wholes are variously understood and impact on people's lives. Regardless of the vast differences in meanings, each chapter demonstrates the physical activities of what Eduardo Kohn called forms.[10] Ilaria Cristofaro explores the sunlight on the sea, Bernadette Brady the twist in a river's flow, Alan Ereira and Kim Malville, the shape of a mountain, and Stanislaw Iwaniszewski the rise of the moon. These phenomena are not just beautiful but are influencers and instrumental partners or associates in life's endeavour that together co-create personal actions and the conclusions that individuals and cultures use to explain life. Importantly, the chapters also work to demonstrate the fundamental connections that run between, and hold, all things – including people – together in a vast, impacting web of influences, meanings and physical possibilities. Adopting this focus dethrones the human as the sole creator of meaning, and reveals the activity, agency and role of substances, materials and life forms in the collaborative processes of life.[11] Moreover, it uncovers some of the problems associated with making intellectual distinctions that depict certain entities as of little significance, others as lifeless and all as existentially separate from each other: as part of these 'confederations' of 'variously composed materiality', we are entangled with their material agency and emerge together.[12]

Therefore, the chapters in this book illustrate how worldly substances, locations, entities and lives-lived are not only fortuitously or even homeostatically contiguous but are fundamentally and materially bound to, or tangled with, each other in co-productive unity.[13] Rather than a world full of individualities, every 'thing' is in perpetual existential relationship and therefore need each other and are *of* each other. Consequently, the perspective adopted by this volume demonstrates that neither actions nor ideas can sidestep the basic elemental physicality of existence, and that any such notion that they can do so does not bear out in accounts of lived experience: people sense, and have sensed, a fundamental connection to the landscape around the world and across all times. As a result, this volume offers a series of examples that illustrate not just the important truth that the substances that comprise life are co-creative partners variously living as humanity and then with humanity, but also show how a range of worldly substances' behavioural capabilities are substantially and significantly implicated in the ways that lives can be lived at all.[14]

The conference took as its starting point the notion that many contemporary conceptions of human lives almost circumvent, and certainly pay scant attention to, the existential, even earthy, connections that inform people's lives. For many, lives are lived with little reference to the complicated shifting material processes out of which bodies, structures, tools, objects, and creatures form and fold. The elemental forces that are responsible for much of existence are all but forgotten in the high-rise, cramped, concreted urban lives so many people now live. Indeed, perhaps since the time of the first Enlightenment thinkers, when so called enchanted or magical thinking was heavily frowned upon as unhelpfully superstitious, knowledge in and of the world and its processes has, for many of us, lost its presence, its vitality and aliveness.[15] Any ability of the entities in the landscape to speak out, to be heard, to hold knowledge and to impart it as sensations, dreams, prophecy, weather conditions and so on has been judged as fanciful and replaced with what might be called a more rational, logical and verifiable approach, where knowledge can only be consider robust and accurate if it can be replicated numerically or under experimental conditions.

This type of modern approach to water, the soil, the sky, the forests and the built environment has redrawn the building blocks of life as essentially inert, mute and dumb, forming into life by chance through some as yet undefined process. This approach not only sucks the life out of the materials around us, but also paints a picture of existence as a setting or arena where personality and personhood are restricted to only certain species and in particular ways, and where life is primarily a process motivated by genetic perpetuation – all of which is framed by and securely coupled to the notion of accumulation (accumulation of wealth, in the case of human beings) as the basic measure of success. Knowledge, in this world, must be found through reductionism, dissection and taking bits apart; imagination that conjures animated landscapes are no more than frivolous flights of fancy – fun for kids, maybe – but certainly not 'the truth'. Using this as the governing perspective to explain life means that bio- and geo-diversity becomes little more than the backdrop and stage upon which human lives are enacted, with the water, the air, forests and other non-human entities retained, controlled, and engaged with solely as props for human use in their never-ending dramas.

However, the depiction of the earth as comprised of inert material substances and merely reactive entities is seriously countered by the immense body of cultural and phenomenologically focused literature that can be found in the world's libraries.[16] These accounts provide compelling alternative perspectives with which to appreciate and understand the multitude of other-than-human forces and beings that actively shape human existence. Together, they demonstrate that material, in its many forms, rather than being mute, *is* experienced as communicative, affective and, importantly, storied; each entity, every 'thing', every part, whether natural or artificial, and even the totality – 'the whole', as Haraway reminds us – has a story to tell.[17] Moreover, materiality is also regularly presented as persons (not people) with dispositions and individual temperaments that cannot be successfully categorised using orthodox typologies.[18]

Expanding the notion of personhood out from people to include other entities accepts that the world is comprised of blending subjectivities that similarly need to be cared for and that have comparable abilities – to broadcast messages, learn and even teach – as the works of Frantisek Baluska, Stephano Mancuso, Monica Gagliano, Charles Abramson, Martial Depczynski, Susan W. Simard and Steve Beyer have amply demonstrated.[19] Consequently, to live with these others they must not be used recklessly, nor should entities be moved, destroyed, or inconsiderately ignored without understanding that such changes by definition will alter the totality,[20] and with that, could bring detrimental consequences for how life can live. As Nurit Bird David and Naveh wrote,

> To cut such 'green' branches is considered *tapu* (wrong conduct toward others; Bird-David 2004b: 332-4) because, they explained, this 'hurts' the tree, which 'like us has a soul'. One Nayaka further explained that 'every [forest] tree is a living being, a tree has a soul. Like people have blood, trees have water'.[21]

As a result, and despite the dominant and loud claims that continue to insist matter is lifeless, it is not always obvious that plants are unable to communicate with us.[22] Nor is it obvious that we cannot be related to a red macaw.[23] People around the world persist in experiencing the world as alive, bursting with personalities, and from this draw various assorted conclusions about how to behave, who is kin and where and how one finds knowledge about existence, as the following quote from Chumpi, a Kawapi individual from the upper Amazonia, explains.

> Woolly monkeys, toucans, howler monkey… are persons, just as we are. The jaguar is likewise a person. … for they are, as it were, our relatives by marriage. They live together among their own relatives; nothing they do is by chance; they talk among themselves; they listen to what we say; they intermarry in a proper fashion. In vendettas, we too kill relatives by marriage, but they are still relatives. They too can wish to kill us.[24]

In a similar vein, the Nayaka not only share the forest with the other-than-human dwellers, but they also communicate directly with them too, as the following short vignette demonstrates.

> Out walking with Naveh, Chathen encountered an elephant. As they approached the elephant 'Chathen repeatedly said to the elephant:

'You are living in the forest, we are also living in the forest; you come to eat here, we are coming to take roots ... we are not coming to do you any harm'[25]. In his words, Chathen emphasized co-dwelling in the forest and points of similarity in an attempt to pre-empt confrontation.

As this passage illustrates, ethnographies have gone a long way to inspiring conversation about how to approach the wealth of differing perspectives and ontologies that populate the world today. Scholars' arrogant habit or tendency towards translating these vivid accounts away or concluding that ideas such as forests being persons or possums being cousins to humans must be merely symbolic devices, as Gilbert Herdt argued, are, thankfully, as Sam Hurn has shown, becoming a thing of the past.[26]

In tandem with the ontological turn in anthropology, which asked the question, 'what if these alternative understandings about the world were embraced as reality?', scholarship is moving away from the limitations associated with the adjudicating, colonial and rational mindset of modernity and is moving towards contemplating not just a lively world but also a world where different perspectives can co-exist without contradiction. Numerous cultural ontologies (accounts that explain reality) offer an animated picture of another world utterly dissimilar to the one lacking in vitality and personality presented earlier. In contrast, these accounts demonstrate that the soils, plants and rocks are not only alive with purpose, but also provide insight, knowledge and wisdom, and in consequence forge significant relationships with people – relationships that enable people to be taught by and have informative friendships with the things around them.[27] As Monica Gagliano wrote,

Each plant has its own song and its own language to sing it... these songs are not metaphors but tangible gestures of a plant's fondness to communicate and relate to the human through kinship. They are a blessing that grants the human person access to the enriching powers of the plant person, an invaluable gift.[28]

The notion of other-than-human wisdom is often associated with animist ontologies, which tend to avoid the assumption that physical appearance is an indicator of internal identity. Rather, following Vivieros de Castro's 'perspectivism', physical appearance is conceptualised as almost a covering that disguises the fundamental physical or material similarities within.[29] This means that categorisations which rely on exteriors fail to appreciate the inner individualities of worldly items. To fail to recognise inner states establishes a landscape occupied by disparate random entities who are often represented as at odds with each other, fighting for survival, rather than working together cooperatively, or negotiating similar events and dealing with analogous concerns. When conceptions of nature depict it as reduced to haphazardly scattered or clustered 'bits', one is taught, even forced, to understand things in isolation. Using this reductive approach positions entities as disassociated from the wider whole.[30] This makes it easy to disregard specific bits as possibly insignificant and thereby maybe reject or eradicate them. On the other hand, animist systems perceive a continuity beyond, or running through, the outward appearance of difference. Any differences in form belie or disguise the inner resemblances in 'motivation, feeling and behaviour' that animate, as Descola puts it.[31]

Numerous communities around the world appreciate life in this way, be it in the form of animism or pantheism; aliveliness runs through the forms that shape the landscape. Neo-, eco- and traditional pagans experience this similarly, as do adherents of probably all traditional religions around the world. According to Surrallés, in Peru a universal vein of potentiality runs through all materiality.[32] Comparably, in Canada, it is only the skin that hides the underlying humanity in every being and, according to the Kasua in Papua New Guinea, 'the bodies of humans, trees, and animals are all filled with the same substances: *bebeta* (blood), *ma* (a vaginal humour), and above all the omnipresent *ibi* (which means 'stomach fat' but also 'tilth' and 'latex'), which is the source of the materiality of all organic and abiotic bodies'.[33]

Phenomenological accounts also provide a wealth of experiences that demonstrate how engagement with the landscape provides an interactive, visceral field of co-creative significances, rather than a backdrop, stage, or location on which to enact human lives. These experiences not only generate sensorial conclusions but also reveal that the sensations produced are a result of being in relationship with, or becoming-with, the world, and as such provides knowledge *from* (rather than about) the mountains, lakes, or moonlight in the way of feelings, connections and associations. Feelings or sensations therefore are generated by, in and through relationship and hence, when careful personal attention is afforded to them, they encourage novel realisations, prompt significations, and create meanings that are valued as noteworthy moments and life lessons – stories to be told that continue and persist as ways to think about the world.[34] People, just like other animals, sense the world in multiple ways – from visual, haptic and tactile contacts and through the changes in physical sensations that these engagements engender within. This might simply include conclusions about the air temperature, the wind direction, or the effects of recent meteorological conditions on the garden, but can also include sensations such as the mud squelching under foot or between one's toes, one's fluttering heartbeat and a sharp intake of breath on contact with the icy chill of stream water, a surge of gratitude as the juice of a freshly picked strawberry dribbles down your chin on biting into it, or the sharp pain from the stabbing received by grabbing a thorny plant stem. Either way, the world is constantly drawing our attention and causing sensations to viscerally rise and fall. This is the conversation from body to body: the world is talking if we are just prepared to pay attention and listen.[35]

The abundance of literature that describes or outlines alternative methods, ways of knowing and ways of being with the world, provide interesting novelties that tend to captivate and fascinate. Perhaps more importantly, they also endure and may be attempting to take root again. While the deadening mechanistic thoughts of industry and geo-politics advance across the now globalised landscapes, a sense of dis-ease about its systems and devices is growing. And not as a reversion to spirituality,[36] where ghostly authorities' wishes are attended to, but as a way to recognise, respect, and celebrate how one exists as part of a vast, pulsing network of influences that stretch out, down and deep into the earth and through other animated worldly entities.[37] And to embrace alternative ontologies where those things that are not human are considered persons and kin, and where knowledge can be given by birds or valleys or fish to people.[38] One is not alone.

The land we walk on *is* the bones of our ancestors

In association with an openness, even resurgence of, these ideas, we may argue that a gentle wave of something Jane Bennett (following Max Weber's earlier warnings regarding modern life) or Patrick Curry might call re-enchantment is tentatively in progress.[39] The expansion of personhood to incorporate non-human entities – including the entire planet – demonstrates how barriers to accepting an animated or alive world are receding.[40]

Personhood, like agency, is often assumed to be something only humanity possesses. Human focused definitions associate personhood with the ability to be rational, to choose and to communicate, and provide persons with civil liberties and rights. However, these definitions have not always included all humans, as the right to own slaves sadly illustrates. Nevertheless, one might suppose that it is only people who can legally have personhood, but this is not the case, as entities such as corporations are given the status of personhood and therefore have rights under the law. Consequently, the notion of personhood extends out from people and in so doing establishes other things as persons with rights for protection.

The concept of environmental personhood is fairly new, having emerged in 1972 from a book titled *Should Trees have Standing?*. The author, Christopher Stone, argued that elements of the environment should have the capacity to bring action to court if aggrieved. Concerned about the destruction that industrial developments were producing, Stone asserted that people who retain purposeful relationships with any aspect of the environment should be able to advocate for and legally defend that entity.[41] Remarkably, his call for the environment to be recognised in this way generated considerable discussion and is now regularly used in the courts to protect aspects of the landscape around the world.[42]

In 2014, after decades of disputes, the Whanganui River in New Zealand (*Te Awa Tupua*) was the first river in the world to be established in law as alive and as a legal person. The attribution of personhood has not only provided the river with rights, but it has also delivered human guardians to ensure all rights are upheld. Giving the water rights was deemed necessary to ensure its wellbeing, partly because of fears about pollutants in factory effluent waste being released into the river.

According to Maori ontology, the source of Whanganui River are the mists that surround the top of the nearby mountains and birth an alpine stream on Mount Tongariro and other tributaries, which then feed the river. Local indigenous thought does not restrict the river's presence to the water channel, but rather considers the entity to be almost boundary-less, contiguous with the surrounding mountains and the sea.[43] This conception extends its influence out from a particular location, as there are no boundaries to the whole world.

The Iwi people explain that the river's existence is the result of ancestors arguing. The ancestors, in this case, are not people; they are mountains. The path that the water runs through was created as one of the mountain ancestors, fighting and hot with rage, took flight – fleeing towards the sea, scattering parts, and altering the landscape. Consequently, the entire area is this ancestor, and the mists, valley, water, and plants of the area are how the ancestor manifests today. On hearing that the status of the river was successfully changed to that of 'person', Tūtochu Whakatupua said, 'Ko au te awa, Ko te awa ko au - I am the river, the river is me', thus highlighting not only how the 'bones' of all ancestors form the ground we walk on, but also the fundamental, ongoing material association and connectivity between human bodies and the landscape.[44] The changing status has also simultaneously rebalanced Maori sovereignty over the area.

Relatedly, animal sentience is now also being reconsidered in several countries. Current debates, echoing those above, focus attention on animals as property, particularly in association with moral positions on the pain and suffering inflicted by industrial or intensive livestock production; these debates are also calling for animals to be recognised as subjects rather than objects.[45]

The idea that things can become persons may seem alien to some, but Naveh and Bird-David reminded us of its deeper roots when they recently posed the question, 'How did persons become things?'[46] Using ethnographic information from the animist hunter gatherer culture of the Nayaka in India, who are increasingly changing their life ways to include selling produce, they set out to 'explore how domesticated animals, plants, and land [are beginning] to "come into being" as objects amidst a Nayaka "world of persons"'.[47] In European history, therianthropy (the belief that humans can metamorphose into animals) and the experience of the aliveness of the landscape, gradually disappeared. Tim Ingold considers that the kind of domination necessary to cultivate or engage in animal husbandry was responsible for the shift in perspective.[48] Comparably, Descola concluded that the development of hierarchies within social relations is to blame.[49] Danny Naveh and Bird David, on the other hand, noted that it is possible to employ what might be considered contradictory ontologies, simultaneously: that is, to see some aspects of the world as animated and alive and others as objects lacking any kind of life. Using the Nayaka experience as illustrative, they note that a change in perceived utility provides the impetus to accept some subjects as transformed into objects. Consequently, Nayaka individuals hold two categories of animals, plants and land concurrently these days: those in the forest are 'sentient co-subjects who think, feel, make decisions, and, to an extent, understand what is said to them',[50] while '[u]nlike their forest counterparts, domesticated animals and plants are treated, sometimes quite aggressively, as objects, framed according to their use value and often according to their exchange value as well'.[51] One does not live with domesticated entities as equals and therefore their status shifts accordingly.

Establishing that things are *for* something appears to be connected to the kind of objectification that is now dominant across the world today. However, cautioning a tidy dichotomy between 'forest "persons"' and 'domesticated "things"', Naveh and Bird-David explain that persons slowly become things when put in different contexts, specifically in economic contexts where items are commodified and quantified.[52] They also remind us that the world uses multiple perspectives contemporaneously without recognising any contradictions – 'the professional logger who privately cares for his garden, or the industrial butcher who privately cares for his dog' are cited as examples of how diverse identities are regularly employed without ambiguity.[53]

The Anthropocene: do we have time?

'It is later than you think' (W. H. Auden)[54]

There is a sense of urgency filtering through public narratives these days – a sense of urgency articulated in the many missives the public around the world are confronted with daily, as almost every news outlet provides yet another example of how one area after another is suffering as a result of the climate changing. These now regular events, having conclusively diffused across the public imagination and discourse, for many, unquestioningly demonstrate how the current global situation – that is, the shifting geo-meteorological and environmental events – are the result of human activity. Taken to a logical conclusion, these events suggest planetary life as we know it is seriously threatened, and in association, numerous global and national organisations have been slowly formed with a view to find solutions to address the problems.

In keeping with the name now given to the Anthropocene Age, any blame for substances like water altering their behavioural patterns falls squarely in the lap of human activity.[55] From the melting glaciers or pollution in the oceans, to the floods, droughts and damaging storms, to the highest recorded temperatures, to the soil's infertility and the air's toxicity and to the decline in biodiversity – it is the vast array of industrialised activities, emerging as they have from the mindset of accumulation, objectification and resource use, that have provided the conditions for these changes. This is not news to any of us. And as the world is being presented as teetering on the edge of becoming a nightmarish dystopia that generates monsters out of the mutating materials that life forms itself from, for increasing numbers, enough is enough.[56] Human exceptionalism must end its rule.

However, solutions are not straightforward. Innovations tend to be rooted in economics and politics in support of the overarching aims of modernity. Typically, powered by the fantasy of growth, the voice of the economist, the data technologist, the mathematician and the engineer now sit at the top table, guiding, informing, and choosing. Appeals to other 'gods' is often deemed eccentric– interesting, but insufficient – and any other knowledge, while charming, is filed under 'story' not 'fact'. But as every cosmologist knows, every account is just another story, every fact can only be considered truthful through the lens of the cultural ontology it emerges from. This then is not a matter of truth, but of truths, of multiple simultaneous worlds, where each knowledge system holds its own in context, which means that other voices must be drawn into discussion if whatever solutions are reached can be holistically and harmoniously applied. This volume provides alternative voices and perspectives and brings ancient but also simultaneously new ideas to the table.

The chapters

The individual chapters variously consider the role of the landscape and its features in shaping human lives, and explore how the conclusions reached provide a picture of the world worlding, with life as a cohered, if differentiated, organic vitality actively co-creating existence in unison, and where people are just one aspect of this wider motivating whole.[57] Each author has approached this from a novel perspective to provide an overarching picture of how all lives living impact each other materially, not incidentally or in ways one can ignore – and in doing so act as a reminder of the physical ties that, from one perspective, can be thought of as binding lives together and, from another, demonstrates that every item, thing and force happening in the world is an aspect of a vast, influencing oneness.

The book is loosely subdivided into three merging subject areas – land, water and sky. The section on land provides a variety of perspectives on how the soil, the landscape, and the environment shape and are shaped by human lives.

Kim Malville's chapter provides us with a vivid picture of the life of mountains. He reminds us of key links between the landscape and environmental features by showing how they are the co-created work of numerous forces including human activity. As such, he demonstrates that the landscape, rather than being simply inert and driven by geo-physical forces, is active with personalities and preferences. Most importantly, the chapter illustrates how the landscape – particularly mountains, in this case – is not an inert and altogether benign sphere, and therefore, must be approached with sensitivity and care in order to avoid dangerous consequences. Using a historical perspective, Malville illustrates the role that specialised practitioners have played in the creation and maintenance of the landscape in Tibet. Following the path of the great Buddhist teacher and magician Padmasambhava, Malville illustrates how the influences of the demons of earthquakes and avalanches were subdued by planting spiritual treasures, sacred texts and teachings around Mt Everest for future generations.

Glenda Tinney, an ecologist turned early years teacher, uses personal childhood memories of sploshing about with tadpoles and mud in Wales to think about the value of changes in the conceptions of and interactions with the environment in the global North. Using Harmony Principles, Tinney explores the links between 'right thinking' and 'right action' and, by using experience of climbing a tree, explores how the environment can teach us about how we want to be human. Her chapter illustrates how the living and inert things around us play an active role in providing life-lessons that may be missed on most curricula in current times.

Suzanne Klein and Lilith Goldschmidt continue to explore the construction of landscapes by turning our attention to the history and development of photography as a method to record 'nature'. Their work outlines the role representations of the other-than-human world using this medium have constructed nature into a series of comprehendible frames for viewers. Rather than providing true likenesses of reality, as the technology suggests, this chapter demonstrates how the 'photographic act' disguises – almost makes invisible – the choices and presence of a photographer in the process, and how memories and conceptions of nature have been carefully crafted through this lens.

Alan Ereira's chapter challenges orthodox ecological conclusions by providing a rich ethnographic picture of the Kogi or Kaggaba in Colombia, a small-scale society existentially and intimately occupied with caretaking the Earth using complicated, dense and secret material and psychic practices. He outlines how conceiving of a landscape as comprised of distinct 'things' is alien to this indigenous group and reminds readers that, while it may appear axiomatically accurate to imagine that things must have edges to exist, from a New Materialities perspective, the notion of edges or boundaries is problematic; things materially blend and seep into each other, and so therefore should not be thought of as individualities. Using this as a springboard into a discussion on the Kogi's perception of the landscape as a singular, living entity, the chapter advances a picture of a people who live in dialogue with the Earth. Chiming with the numerous examples of small-scale societies around the world who continue to live in an animated world, this chapter offers a strong counterpoint to the view of a world made up of separate, competing things.

The next section concerns itself with how water plays a role in human lives.

Ilaria Cristofaro adopts an anthro-archaeological perspective on the immateriality of materiality to continue the discussion. Cristofaro's chapter explores conclusions and the social significances of the shimmering play of light cast from the moon or sun on the sea. Using a phenomenological approach, Cristofaro demonstrates how these glittering paths provide inspiration, even persist in urging people to think through complex and emotionally potent aspects of existence – specifically how death is negotiated and understood. By using these beautiful visual signs almost as clues in the landscape, Cristofaro reminds us how people have engaged with and represented the story of death.

Bernadette Brady's chapter is inspired by the pre-Christian Celtic mythology provided by a rich compilation of manuscripts called the *Mabinogion*. The *Mabinogion*, written in the 12th-13th centuries in Welsh, is a collection of stories about ancient Wales. Brady focuses on the connections between the mythological accounts in the text and the geographical locations as they appear in the landscape, to make conclusions about the cosmology as presented by the stories. She does this by focusing specifically on the Afon Cynfael river in Gwynedd in the north of Wales, as the river is named in the fourth branch of the mythological collection, and by paying careful attention to the construction of the story, illustrates how it provides clues to understand the calendar and seasons.

Alexander Scott is concerned with elucidating the complex network of materials and meanings that collect, seep, and spread out to, and from, places. Attending to water in Liverpool, he shows how any sense of place is not restricted to that location but rather almost breathes, and certainly flows, in and out in concert with multiple localities, forces and ideas that gather, muster, and amass. Scott notes that identities are relational and referential, and demonstrates how places – in extending out from any geographical location in multiple tangled, even spiralling ways – co-produce their identities in association with numerous other spaces, impacting in material and immaterial ways.

Moragh Feeney-Beaton also plunges into water to think about how swimming might be helpfully conceived of as a liminal act. Explaining her experiences of 'wild swimming', she explores how engaging with water in these settings provide a space where the notions of the 'ordinary' and the 'extraordinary' entwine to produce significant numinous experiences in the everyday. Feeney-Beaton maintains humanity is occupied in a constant 'search for uplifting', and this chapter reveals water's part in realizing that.

Melanie Long offers an ethnography of living on house boats and details the kinds of practical negotiations one must make with the water, and the other animals that live with the water, to ensure a workable relationship in what she positions as a liminal space. The liminal, as established by Arnold van Gennep and developed by Victor Turner, is a concept that describes a creative, unpredictable, unsettled zone between two more normative ones.[58] For Long, boats as homes provide a portion of 'dry land' floating on the fluid changeability of the river and as such can be understood as troubling the boundaries of the more common practice of living on the soil. Choices to live this way are numerous, but Long importantly demonstrates how this choice emerges through a sense of kinship with, or connection to, both the river and also the boats.

The final section draws on cosmological features to illustrate that the connectivity of existence moves out from the 'edges' of the atmosphere past the night sky and further into the universe. It draws spirituality 'down to earth' and provides a series of examples that demonstrate how earthly spaces offer and create places of worship.

Stan Iwaniszewski's work provides a detailed account of the significance of celestial bodies for human lives. Outlining the many correspondences between activities in the heavens with those below, the reader is shown how the cosmological meanings enable culturally significant knowledge to be generated and lived by. Using ethnographic information from the Aztecs, Iwaniszewki problematises and extends any orthodox notion of personhood out from humanity to both encompass features in the landscape and above, and also to allow aspects of 'the person' to seep and be distributed through the environment.

For Selma Faria, current times demand a shift in paradigm away from the dated focus on survival towards one that proposes an ecologically integrative model – one that attends to equilibrium and interconnectivity over accumulation. And that draws together the bodies of people with the rest of the environment so that all existential connections, from cosmological features to the chemical composition of our own bodies, are taken into account.

Fenella Dean approaches the slippery concept of the sacred to untangle some of its complications and considers how spaces qualify for the title 'sacred' by using the example of the O2 building, a fairly new construction built on a disused site over 20 years ago in London. By attending to the materiality, function, use and construction of the O2 arena in London, Dean demonstrates how spaces develop their sacred status in association with human experiences, rather than in isolation or intrinsically, and that this process of almost, what one might call, sacredisation relies on conscious attention to how objects, spaces and things enact their place within the profane or mundane of daily life. Again, tying in cosmological activities, Dean's chapter provides another example of how spaces materialise spirituality through the construction of ideas into earthly forms and how any human connection or links to the cosmos can be made tangible in built-up areas.

For too long the standard Euro-American view of the world as an inert resource to be exploited for human benefit has held most of the world in an economic, profit-driven stranglehold. Current conditions suggest that the increasingly ruthless sophistication of industrialised methods is responsible for the slowly unfolding alterations in environmental conditions, as we hear regular reports on how the processes of worldly materiality are altering the way they function. The weather patterns are changing in almost every region, often causing previously unimaginable, even mythic destruction: towns are washed or burnt away overnight, oceans are part plastic, and the air we all breathe is heavy with particulate matter.

With few effective adaptation strategies in place, it appears that the route to global disaster is being set. The Euro-American mindset and the mythical creation – 'the market', interested only in competition, consumerism and accumulation – is blamed. Small waves of activism in the social, economic and political spheres around the planet seek to change this perspective, with some moments of success. This book represents our contribution to add to the voices that are calling out for change. In this case, we want a change of mind and heart, a change that realizes – makes real – the connections between us and our material partners. However, it is also important to challenge the view of the world as meaningless by reasserting its role as meaning-full, and to recognise the human role as not above and beyond nature, but fully within and a part of nature. We therefore need to understand, respect and explore our relationship with world around us and this book, in its own way, is a part of this much larger mission.

Notes

1. Luci Attala, *How Water Makes us Human* (Cardiff: University of Wales Press, 2019), p.4.

2. 'Materialities in Anthropology and Archaeology', https://www.uwp.co.uk/series/category/Materialities-in-Anthropology-and-Archaeology/ [accessed 18 July 2021].

3. Darrelyn Gunzburg and Bernadette Brady, eds, *Space, Place and Religious Landscapes: Sacred Mountains*, Bloomsbury Studies in Material Religion (London: Bloomsbury, 2020).

4. Karen Barad, *Meeting the Universe Halfway: Quantum Physics and the Entanglement of Matter and Meaning.* (Durham, NC, and London: Duke University Press, 2007); Donna Haraway, *Staying with the Trouble: Making Kin in the Chthulucene* (Durham, NC: Duke University Press, 2016); Fritjof Capra, *The Hidden Connections: A Science for Sustainable Living* (London: Harper Collins, 2002).

5. Luci Attala, *The Role of Water in Shaping Futures in Rural Kenya: Using a New Materialities Approach to Understand the Co-productive Correspondences Between Bodies, Culture and Water* (PhD Thesis, Exeter University, 2018).

6. The Sophia Centre, https://www.uwtsd.ac.uk/sophia/ [accessed 23 May 2022]; The Harmony Institute, https://www.uwtsd.ac.uk/harmony-institute/ [accessed 23 May 2022].

7. David Cadman, 23 May 2017, cited in Nicholas Campion, Introduction, in Nicholas Campion, ed., *The Harmony Debates: Exploring a practical philosophy for a sustainable future* (Lampeter: Sophia Centre Press, 2020), pp.17–29, p.22.

8. Arne Naess, 'The Shallow and the Deep, Long-Range Ecology Movement', *Inquiry* 16, no. 1–4 (1973): pp.95–100.

9. Naess, 'The Shallow and the Deep, Long-Range Ecology Movement', p.95.

10. Eduardo Kohn, *How Forests Think: Towards an Anthropology of Beyond the Human* (Berkeley and Los Angeles, CA, and London: University of California Press 2013).

11. Jane Bennett, *Vibrant Matter: A Political Ecology of Things* (Durham, NC, and London: Duke University Press, 2010).

12. Serenella Iovino and Serpil Oppermann, eds, *Material Eco-criticism* (Bloomington and Indianapolis, IN: Indiana University Press, 2014), p.8.

13. James Lovelock, *The Ages of Gaia: A Biography of our Living Earth* (Oxford: Oxford University Press, 1988).

14. Luci Attala, *How Water Makes us Human*; Luci Attala and Louise Steel, eds, *Body Matters: Body Matters: Exploring the Materiality of the Body* (Cardiff: University of Wales Press, 2019).

15. Max Weber, *From Max Weber: Essays in Sociology*, H. H. Gerth and C. Wright

Mills, eds and trans (Oxford University Press, 2005); Jane Bennett, *The Enchantment of Modern Life: Attachments, Crossings and Ethics* (Princeton, NJ: Princeton University Press, 2016).

16. See: David Abrams, *The Spell of the Sensuous: Perceptions and Language in a More-than-Human World*. (New York: Vintage, Random House, 1996); Monica Gagliano, *Thus Spoke the Plant: A remarkable journey of ground breaking scientific discoveries and personal encounters with plants* (Berkeley, CA: North Atlantic Books, 2018); Sam Hurn, *Humans and Other Animals: Human-Animal Interactions in Cross-Cultural Perspective* (London: Pluto Press, 2012); Iovino and Opperman, *Material Eco-criticism*; Eben Kirksey and Stephen Helmreich, 'The Emergence of a Multispecies Ethnography', *Cultural Anthropology Special Issue: Multispecies Ethnography* 25, no. 4 (2010): pp.545–76.

17. Donna. J. Haraway, *When Species Meet: Posthumanities Vol. 3* (Minnesota, MN: University of Minnesota Press, 2008).

18. Iovino, and Opperman, *Material Eco-criticism*.

19. Frantisek Baluska and Stephano Mancuso. 'Plant neurobiology: From sensory biology, via plant communication, to social plant behaviour', *Cognitive Process* 10 (2009): S3–S7; Monica Gagliano, Charles Abramson, and Martial Depczynski, 'Plants learn and remember: let's get used to it', *Oecologia* 186 (2018): pp.29–31, 10.1007/s00442-017-4029-7; Susan W. Simard, 'Mycorrhizal networks and complex systems: Contributions of soil ecology science to managing climate change effects in forested ecosystem', *Canadian Journal of Soil Science* 89 (2009): pp.369–82; Susan W Simard, 'The foundational role of mycorrhizal networks in self-organisation of interior Douglas-Fir forests', *Forest Ecology and Management* 258S (2009): S95–S107; and Stephan V. Beyer, *Singing to the plants: A guide to mestizo shamanism in the Upper Amazon* (Albuquerque, NM: University of New Mexico Press, 2010).

20. Alan Ereira, *From the Heart of the World* (London: Jonathan Cape Ltd, 1992).

21. Nurit Bird David and David Naveh, 'Relational epistemology, immediacy, and conservation: Or, what do the Nayaka try to conserve?', *Journal for the Study of Religion, Nature and Culture* 2, no. 1 (2008): pp.55–73, p.67.

22. Luci Attala, 'I am Apple: relationships of the flesh. Exploring the corporeal entanglements of eating plants in the Amazon', in Luci Attala and Louise Steel,, eds, *Body Matters: Exploring the Materiality of the Body* (Cardiff: University of Wales Press, 2019b); and Matthew Hall, *Plants as Persons: A Philosophical Botany* (Albany, NY: SUNY Press, 2011).

23. Hurn, *Humans and Other Animals*.

24. Phillipe Descola, *Beyond Nature and Culture* (Chicago, IL: Chicago University Press, 2013): p.15.

25. Bird David and Naveh, 'Relational epistemology', p.64

26. Gilbert Herdt, *The Sambia: Ritual and Gender in New Guinea* (Marceline, MO: Wadsworth Publishing Co. Inc., soft cover edition,1987); Hurn, *Humans and Other Animals*.

27. Kate Feyers-Kerr, 'Becoming a Community of Substance: The Mun, the mud and the therapeutic art of body painting', in Luci Attala, Louise Steel and Katharina Zinn, eds, *Body Matters: Exploring the Materiality of the Human Body* (Cardiff: University of Wales Press, 2019), pp.109–133; Beyer, *Singing to the plants*; Nurit Bird David, 'Puja or sharing with the gods? On ritualized possession among Nayaka of South India'. *Eastern Anthropologist* 49 (1996): pp.259–75.

28. Gagliano, *Thus Spoke the Plant*, p.24.

29. Eduardo Vivieros de Castros, Cosmological deixis and Amerindian perspectivism. *The Journal of the Royal Anthropological Institute* 4, no. 3 (1998): pp.469–88.

30. Gagliano, *Thus Spoke the Plant*.

31. Descola, *Beyond Nature and Culture*, p.69.

32. Alexander Surrallés, 'Human Rights for Nonhumans', *Hau: Journal of Ethnographic Theory* 7, no. 3 (2017): pp.211–235, https://www.journals.uchicago.edu/doi/epdf/10.14318/hau7.3.013 [accessed 14 October 2022].

33. Surrallés, 'Human Rights for Nonhumans', p.69.

34. Tim Ingold, 'The Art of Paying Attention', YouTube Channel *The Art of Research*, 22 February 2018, https://www.youtube.com/watch?v=2Mytf4ZSqQs [accessed 14 October 2022].

35. Ingold, 'The Art of Paying Attention'; Gagliano, *Thus Spoke the Plant*.

36. Graham Harvey, *Animism: Respecting the Living World* (New York: Columbia University Press, 2005).

37. Lambrous Malafouris, *How Things Shape the Mind: A Theory of Material Engagement* (Cambridge, MA: MIT, 2013).

38. Hurn, *Humans and Other Animals*.

39. Max Weber, *From Max Weber: Essays in Sociology*, H. H. Gerth and C. Wright Mills, eds and trans (Oxford: Oxford University Press, 2005); Patrick Curry, *Enchantment: Wonder in Modern Life* (Edinburgh: Floris Books, 2019); Jane Bennett, *The Enchantment of Modern Life: Attachments, Crossings and Ethics* (Princeton, NJ: Princeton University Press, 2001).

40. 'The Universal Declaration of the Rights of Nature', Homepage, *Global Alliance for the Rights of Nature*, 2018, https://www.garn.org/rights-of-nature/ [accessed 15 October 2022]; James R. May and Erin Daly, *Global Environmental Constitutionalism* (New York and Cambridge: Cambridge University Press, 2015).

41. Christopher Stone, *Should Trees have Standing: Law, Morality and the Environment*, 3rd edn (Oxford: Oxford University Press, 2010).

42. Sanket Khandelwal, 'Environmental Personhood: Recent Developments and the Road Ahead', *Jurist: Legal News and Commentary*, 24 April 2020, https://www.jurist.org/commentary/2020/04/sanket-khandelwal-environment-person/ [accessed 14 October 2022].

43. Water Alternatives, *I am the river. the river is me*, 2021, https://www.water-alternatives.org/index.php/cwd/item/99-river; and MEL Films, *The River is Me*, 2018, https://vimeo.com/288119812. [Accessed 14 October 2022].

44. Elaine Hsiao, 'Whanganui River Agreement: Indigenous Rights and the Rights of Nature', *Environmental Policy and Law* 42, no. 6 (2012): pp.371–75.

45. Wendy. A. Adams, 'Human Subjects and Animal Objects: Animals as 'Other' in Law'. *Journal of Animal Law and Ethics* (2010).

46. Danny Naveh and Nurit Bird-David, 'How did Persons Become Things: Economic and Epistemological Changes Among Nayaka Hunter-Gatherers', *Journal of the Royal Anthropological Institute* 20 (2014): pp.74–92.

47. Naveh and Bird-David, 'How did Persons Become Things?', p.76.

48. Tim Ingold, *Perceptions of the Environment*.

49. Descola, *Beyond Nature and Culture*.

50. Naveh and Bird David, p.76.

51. Naveh and Bird David, p.76.

52. Naveh and Bird David, p.81.

53. Naveh and Bird David, p.83, citing Alf Hornborg, 'Animism, fetishism, and objectivism as strategies for knowing (or not knowing) the world', *Ethnos* 7 (2006: pp.22–32, p.24.

54. W. H. Auden, 'Consider This and In Our Time', *Poems* (London: Faber and Faber, 1930).

55. Luci Attala *How Water Makes us Human* (Cardiff: University of Wales Press, 2019), line 51.

56. Haraway, *Staying With The Trouble*.

57. Haraway, *Staying With The Trouble*.

58. Arnold van Gennep, *The Rites of Passage* (London and New York: Routledge, 2004); Victor Turner, *The Forest of Symbols: Aspects of Ndembu Ritual* (Cornell, NY: Cornell University Press, 1970).

References

Abrams, D. *The Spell of the Sensuous: Perceptions and Language in a More-than-Human World.* (New York: Vintage, Random House, 1996).

Adams, Wendy, A. Human Subjects and Animal Objects: Animals as 'Other' in Law. *Journal of Animal Law and Ethics* (2010).

Attala, L. *The Role of Water in Shaping Futures in Rural Kenya: Using a New Materialities Approach to Understand the Co-productive Correspondences Between Bodies, Culture and Water.* PhD Thesis, (Exeter University, 2018).

Attala, L. *How Water Makes us Human* (Cardiff: University of Wales Press, 2019).

Attala, L., and Steel, L. (eds.), *Body Matters: Body Matters: Exploring the Materiality of the Body* Cardiff: University of Wales Press, 2019).

Attala, L. "I am Apple: relationships of the flesh. Exploring the corporeal entanglements of eating plants in the Amazon" in Attala, L., and Steel, L. (eds) *Body Matters: Exploring the Materiality of the Body.* (Cardiff: University of Wales Press, 2019).

Auden, W. H. 'Consider This and In Our Time' *Poems* (London: Faber and Faber, 1930).

Barad, K. *Meeting the Universe Halfway: Quantum Physics and the Entanglement of Matter and Meaning.* (Durham (NC) and London: Duke University Press, 2007).

Baluska, F., and Mancuso, S. 2009. "Plant neurobiology: From sensory biology, via plant communication, to social plant behaviour." (*Cognitive Process* 10: S3-S7, 2009).

Bennett, J. *Vibrant Matter: A Political Ecology of Things.* (Durham and London: Duke University Press, 2010).

Bennett, J. *The Enchantment of Modern Life: Attachments, Crossings and Ethics* (Princeton University Press, 2016).

Beyer, Stephan. *Singing to the Plants: A Guide to Mestizo Shamanism in the Upper Amazon.* (Albuquerque: University of New Mexico Press, 2009).

Bird David, N. 'Puja or sharing with the gods? On ritualized possession among Nayaka of South India'. *Eastern Anthropologist* 49, 259-75 (1996).

Bird-David, N., and Naveh, D. Relational epistemology, immediacy, and conservation: Or, what do the Nayaka try to conserve? *Journal for the Study of Religion, Nature and Culture* 2(1):55-73. (2008).

Capra, F., *The Hidden Connections: A Science for Sustainable Living* (London: Harper Collins, 2002).

Descola, P. *Beyond Nature and Culture* (Chicago: Chicago University Press, 2013: p15).

Ereira, A., *From the Heart of the World.* (London: Jonathan Cape Ltd, 1992).

Feyers-Kerr, K. "Becoming a Community of Substance: The Mun, the mud and the therapeutic art of body painting". In Attala, L, Steel, L & Zinn, K. (eds.) Body Matters: Exploring the Materiality of the Human Body. (University of Wales Press, pp. 109-133, 2019).

Gagliano, M. *Thus Spoke the Plant: A remarkable journey of ground breaking scientific discoveries and personal encounters with plants*, (Berkeley, California: North Atlantic Books, 2018).

Gagliano, M., Abramson, C., and Depczynski, M. Plants learn and remember: let's get used to it. *Oecologia*. 186. 29-31. 10.1007/s00442-017-4029-7. (2018).

Gunzburg, D and Brady, B., (eds), *Space, Place and Religious Landscapes: Sacred Mountains*, Bloomsbury Studies in Material Religion (London: Bloomsbury 2020).

Hall, M. *Plants as Persons: A Philosophical Botany.* (Albany (NY): SUNY Press, 2011).

Haraway, D. J. *When Species Meet: Posthumanities Vol 3* (Minnesota: University of Minnesota Press, 2008).

Haraway, D. J. *Staying with the Trouble: Making Kin in the Chthulucene* (Duke University Press, 2016).

Harvey, G. *Animism: Respecting the Living World* (Columbia: Columbia University Press, 2005).

Herdt, G. *The Sambia: Ritual and Gender in New Guinea* (Wadsworth Publishing Co Inc; Soft Cover edition,1987).

Hornborg, A. Animism, fetishism, and objectivism as strategies for knowing (or not knowing) the world. *Ethnos* 7, 22-32 (2006).

Hsiao, E. "Whanganui River Agreement: Indigenous Rights and the Rights of Nature." *Environmental Policy and Law* 42 (6): 371–75 (2012).

Environmental Policy and Law 42 (6): 371–75.

Hurn, S. *Humans and Other Animals: Human-Animal Interactions in Cross-Cultural Perspective.* (London: Pluto Press, 2012) .

Ingold, T. *Perceptions of the Environment: Essays on Livelihood, Dwelling and Skill* (London: Routledge, 2010).

Ingold, T. 'The Art of Paying Attention' at *The Art of Research* [online] Available at https://www.youtube.com/watch?v=2Mytf4ZSqQs (2018).

Iovino, S., and Opperman, S. (eds), *Material Eco-criticism.* (Bloomington and Indianapolis: Indiana University Press, 2014).

Kirksey, E., and Helmreich, S. The Emergence of a Multispecies Ethnography. *Cultural Anthropology Special Issue: Multispecies Ethnography* 25: 4, pp. 545–76 (2010).

Khandelwal, S. 'Environmental Personhood: Recent Developments and the Road Ahead' *Jurist: Legal News and Commentary* [online] Available at https://www.jurist.org/commentary/2020/04/sanket-khandelwal-environment-person/, 2020.

Kohn, E. *How Forests Think: Towards an Anthropology of Beyond the Human.* (Berkeley, Los Angeles, London: University of California Press, 2013).

Lovelock, J. *The Ages of Gaia: A Biography of our Living Earth* (Oxford: Oxford University Press, 1988).

Malafouris, L. *How Things Shape the Mind: A Theory of Material Engagement* (Cambridge MA: MIT, 2013).

'Materialities in Anthropology and Archaeology', https://www.uwp.co.uk/series/materialities-in-anthropology-and-archaeology/ [accessed 18 July 2021].

May, J. R., and Daly, E. *Global Environmental Constitutionalism* New York, (Cambridge: Cambridge University Press, 2015).

MEL Films, *The River is Me* https://vimeo.com/288119812 (2018).

Simard, S. W. "Mycorrhizal networks and complex systems: Contributions of soil ecology science to managing climate change effects in forested ecosystem." *Canadian Journal of Soil Science* 89:369-382, (2009).

Simard, S. W. "The foundational role of mycorrhizal networks in self-organisation of interior Douglas-Fir forests." *Forest Ecology and Management* 258S: S95-S107, (2009).

Stone, C. *Should Trees have Standing: Law, Morality and the Environment* (3rd ed.) (Oxford: Oxford University Press, 2010).

Surrallés, A. "Human Rights for Nonhumans" *Hau: Journal of Ethnographic Theory* 7 (3), 211–23 (2017).

Turner, V. *The Forest of Symbols: Aspects of Ndembu Ritual* (Cornell, University Press, 1970).

The Universal Declaration of the Rights of Nature Global Alliance for the Rights of Nature. *Global Alliance for the Rights of Nature Home Page* [online] Available at https://therightsofnature.org (2018).

Vivieros de Castros, E. Cosmological deixis and Amerindian perspectivism. *The Journal of the Royal Anthropological Institute* 4(3), 469–88. (1998).

Van Gennep, A. *The Rites of Passage.* (London, New York: Routledge, 2004).

Weber, M. (H. H. Gerth and C. Wright Mills (trans and eds.)), *From Max Weber: Essays in Sociology*, (Oxford University Press, 2005).

Water Alternatives, *I am the river. the river is me.*[online] Available at https://www.water-alternatives.org/index.php/cwd/item/99-river (2021).

2

SACRED AND COSMIC MOUNTAINS IN THE HIMALAYA AND ANDES: ASCENT AND CIRCUMAMBULATION

J. McKim Malville

Introduction

This chapter explores the meaning behind two completely different kinds of human interaction with mountains as a way of understanding the power and agency of mountains. In the Himalaya, sacred mountains were circumambulated and not climbed, whereas in the Andes, especially during the Inca empire, mountains were ascended and not circumambulated. Each of these cultural traditions has the characteristics of a *meme*, a term coined by Richard Dawkins and developed further by E. O. Wilson to describe a unit of cultural heritage.[1] In the context of this chapter, South Asian circulation around a centre and Andean ascent are units of culture, which are self-replicating as they pass from individual to individual, both horizontally through culture and vertically across centuries. These units of culture are exposed to evolutionary processes as they replicate vertically between generations, such as genes that pass from parent to child and, like viruses or bacteria, as they may pass horizontally across cultures. In the Andes, as I have suggested in previous research, the meme of ascent may have arrived with migrants from Asia carrying shamanic traditions: it appears archaeologically in the truncated pyramids and monumental staircases of Caral, the Sechin complex of the Casma Valley and Chavin de Huantar.[2] In the Inca world, according to Johan Reinhard and J. Constanza Ceruti, the meme of ascent appears to be expressed in elaborately carved huacas and in shrines on the summits of over 100 Andean peaks higher than 5000 meters, culminating with the world's highest known archaeological site on the summit of Mount Llullaillaco.[3] Andean people also engaged in reciprocal relationships with mountains. Life could be fragile in the Andes with the constant threat of drought, floods, avalanches, and earthquakes. Mountains could, also, be agentive and responsive to gifts, offerings, and prayers.

In India and Tibetan regions, the meme of circumambulations is found practically everywhere, such as pilgrims walking around Mount Kailash, and devotees encircling the spires of temples and stupas as representations of the cosmic mountain whilst themselves spinning prayer wheels. Known as Mount Meru or Mount Sumaru, the cosmic mountain represents for Indo-Tibetan traditions the *axis mundi*, the centre around which the cosmos revolves.[4]

Intertwining these two memes is the phenomenon of scale invariance, a characteristic of many features of the natural world ranging from snowflakes and cauliflowers to stars orbiting the centres of galaxies, such that elements at different scales are identical except for size. The scale invariance of the cosmos, which is expressed in a belief in the parallelism of microcosm and macrocosm, is a fundamental feature of the worldviews of the major religions of Asia. Such presumed homology of the large and small, of the cosmic and the human, gives meaning and significance to the individual human life. In these world views, to walk around a person, temple, city or mountain not only honours the centre but is similar to encircling the entire universe.[5]

Systems that are scale invariant are characterized by power law distributions. In these systems the number of elements of a particular size r is given by the equation $N = Ar^{-D}$ where D is defined as the fractal dimension.[6] Scale invariance is demonstrated by changing the scale of the structure or of the event from r to kr, where k is a scaling factor. The power law behaviour remains unchanged and becomes $N = Ak^{-D} r^{-D}$. Only the constant has changed not the fundamental behavior of the equation.

The Sierpinski Triangle (Fig. 1) is a classic fractal, showing scale invariance and a power law distribution. If one counts the number of triangles with different sizes and plots them, the result is a power law distribution as is shown in Figure 2. The parts of the fractal are clearly interconnected, differing only by size. The parts are also non-separable: removing a section renders the pattern no longer a fractal.

The physicist Per Bak has used avalanches in a sand pile to illustrate the process by which a system can achieve scale invariance. When sand is poured onto a pile with a slope less than the angle of repose, sand grains act as isolated and independent objects. But, when the slope achieves the angle of repose, the system achieves self-organized criticality (SOC) and the sand grains behave cooperatively. Avalanches begin to occur, the sizes of which follow a power law, such that there are more small avalanches than large ones and the system acquires the characteristics of a fractal. The essential element in this case of self-organized criticality is cooperative behaviour of the sand grains.[7] In the realm of human experience, when groups of people, such as pilgrims reach SOC due

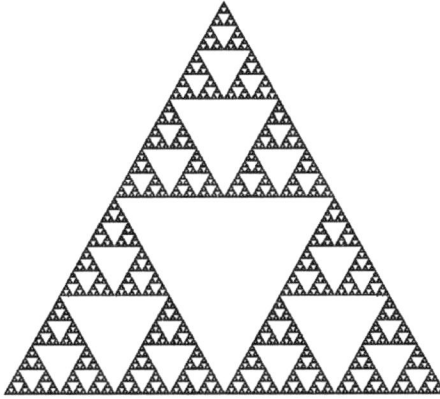

Figure 1. Sierpinski Triangle. Wikimedia Commons.

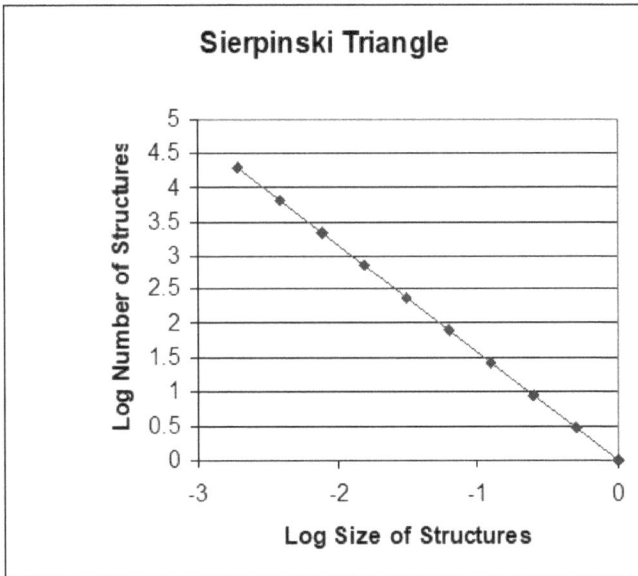

Figure 2. Plot of the number of triangles of different sizes showing a power law $N = r^{-1.585}$. Note the numbers increase with smaller sizes.

to their cooperative behaviour and mutual interaction, they begin behaving like fractals.

An aspect of scale invariance that is found in archaeology has been called symbolic resonance by the archaeologist John Fritz.[8] In his interpretation of sacred spaces such as the great city of Vijayanagara, the largest ruined city in the world, and the ancestral pueblo structures of Chaco Canyon, he suggested that a resonance develops in the minds of people who live in and move through these multi-dimensional spaces. Resonance means a coupling between an individual and another phenomenon in the cosmos. Experiences at one scale can couple with experiences at other scales. The consequence is a sense of the interconnectedness of the universe.

Scale invariance establishes a universality of meaning that transcends size and place. If an encounter with the sacred involves a sense of what lies beyond oneself, then participation in pilgrimage around a sacred mountain such as Mount Kailash provides entry into the sacred realm. The field research described in this chapter was initiated to learn more about the ways in which mountains influence people and have the power to establish religious or spiritual interactions with those who live within them or are drawn to them.

The centre

To begin this exploration of human interactions with mountains, this chapter will consider the concept of the centre of space in South Asia. Ancient cosmologies, both eastern and western, assert that the centre of space is everywhere.[9] For somewhat different reasons, modern astrophysics provides a similar insight. According to our understanding of modern cosmology, the centre of the expanding cosmos is everywhere; no point of space, no planet, no star, no galaxy is the sole and unique centre.[10] Similar to the surface of an expanding balloon, every place is a centre from which matter is receding. Regardless of where a person may stand or which galaxy is called home, the movement of space away from each person is precisely the same.

There is a popular story in Hinduism describing a competition involving the two sons of Parvati and Shiva, who are Ganesh, the elephant headed god, and Kartikeya, the handsome and ambitious god of war, also known as Skanda or Murugan. Ganesh rides a small mouse while Kartikeya has a beautiful peacock as his vehicle.[11] In order to win from their parents a special mango that grants knowledge and wisdom, the two boys set off on a race to see who could first circle the entire universe. Karttikeya climbed on his peacock and began racing to the edge of the universe, confident that he would beat his brother and his mouse. Meanwhile, Ganesh circumambulated his father and mother who, for him, were the entire universe. Two cultural traditions appear in the story, circulation and scale invariance, which reappear again and agin in various forms in India and Tibet.[12]

In south Asia, the mountain that is most often identified as the centre of the world is Mount Kailash in western Tibet. High on the Tibetan plateau, it is unque in its location and in the traditions with which it is associated. By tradition, the first and only person to have reached its summit was the sage Milerapa when he rode a beam of sunlight in a competetion with the Bonpo shaman Naro Bonchung, who rode his drum. Traveling by sunlight is faster than by a shaman drum, and Milerepa reached the summit first.[13] This magnificant snow covered peak has never felt the feet of modern mountaineers. The description by Mircea Eliade of sacred space comes close to capturing the nature of the neighbourhood of Mount Kailash, and, indeed, also that of Mount Everest, referred to as Sagarmatha in Nepalese and Chomolungma in Tibetan: '...the place becomes an inexhaustible source of power and sacredness and enables man, simply by entering it, to have a share in the power, to hold communion with the sacred.'[14] Such a place, according to Eliade, is never chosen but is discovered. There are many mountains in the Himalayas that are held to be sacred by those who live near them. The summits of only a few have remained untouched because of their sacredness. Other sacred mountains in the Himalaya, for which climbing is prohibited, are the dramatic spire of Machapuchare (6993 m, 22942 ft) in Nepal and Gangkar Puensam (7570 m, 24836 ft) in Bhutan, which may be the highest unclimbed mountain in the world.

Sacred valleys

Valleys in Tibet became sacred due to the activities of Buddhist teachers and monks and nuns.[15] This tradition started in the eighth century when, according to the Tibetan historical accounts known as 'The Blue Annuals' (1476), the Tibetan king Trisong Detsen invited the abbot of the great Indian Buddhist university of Nalanda, Shantarakshita, to bring Buddhism into his country.[16] Unfortunately, the demons of Tibet such as those of earthquakes, droughts, and floods defeated the abbot. Next, the king invited the renowned teacher and great tantric practitioner, Padmasambhava, also known as Guru Rinpoche, to vanquish these demonic forces.

The demons were either subdued and/or converted to assist in the spiritual awaking of Tibet. Some of these indigenous deities became fierce protector deities in Tibetan Buddhism, and are able to destroy the obstacles to enlightenment. Padmasambhava's conversion of chaos to order in Tibet is depicted in the religious masked dances of Mani Rimdu, which were initially performed in

Rombuk Monastery on the north face of Mount Everest and are now performed annually in the Tengboche, Thame, and Chiwong Monasteries of Nepal.[17] In the courtyard of these monasteries, the dancers move clockwise, encircling the central pole and Padmasambhava appears in his eight forms, including the fierce form Dorje Drolo, who challenges demons with ritual daggers, converting chaos to order and the mundane to the sacred (Fig. 4). As Wade Davis noted, the British mountaineers, not understanding what they were watching in 1924 at Rombuk, called the performance 'devil dances, whereas they were the most fundamental expression of the sacredness of the local landscape'.[18]

According to tradition, as he moved through the valleys of Tibet, Padmasambhava planted spiritual treasures, sacred texts and teachings. Some were sealed in chortens and caves around Mount Everest for future generations. He reportedly spent seven months in the Rongbuk valley at the northern base of Mount Everest, which became a place of great holiness for Tibetans. These valleys became the places to be born or reborn; places to be liberated from the cycle of life and death. These were refuges, dominated by protective mountain deities, where pilgrims could flee violence. Merely to walk through such a landscape was to gain merit and obtain realization provided one's intentions were pure and the time was right. To climb a mountain such as Everest seemed to the monks at the Rongbuk Monastery when they encountered the British climbers in 1921 to be meaningless work.[19] In 1921 there were twenty monks spending the year at Rongbuk monastery; hundreds visited the monastery in the summer, and in caves and cells throughout the serene, quiet, and peaceful valley there were another 300-400 hermits.[20] To them the British climbers were great enigmas: risking one's life in order to struggle over rocks and ice seemed to be the height of ignorance and delusion. For the Buddhist monks, life was a precious gift, an opportunity to obtain enlightenment. Why waste that opportunity by chancing death on a mountain? The British climbers were drawn to the mountain by a combination of British pride, the challenge to conquer, and, for some such as George Mallory, a life-threatening obsession. In 1924, when the British returned to Rongbuk Monastery after two unsuccessful attempts on the mountain, they discovered an extraordinary mural inside the monastery, which had been painted sometime after 1922, which expressed the view of the Rongbuk monks of the British who wished to conquer the mountain that dominated the head of their valley. Davis has provided the description given by John Noel who sketched and photographed the mural:

Cloven-hoofed devils armed with pitchforks casting a party of climbers into a vortex that spun ever deeper into a cold abyss, a zone of hell...

of ice, snow, and murderous winds. Ferocious dogs guarded the flanks of Everest while at its base lay prostrate a single white body, speared and ravaged by horned demons.[21]

Tibetan names for Mount Everest were *Chomolungma*, the Goddess Mother of the World, and *Miyolangsangma*, one of the Sisters of Long Life, who had been subdued by Padmasambhava and transformed into 'protector goddesses of the Buddha dharma'.[22] These contradictory interactions with the great mountain were painful violations of the contemplative lives of the Rombuk monks and the sacredness of their landscape.

Figure 4. Dorje Drolo – The fierce emanation of Padmasambhava at Tangboche Monastery carrying ritual daggers, Purbas and Vajras. Drawing by Megan Yalkut with permission; photo by author- mask of Dorje Drolo by Purba Sonam Sherpa, Tengboche Monastery

Methodology

In order to test for scale invariance of pilgrims coming to Varanasi, India and Tibet, my research partner Professor Rana Singh from Benares Hindu University and I organized a collaborative program involving the University of Colorado and Benares Hindu University. Under the direction of Rana Singh, visitors to Asi Ghat, the southernmost ghat of Benares, were counted for 600 days between 31 October 1998 and 21 June 2000 from 6 am through 9 am. In addition, we measured the GPS locations of every shrine on the major pilgrimage circuits around Varanasi using two Garman GPS75 receivers. A stationary receiver was fixed on the roof of the Ganges View Hotel in Asi Ghat. The second receiver was mobile. Measurements were based upon the World Geodetic System 1984. The base station was operated over a period of six weeks, producing more than 14,000 measurements of latitude and longitude resulting in a precision of 1/100 arc second. In the field, measurements were recorded every 10 seconds for a minimum of 10 minutes at each site. For those shrines and temples that were located deep within the narrow streets of Varanasi, GPS measurements were made on the roofs of nearby buildings. In Tibet, I used one GPS receiver to measure the locations of shrines on the pilgrimage kora around Mount Kailash. What follows are the results of our fieldwork at Mount Kailash and Varanasi.

Mount Kailash

Lying to the north of Varanasi, Mount Kailash has been a major pilgrimage site for more than 2500 years. It has the distinction of being the most venerated but the least visited of Asia's sacred places. Because of its remote location and the high altitude of far western Tibetan plateau, it is visited by a few thousand pilgrims each year. Circulation about the mountain can be a daunting experience in which the 18,400 ft pass north of the mountain, the Drolma La, must be crossed.

The vicinity of the mountain is the source of four of South Asia's major rivers, the Indus, the Brahmaputra, the Karnali, which feeds the Ganga, and the Sutlej. Mount Kailash is revered by four different religions as one of the most sacred pilgrimage destinations in Asia. Hindus regard Mount Kailash as the manifestation of Mount Meru, the axis of the world, around which revolve the sun, Moon, planets and stars. It is considered to be a bridge between the celestial and terrestrial realms. Lord Shiva and his consort Parvathi reside on its summit The Jains view the mountain as the place where their first prophet obtained enlightenment. Tibetan Buddhists also view the mountain as Mount Meru, like an axis of a milling stone, the centre around which all revolves. Pilgrimage to Mount Kailash has been described as the 'ultimate pilgrimage', probably the most difficult in Asia and perhaps in the world, covering great distances at high altitudes and harsh conditions. The Bonpo and Jains circle the mountain in a counter-clockwise direction, while Buddhists and Hindus follow it in a clockwise manner, paralleling the apparent diurnal motion of the sun, Moon, planets, and stars.

The major festival in the vicinity of the mountain is Saka Dawa, which occurs on the full Moon of May-June. At that time an 80' tall flagpole, festooned with prayer flags is raised, celebrating the Buddha's birthday. Not just a celebration,

Figure 5. Three forms of human interaction with mountains: (left) Mount Kailash (6714 m, 22028 ft) and Chorten Kangri, the entry into the pilgrimage kora at Tarboche (photo by the author). (right) Structures on the summit of Cerro Llulliallaco (6739 m, 22,100 ft) (photo by Grahm Zimmerman with permission). (lower) Gandaran Frieze of Buddhists circumambulating a stupa, Northwest Pakistan, 2nd Century, CE (Creative Commons, Bitish Museum)

the festival is the time when the 'axis of the universe' is symbolically renewed and order of the cosmos is reaffirmed. The festival is a mixture of ritual, trade fair, and social gathering, to which Tibetans come from great distances. The first act of the circling of the mountain, the *kora*, after leaving the starting point at Darchen (4675m) is the circumambulation the flagpole.

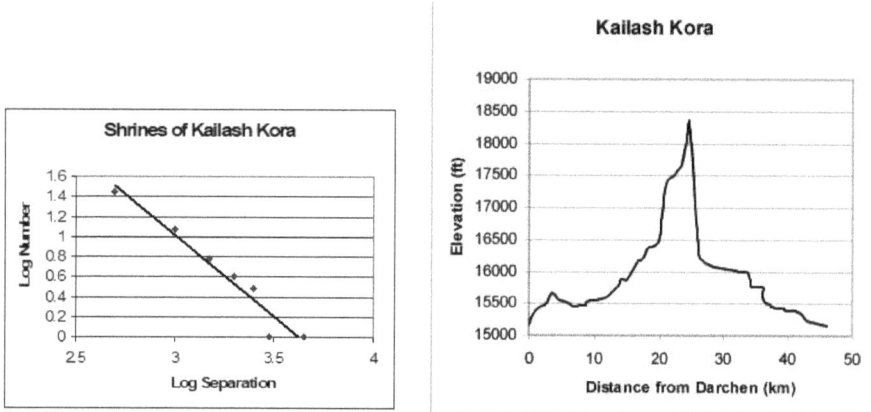

Figure 6. The Kora around Mount Kailash. (left) Log-log plot of the separation of shrines. (right) Profile of the kora.

Considering the multiplicity of religious traditions associated with Kailash as well as its isolation and challenging environment, it is unlikely that the pathway was created in its entirety by any single religious authority. Many people over many generations must have walked the path and established its cumulative meaning. Once thus established, the kora would have become frozen in time to become the pilgrim path experienced today. The separation of the shrines of the kora follows a power law distribution, $N = r^{1.63}$, which is evidence of scale invariance and suggestive of cooperative behaviour of the pilgrims or fractal spacing of land forms around Mt. Kailash. Equal spacing of these shrines is unlikely given their remoteness and the lack of any administrative authority. Random spacing, would, at first glance, seem likely, however that distribution would show a bell-shaped curve, which is not indicated by the measurements (Figure 7). In contrast, the distribution of shrines shown in Figure 6, contains many smaller separations than large ones, consistent with a power law. Features of the natural world, such as braided streams, lakes, coastlines, and faults often are scale invariant. The processes that led to the selection of certain shrines along the Kailash kora involved local geology, established by unusual rock formations and noteworthy views. The resulting scale invariance would then reflect the self-organized criticality of the surrounding physical landscape. However, not all the Kailash shrines are associated with unique landforms. The fundamental process in their establishment suggest a complex interaction between humans and a sacred landscape, an expression the *sacred ecology* of Kailash that couples the vastness of the Tibetan landscape with millennia of Hindu, Buddhist, and Bon traditions.

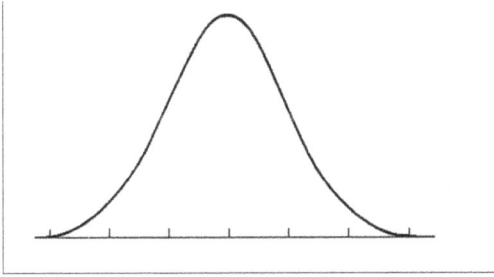

Figure 7. The bell-shaped curve expected for a random distribution.

The pilgrimage circuit of Mount Kailash is a member of a family of nested circular patterns, which range upward and in scale from the clockwise motion of the nine planets around the cosmic mountain to the spinning of Buddhist prayer wheels. These movements are outlined in Table 1. It is possible that some pilgrims do sense that they are participating in a vast network of circular motion. It is extraordinary to see Tibetan pilgrims walking around Mount Kailash, while holding a spinning prayer wheel.

Table 1: Scale Invariant Circulation

1. Revolution of sun, Moon, planets and stars around the axis of the universe.
2. Circulation of pilgrims around Mount Kailash.
3. Circulation of people around villages, sacred lands, and the Indian sub-continent.
4. Circulation of people around temples, stupas, and chortens.
5. Circulation of people around flag poles, shrines and sacred stones.
6. Rotation of large and small prayer wheels.

Varanasi

The longest of the five pilgrimage circuits is the Chaurashikrosha Yatra, which circled today's ruined Shiva temple of Madhyameshvara the Lord of the Centre, which was originally the centre of Varanasi. To circumambulate the temple is to encircle Mount Meru, in a manner similar to circumambulating Mount Kailash.[23] Today the centre of Varanasi is the Vishvanatha temple, the Golden Temple, which is visited by pilgrims at the start and completion of their encircling of the city. Adjacent to Visvanatha is the deep Janavapi well, which represents the underworld with its symbolism of water, darkness, death, and rebirth. As Rana. P. B. Singh has noted, the combination of well and temple establishes a powerful axis mundi. The most popular pilgrimage route in Varanasi is the Panchakroshi, which takes five days to complete, involves 108 shrines and covers 88.5 km.[24] As part of our fieldwork, we measured the locations of every shrine on the Pancakroshi as well as those of the two inner pilgrimage circuts with differential GPS receivers. We found that the spacing of shrines follows a power law, $N = r^{-1.47}$ as shown in Figure 8, similar to the distribution of shrines we measured around Mount Kaiash. In both places pilgrims believed they were walking around the axis of the world.

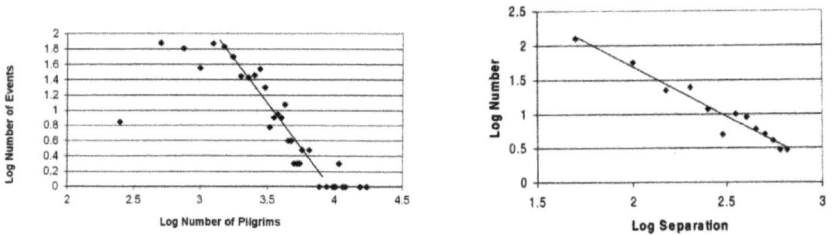

Figure 8. (left) Log-log plot of the numbers of groups of pilgrims of various sizes arriving at Asi Ghat, Varanasi. (right) Log-log plot of the separation of shrines on the Panchakroshi Yatra and the three inner yatras of Varanasi.

In addition, as part of the survey at Asi Ghat, we recorded the gender and approximate ages of over 800,000 bathers and pilgrims. The distribution of numbers of pilgrims follows another power law, $N = r^{2.17}$, as is also shown in Figure 8. Our research reveals the extraordinary fact that the flow of pilgrims around Varanasi as well as around Mount Kailash mimics the behaviour of many other features of the natural world that reach criticality, such as avalanches and trees in a forest.

Cosmic mountains in South Asia are contained in a complex ritual system entangling Hindu and Buddhist temples, the axis of the world, and cosmic cities. Circumambulation rather than ascent is the norm. According to the Buddhists who live there, sacred mountains, such as Mount Kailash, should not be climbed. They believe that they share with sacred cities a uniqueness of location as well association with legendary feats by gods and humans. The gods/goddesses of the mountains are, for Tibetans, embodiments of the mountains and, as such, they are agentive and engage in reciprocal contracts with humans (an example being how the sherpa Tenzin Norgay who climbed Everest with the first Westerner to do so, attributed his safety and success on that voyage to right relationships with the goddess of the mountain). In the valleys where I conducted field research, a ritual festival was held annually for Mountain Gods who interacted with the local communities they protected via spirit mediums. In contrast, mountains in the Andes, especially in south where they may not be snow covered throughout the year, are climbed. In the Inca Empire, mountains like the rest of the physical world were considered to be alive and agentive, capable of influencing human life and engaging in reciprocal contracts with humans.

The Andes

> "And up the ladder of the earth I climbed
> through the dreadful thickets of lost forests
> to you, Machu Picchu." [25]

The Andean theme of ascent between worlds may have arrived with the first migrants to the coast of Chile as early as 14,000 BCE. Not only did those who reached the coastline need to ascend from the narrow coastline to the mountainous interior, but they also may have carried with them the shamanic tradition of spiritual ascent or shamanic flight. Eliade pointed out the evidence for a transfer of shamanic ritual traditions from Asia to South America among the Mapuche of southern Chile.[26] The suggestion of such a transfer is also encouraged by recent studies of mitochondrial DNA by M. Bodner et al.[27] The first archaeological evidence for ritual ascent in the Andes is found in the major pyramid of Caral dating to 2650 BCE, which has a staircase leading upward from a sunken circular plaza to the summit. This may have enabled the ritual passage across the three worlds from the lowest to the highest as well as the transformation of the shaman from a human to a deity.

Apus

In addition to the ascent of mountains, reciprocity between humans and mountains has been a fundamental feature of the Andean world. Humans sought to achieve reciprocal relationships with the powerful forces of the land and sky by making offerings, which they hoped would require a substantial positive response.[28] Mountains, referred to as *apus*, were understood as living beings who were, and still are, capable of being alternately very dangerous or benign, providing water for agriculture or responsible for droughts, avalanches, earthquakes, and fierce weather.

One tradition that predated the Inca and still continues to this day involves *apachetas*, piles of stones that were placed as offering on mountain tops, mountain passes, or other significant parts of a journey.[29] Some *apachetas* were representations of nearby mountains. Other *apachetas* could embody the essence of the mountain, to which offerings were made such as children, coca leaves, shells maize, and stones. These shaped stones ore piles of stones were and are thought to have had the full essence and power of the mountain itself.

Some groups in Peru believed mountains to be their ancestors. Similar to the belief that bears were the ancestors of Basques as well as other early Europeans certain groups in the Andes believed they were descended from mountains, as evidenced by an aspect of mountain worship involving cranial deformation.[30] In the Colca Valley of Peru, skulls of children were molded into the shapes of the mountains which they believed were their ancestors descended. [31] For example the Collagua shaped their heads to resemble their primary huaca, a snow-capped volcano. They bound the heads of their children to make them tall, thin, and slightly tapering, in imitation of the peak's shape. The residents of the Cabana province believed they descended from another holy mountain that was flat, and their children acquired flattened heads. People thus became mountains as some rock *apachetas* became mountains. Mountains became pyramids as early at 3000 BCE at Caral, and stairways became routes of ritual ascent. Stairs appeared at Chankillo, which, with its thirteen towers, provides a clear-cut demonstration of ascent rituals.

Chankillo

Chankillo has become one of the most frequently described sites in the Casma Valley, lying 315 km north of Lima.[32] It is a place of stairways, a celebration of ascent and descent: twenty five sets of stairs connect its thirteen towers. (Figure 11) Ritual processions may have climbed up and down twelve of these towers.[33] These towers are themselves ascending platforms, built successively higher such that, as one moves upward platform by platform, one proceeds to higher and higher worlds. The orientations of the platforms slowly rotate from a terrestrial world (north-south) to alignment with the solstices, as if celebrants are moving from the terrestrial realm to the solar realm. The stairways are steep, making for arduous passage, not inappropriate for pilgrimages, spiritual journeys, and liminal experiences. Only the highest tower has one stairway, on its north side, indicating that it was the final destination for upward ritual movement. These towers may have been miniature mountains associated with the rituals of moving through the three worlds. The controversial suggestion has been made that these towers served as a horizon calendar. However, with their steps ritual processions across the towers must have preceded any use as horizon markers.

Huacas

The Inca ruler, Pachacuti, is credited with establishing Cusco as the capital of the Inca Empire, embarking on a course of imperial expansion, and establishing a system of *huacas* in the Cusco basin and beyond. Running water was understood to be an energizing and animating life force in Andean cultures, associated with the Quechua verb, *camay*. The agent of *camay*, the 'camayer' is known as *camac*. In the cosmology described in the Huarochirí manuscript, life is born from the embrace of feminine earth by masculine water, homologous to the growth of plants from soil when moistened by water.[34] Rocks, like seeds, could become alive with the assistance of water. The circulation of running water and the pouring of offertory liquids could animate certain inanimate objects to become *huacas*, which were then understood to be sentient beings with extraordinary and superhuman powers. *Huacas* were involved in ancestor worship, which was a driving force of the Inca Empire and with water control, which was a vital necessity in the water-challenged Andean world. Mountains and *apachetas* could be *huacas*. Ollantaytambo, one of the royal estates of Pachacuti in the Sacred Valley, contains impressive hallmarks of his reign. Its massive stonework, elaborate stone carvings, and the water shrine of Incamisana with water channels and fountains appear to display the animating power of water.[35] Cliffs on the western side of the Incamisana contain a myriad of carved nonfunctional stairways, waters channels, and niches (Figure 11). The cliff face may have been a massive *huaca*, animated and empowered by sunlight and the flowing water at its base.[36] These non-functional stairs, which are found throughout the Inca empire, are extraordinary, in the words of Pasternosto, in their 'obsessive' abundance.[37] (Figure 11)

Figure 11. (upper left) Stairways at Ollantaytambo. (photo by the author);
(upper right) The Third Stone at Saihuite- note the five scales of steps (photo by S.
Gullberg); (lower) The towers and stairs of Chankillo (left photo by Carlos Aranibar;
right photo by the author)

Machu Picchu and Huayna Picchu

Perched high on a narrow ridge of granite, Machu Picchu, contains more
examples of both functional and non-functional stairways. A remarkable feature
of these stairways, here and elsewhere in the Inca empire, is their multiplicity
of scales.[38] For example, the cave below the Torreon, known as the Royal
Mausoleum contains two adjacent starways with scales, which differ in size
by a factor of two. The huaca near the main gate identified as the Ceremonial
Rock contains multiple scales, as does the River Intiwatana in the canyon below
Machu Picchu.[39] The extraordinary Third Stone of Sayhuite contains steps with
five different sizes (Figure 11). These appear to be examples of scale invariance.
The greatest huaca of Machu Picchu, the rock enclosed by the Torreon, appears
to be a smaller version of Huayna Picchu, with a cave at its base with a solar-
illuminated rock on the summit. It is clear from the manner in which Huayna
Picchu is framed in the major southern gateway to Machu Picchu that the peak
was one of its most significant features of the area, a smaller version, perhaps, of
the nearby sacred mountain of Salcantay, another example of Fritz's proposed
symbolic resonance.

Ritual ascents of Huayna Picchu, from the north, directly from the Urubamba River, may have preceded the establishment of Machu Picchu. The peak may have been the primary sacred feature of the area. Nearly encircled by the Urbamba River, the peak would thus be empowered and animated by water through the process of *camay*. Its precipitous northern stairway ascends 390 m from the largest double jamb doorway of Machu Picchu. Double jamb doorways were characteristically entries into ceremonial areas or residences of Inca nobility. The doorway is adjacent to the cave known as the Temple of the Moon, which contains the most finely crafted niches for the mummies in Machu Picchu, which may have been carried to the summit on special occasions. The stairway may be an explicit metaphor for ascent from the water of the Urubamba River and the cave of the underworld to the upper realms. Once the summit had been reached, the southern stairway would have been descended to reach Machu Picchu. Such ritual ascent and descent of stairs are similar to the ritual double stairways of Chankillo. These precipitous stairways of Huayna Picchu may once have been the principal entry into Machu Picchu for pilgrims and ritual specialists.

Llullaillaco

The most dramatic example of the meme of ascent and the agentive power of mountains was the climbing and the building of ceremonial structures by the Inca on many of their highest peaks, the highest being Llullaillaco with an altitude of 22,110 feet. (Figure 5) It is the seventh highest mountain in the Americas, containing on its summit the world's highest archaeological site, which has been carefully excavated by Johan Reinhard and colleagues.[40] There are more than 100 high mountains with Inca shrines on their summits.[41] Of these, sixteen shrines containing mummies have been documented and most of these involved child sacrifice.

Llulliallaco can be climbed only during the southern summer, between November to March. The most likely times for pilgrimage would be days around December solstice, the time of the major Inca celebration of Capac Raymi. The timing of this celebration would have required planning and precision. Everything on the mountain had to be ready for the participants. Weather would have added additional uncertainty, but since the sun does not move appreciably for a week around solstice, the date of the celebration was flexible. The route upward contains a number of resting places (*dharamsalas* in India) for pilgrims, priests, and sacrificial victims.

The summit platform, thirty feet long, twenty feet wide, contained the bodies of three children, a thirteen-year-old girl and a boy and girl aged four-

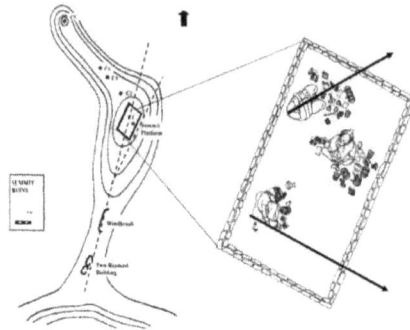

Figure 12. Summit platform showing the orientation of burials. The lower, southern, burial faced December solstice sunrise and the upper faced June solstice sunrise. The platform is at the northern end of the summit ridge. Diagram modified from Reinhard and Ceruti, *Inca Rituals and Sacred Mountains*: pp. 63 and 71.

to-five years. (Figure 12) The platform is rotated a little more than 10 degrees away from the natural ridge line suggesting an intention to orient it to December solstice sunrise. Estimating atmospheric refraction from the summit of the mountain, it appears the upper edge of the sun would appear about one and a half degrees from the orientation of the platform.[42] The young boy may thus have been intentionally placed facing the first gleam of the sun on a date near December solstice.

The thirteen-year-old girl was facing northeast, approximately 53° north of the boy, to within 0.6° of the first gleam of June sunrise. However, the mountain cannot be climbed during the winter month of June in the southern hemisphere. There are two methods that could have been used to estimate the point on the horizon where the June solstice sun first appears. After reaching the summit, a member of the climbing party who reached the summit before sunset may have noted the direction of the last gleam of the setting sun on December solstice. Turning the exact opposite direction he would have faced the approximate position of the rising sun at June solstice. A second approach would have been to measure ahead of time the angular separation of sunrise on summer and winter solstice somewhere near the base of the mountain and use that to establish the orientation of the girl. Both of these approaches to determine the direction of June solstice on the mountain appear feasible, and, consequently, it is not unreasonable to suggest that the burials in the summit platform marked the two major solar festivals of the Inca. The third child is approximately facing the major summit, perhaps honoring the mountain deity or, in fact, becoming the bride of the mountain. Llulliallaco remained the highest mountain that was climbed by humans for nearly four hundred years. It was only until Matthias Zurbriggen climbed Aconcagua (6962 m, 22841 ft) in 1897 that humans set foot on a higher mountain.[43]

Conclusions

The field research described in this chapter was initiated to learn more about the ways in which mountains influence people and have the power to establish religious or spiritual interactions with those who live within them or are drawn to them.

The mountains of the Himalaya seemed to be primarily platforms or manifestations of the gods or *axes mundi*. In the Andes, mountains were alive, could influence people living around them with whom people could establish reciprocal compact. Especially in southern Peru where the summits were not snow covered during the southern summer, the mountains could be climbed and offerings left on their summits. Mountains shared with the sun the distinction of being powerful agentive features in the Inca World. Associated with dangerous weather, droughts, avalanches, and rock falls, mountains could influence human life for ill or good. Of the three shamanic realms, they were the highest that could be reached through the meme of ascent.

Circumambulation of Mount Kailash, not attempts to reach its summit, established the base of the mountain as a sacred space. Likewise, time spent by Padma sambhava in the vicinity of Mount Everest blessed its valleys, which became immensely more valuable for pilgrims and local residents than attempting to reach its summit. While pilgrims continue to circle unclimbed Mount Kailash, the bond between people and sacred mountains of the Himalayas has been broken, first in 1907 with the ascent of Trisul (7120m) by Tom Longstaff. British climbers first attempted Mount Everest in 1921, to the dismay of Tibetans who considered it beyond comprehension to court death by attempting to climb a high mountain.[44] After many attempts, the British with significant support by Sherpas, succeeded in reaching the summit of Mount Everest in 1953.

In spite of numerous requests to the contrary by local communities practically all the high peaks of south Asia have been climbed. The third highest mountain in the world, Kangchenjunga, is considered by the Sikkimese as the divine protector of their land. In 1955, when a British expedition announced their plans to climb the mountain, the Indian, Sikkimese, and Nepali governments requested that they cancel their plans for fear of provoking the mountain deity. An agreement was made that climbers would stop short of the summit. The climbers kept their word, turning back twenty feet from the summit, 'leaving no foot mark on the summit'.[45] Since that time, however, over 200 climbers have reached the summit, and judging from many published photos, the initial promise has not been kept. On another 8000-meter peak, Manaslu, in 1964 Japanese climbers encountered hostile villagers, who claimed that previous expeditions had displeased the gods, causing avalanches that destroyed a monastery and killed 18 villagers. The expedition was forced to retreat, but the mountain was climbed two years later.

Commercial climbing of Mount Everest began in the 1990s, and by the end of 2018 Mount Everest has been climbed an astonishing 8306 times from both the Nepalese and Tibetan sides. During the climbing season the once remote, quiet, and sacred valley of Rombuk is overrun with climbers, porters, guides and mountains of garbage. The Chinese, certainly no fans of Tibetan culture, are developing the valley as a major tourist destination, with a paved road from Lhasa to the monastery and basecamp. They are also building a huge climbing center, museum and hotel in Old Tingri, some forty miles from the Rongbuk Valley. Although mountaineering in the Himalayas has become a very popular sport, Hindu and Buddhist pilgrims continue to circumambulate Mount Kailash as well as countless other temples that are representations of Mount Meru. On the other side of our planet, travelers still toss rocks onto Andean *apachetas*, creating their own versions of mountains.

Notes

1.   Richard Dawkins, *The Selfish Gene* (Oxford: Oxford University Press, 1977), p.192; Edward O. Wilson, *Consilience- the Unity of Knowledge* (New York: Knopf, 1998), p.352.

2.   J. McKim Malville, 'Passages between Worlds: Heaven, Earth, and the Underworld in the Andean Cosmos', *Culture and Cosmos* 20 (2017): pp.31–58.

3.   Johan Reinhard and Maria Constanza Ceruti, *Inca Rituals and Sacred Mountains: A Study of the World's Highest Archaeological Sites* (Los Angeles, CA: Cotsen Institute of Archaeology, 2010), pp.33–98.

4.   J. McKim Malville, 'Astrophysics, Cosmology, and the Interior Space of Indian Myths and Temples', in K. Vatsyayan, ed., *Concepts of Space: Ancient and Modern* (New Delhi: Indira Gandhi National Centre for the Arts, 1989), pp.123–44, p.138.

5.   George Michell, *The Hindu Temple* (Chicago, IL: The University of Chicago Press, 1977), p.66.

6.   Ali Bulent Çambel, *Applied Chaos Theory: A Paradigm for Complexity* (Boston, MA: Academic Press, Inc., 1993), p. 180.

7.   Per Bak, *How Nature Works: The Science of Self-Organized Criticality* (New York: Copernicus, 1996), p.1–64.

8.   John M. Fritz, 'Paleopsychology today: Ideational systems and Human Adaptation in Prehistory', in C. Redman, ed., *Social Archaeology: Beyond Subsistence and Dating* (New York: Academic Press, 1978), pp.37–59; John M. Fritz, 'Chaco Canyon and Vijayanagara: Proposing Spatial Meaning in Two Societies,' in E. Ingersoll and G. Bronitsky, eds, *Mirror and Metaphor* (Lanham, MD: University Press of America, 1987), pp.314–49.

9.   F. Stahl, 'The Centre of space: Construction and Discovery', in K. Vatsyayan, ed., *Concepts of Space, Ancient and Modern* (New Delhi: Indira Gandhi National Centre for the Arts, 1991), pp.83–100, p.83.

10.   Bradley W. Carroll and Dale A. Ostlie, *An Introduction to Modern Astrophysics,* 2nd edn (Cambridge: Cambridge University Press, 2018), pp.1144–1229.

11.   Robert L. Brown, *Ganesh: Studies of an Asian God* (Albany, NY: State University of New York Press, 1991).

12.   Surinder M. Bhardwaj, 'Circulation and Circumambulation', in J. McKim Malville and B. Saraswati, eds, *Pilgrimage: Sacred Landscapes and Self-Organized Complexity* (New Delhi: Indira Gandhi National Centre for the Arts, 2009), pp.47–58, pp.52–53

13.   John Snelling, *The Sacred Mountain* (London: East-West Publications, 1990), pp.25–35.

14.   Mircea Eliade, *Patterns in Comparative Religion* (New York: New American Library, 1974), p.368.

15.   Hugh Richardson, *A Cultural History of Tibet* (Boulder, CO: Shambhala, 1995).

16.   Donald S. Lopez Jr, Introduction, in Donald S. Lopez Jr., ed., *Religions of Tibet in Practice* (Princeton, NJ: Princeton University Press, 1997), p.7.

17.   Richard J. Kohn, *Lord of the Dance: The Mani Rimdu Festival in Tibet and Nepal* (Albany, NY: New York University Press, 2001), pp.35–48.

18.   Wade Davis, *Into the Silence: The Great War, Mallory, and the Conquest of Everest* (New York: Vintage. 2011), p.446.

19.   Davis, *Into the Silence*, p.400.

20.   Davis, *Into the Silence*, p.269.

21.   Davis, *Into the Silence*, pp.499–500.

22.   Davis, pp.310-311.

23.   J. McKim Malville and Rana B. P. Singh, 'Astronomy in the Mythology and Ritual of India: The Sun Temples of Varanasi', *Vistas in Astronomy* 39, no. 4 (1995): pp.431–49.

24.   Rana P. B. Singh, 'Sacred Geometry of India's Holy City, Varanasi: Kashi as Cosmogram', in Rana P. B. Singh, ed., *The Spirit and Power and Place: Human Environment and Sacrality* (Varanasi: National Geographical Society of India, 1993), pp.189–216.

25.   Pablo Neruda, *Alturas de Machu Picchu*, 1950; English translation by Lito Tejada-Flores, 1998, p.15.

26.   Mircea Eliade, *Shamanism: Archaic Techniques of Ecstasy* (Princeton, NJ: Princeton University Press, 1964), p.53, pp.122–25.

27.   Martin Bodner, Ugo A. Perego, Gabriela Huber, Liane Fendt, Alexander W. Röck, Bettina Zimmermann, Anna Olivieri, Alberto Gómez-Carballa, Hovirag Lancioni, Norman Angerhofer, Maria Cecilia Bobillo, Daniel Corach, Scott R. Woodward, Antonio Salas, Alessandro Achilli, Antonio Torroni, Hans-Jurgen Bandelt, and Walther Parson, 'Rapid Coastal Spread of First Americans: Novel Insights from South America's Southern Cone Mitochondrial Genomes', *Genome Research* 22 (2012): pp.811-20.

28. Lawrence A, Kuznar, 'An Introduction to Andean Religious Ethnoarchaeology: Preliminary Results and Future Directions', in Lawrence A. Kuznar, ed., *Ethnoarchaeology of Andean South America* (Ann Arbor, MI: International Monographs in Prehistory, 2001), pp.42–43.

29. Carolyn J. Dean, *A Culture of Stone: Inka Perspectives on Rock* (Durham, NC: Duke University Press, 2010), pp.56–61.

30. Roslyn M. Frank, 'A status report: A review of research on the origins and diffusion of the belief in a Sky Bear', in Fabio Silva, J. McKim Malville, Tore Lomsdalen, and Frank Ventura, eds, *The Materiality of the Sky: Proceedings of the 22nd Conference of the European Society for Astronomy in Culture*, University of Wales (Lampeter: Sophia Centre Press, 2016), pp.79–87, p.80.

31. Deborah E. Blom, 'Embodying borders: human body modification and diversity in Tiwanaku Society, *Journal of Anthropological Archaeology* 24 (2005): pp.1–24, p.4.

32. J. McKim Malville, 'Astronomy and ceremony at Chankillo: An Andean Perspective', in Clive Ruggles, ed., *Archaeoastronomy and Ethnoastronomy: Building Bridges between Cultures, Oxford IX International Symposium on Archaeoastronomy* (Cambridge: Cambridge University Press, 2011), pp.154–61.

33. Shelia Porzorski and Thomas Porzorski, *Early Settlement and Subsistence in the Casma Valley, Peru* (Iowa City, IA: University of Iowa Press, 2002), p.99.

34. Frank Solomon and George L. Urioste, trans, *The Huarochirí Manuscript* (Austin, TX: The University of Texas Press, 1991), p.16.

35. Kenneth R. Wright, Arminda .M. Gibaja Oviedo, Gordon F. McEwan, Richard W. Miksad, and Ruth M. Wright, *Incamisana: Engineering an Inca Water Temple*. Weston: American Society of Civil Engineers, 2016), pp.71–80.

36. J. McKim Malville, 'Animating the Inanimate: Camay and Astronomical Huacas of Peru', in J. Alberto Rubiño-Martín, Juan Antonio Belmonte, Francisco Prada and Anxton Alberd, eds, *Cosmology Across Cultures* (San Francisco, CA: Astronomical Society of the Pacific, 2009), pp.261–66.

37. César Paternosto, *The Stone and the Thread: Andean Roots of Abstract Art* (Austin, TX: University of Texas Press, 1996), p.71.

38. J. McKim Malville, 'Passages between Worlds: Heaven, Earth, and the Underworld in the Andean Cosmos', *Culture and Cosmos* 20 (2017): pp.31–58.

39. Steven Gullberg and J. McKim Malville, 'The River Intiwatana: Huaca Sanctuary on the Urubamba', *Mediterranean Archaeology and Archaeometry* 14 (2014): pp.179–87.

40. Johan Reinhard and Maria Constanza Ceruti, *Inca Rituals and Sacred Mountains: A Study of the World's Highest Archaeological Sites* (Los Angeles, CA: Cotsen Institute of Archaeology, 2010), pp.61–85.

41. Constanza Ceruti, 'Human Bodies as Objects of Dedication at Inca Mountain Shrines (North-Western Argentina)', *World Archaeology* 36 (2004): pp.103–22, p. 103, p. 119.

42. J. McKim Malville, 'The Archaeostronomy of High Altitude Inca Ceremonialism', *Mediterranean Archaeology and Archaeometry* 18 (2018): pp.199–204, p. 202.

43. Richard Sale and John Cleare, *Climbing the World's 14 Highest Mountains: The History of the 8000-Meter Peaks* (Seattle, WA: Mountaineers Books, 2000), p.24.

44. Davis, *Into the Silence*, pp.269–73.

45. Charles Evans, *Kanchenjunga, The Untrodden Peak* (New York: E. P. Dutton, 1957), pp.127–128.

3

NATURE, ECOLOGY AND EARLY YEARS EDUCATION

Glenda Tinney

Introduction

As someone who trained and worked as an ecologist and now works as an early years' lecturer I have often pondered how children and adults (including myself) have become disconnected from the natural cycles of the environments on which we depend. In recent discussions with colleagues interested in Harmony principles and the consequences for the wider sustainability crisis, I am increasingly drawn to consider the implications of this where supporting early childhood education and care are concerned.[1]

The focus provided by the notion of 'Harmony' on holism, interdisciplinary approaches, wellbeing and love has several parallels with the aims of early years' policy and practice in Wales, as well as the wider international context.[2] Recent new curriculum developments in Wales within the formally-maintained education sector also provide evidence of a focus on a more holistic approach to education and a central place for wellbeing, ethics and citizenship.[3] Harmony as outlined by HRH The Prince of Wales, Tony Juniper and Ian Skelly suggests '"right action" cannot happen without "right thinking"'.[4] In this chapter I want to consider the implications of 'right thinking' in the context of young children and the adults that support them in terms of encouraging learning from the non-human environment, a sense of place and connectedness to the world.

Context

I spent many happy springs in my early childhood searching for frog spawn and watching tadpoles in the ponds and ditches of Ceredigion in mid Wales. Like many children of my generation in the 1970s and 1980s, playing and exploring outdoors was a natural part of childhood experiences. However, these fond memories have a parallel counterpoint with the memory of returning to these ponds not long after to find them drained and destroyed. The feeling of intense sadness that the frogs would no longer be able to return have overtaken my earlier, happier memories, even 40 years later. Louise Chawla has discussed 'significant life experiences' in nature as being formative to why adults in later life become involved in roles linked to environmentalism or conservation.[5] For me, this moment of loss has stayed as a significant memory and may explain my own fascination with ecology and sharing this interest with others. The same feelings of loss have often returned in adulthood when listening to people talk about the current climate change crisis or plastic pollution panic. Bob Jickling retells accounts of different people's experiences of anger, loss and sadness when faced with first hand experiences of the damage or destruction of other parts of the natural world.[6] These experiences are highlighted as transformative in terms of changing these people's subsequent behaviours towards the non-human world. In his account, Jickling suggests transformational moments are experiential in that they are experienced first-hand by the person who is transformed and cannot be measured by conventional educational assessments, but involve instead listening to, and learning from more than the human world.[7] This resonates with my own childhood memories where the loss of the frogspawn and tadpoles was a part of my real lived experience. As a child brought up in a small Welsh-speaking rural community, the demise of the frog ponds also ran in parallel with the decline of the same community, with the local school closing, rural depopulation and the decline in the Welsh language, all close to my personal cultural context.

However, there is a danger that these melancholic memories are isolated from wider complexities. I was also part of the community who economically benefited from the agricultural intensification driving the draining of the land in Ceredigion during the 1980s. Despite my growing sadness at the changes in my local and global environment, I was also a member of the generation who embraced single-use plastics, became increasingly dependent on car travel, provided my own children much less freedom to play outdoors, and consumed products that have in some part sustained global inequalities and environmental injustice. Therefore, my discussion in this chapter, which ponders learning from the non-human environment as one way of engendering a sense of place, is not intended as a nostalgic and romanticised view of a better past childhood. In a rapidly changing Euro-American context our opportunities to engage with the non-human world have also changed. I searched for frog spawn, built dens, and made mud pies in a world where mobile digital devices, 24-hour TV and social media were not yet part of my world. Digital media, however, is for many of today's children in Wales the lens from which they interact with their environment and construct their own sense of place. I would argue my early years experiences were through a different lens, one not dominated by the human world.

The pond, the water, the boggy field and soil also changed me and my own interactions with the world. As noted by Robert Michael Pyle in *The Thunder Tree* (p. xvii) '... most people I speak with seem to have a ditch somewhere – or a creek, meadow, woodlot, or marsh... These are places of initiation, where the borders between ourselves and other creatures break down, where the earth gets under our nails and a sense of place gets under our skin'.[8] Could a move away from these first hand experiences– such as that of the frog spawn and pond integral to my own childhood – have implications for young children's development and learning, where their first hand interactions are increasingly technological and are removed from the direct and visceral interactions with the living and non-living parts of the non-human world? As noted by Barad and discussed later in the context of the new materialism, '"We" are not outside observers of the world. Nor are we simply located at particular places in the world; rather, we are part of the world in its ongoing intra-activity'.[9]

Current early childhood education and care context

Early years' education, care literature and practice places an emphasis on learning through play which is reflective of Froebel's view that 'play at this stage is not trivial; it is highly serious and of deep significance'.[10] In its inception, the Welsh early years' curriculum Foundation Phase for 3–7 years old was also based on philosophies and theory which underpin the significance of learning through play.[11] However, recent reports point to a lack of consistency and understanding of learning through play, especially the open-ended, free play which (as in my own childhood experiences) was child-led and I believe, in my own context, supported transformative moments[16] in relation to empathising and learning with the non-human parts of my world. Derby, cited in Jickling, suggests that formal education is '... characterised by fragmentation, emotionlessness and [is] exacerbated by privileging of epistemic foundations such as anthropocentrism, reductionism, linear causality and dualism'.[12] This resonates with the discourse in Wales, with criticism of an overly assessed, didactic curriculum with negative implications for children's wellbeing and rights.[13]

Furthermore, in terms of outdoor learning, data suggests that in the UK children in the 21st century are spending less time outdoors than previous generations.[14] Richard Louv pointed towards 'nature deficit disorder' in relation to the negative health and emotional consequences of children's lack of experiences outdoors in nature, while Peter Gray provided a strong argument for the central importance of free, child-led play for children's learning, with this including independent play outdoors.[15] Gray also argued that the opportunities for independent freely chosen play have been limited in the Euro-American context to the detriment of a child's education.[16] In terms of a sense of place, the ponds, woodlands and fields that were my own play areas have been replaced by digital experiences, with outdoor experiences taking place in more structured play environments such as playgrounds, where free play is increasingly limited.[17]

In the literature there is a consensus that outdoor experiences and engaging with the non-human world offer benefits for children cognitively, physically, emotionally, socially and linguistically.[18] This is underpinned by the work of the earliest pedagogues Johann Heinrich Pestalozzi and Friedrich Froebel in terms of the significant benefits of children learning outdoors.[19] They described an outdoor environment which provided the opportunities for children to explore, discover and be curious, as opposed to structured adult-led activities which happen to take place outside. There is also a focus in early years' sustainability literature that engaging with the non-human environment is significant in supporting an understanding and empathy for the world, which could support better sustainability practice in the future.[20] In Wales, the Foundation Phase curriculum for young children (3–7 years) afforded outdoor learning the same status as indoor learning; however, this aim was not always observed in practice, as outdoor experiences were often adult led and structured, thereby preventing children the opportunity to also interact with the environment independently and according to their own interests and curiosity.[21] Transformative experiences which could change behaviour in terms of using resources more sustainability or respecting the value of the non-human world, according to Jickling , are dependent on hands on, personal experiences and thus I would argue that young children need a diversity of different experiences which allow for transformation, and this includes child-led engagement with the non-human environment.[22]

It is pertinent to note here that I have chosen to refer in this chapter to the non-human world/environment as opposed to 'nature'. Nature is a contested concept.[23] As an ecologist I would have considered nature to represent ecosystems which include the non-living and living environment. Inherent in this representation was a debate whether the human species was separate or simply another constituent part of the ecosystem. Authors such as Bruno Latour argue that separating 'nature' and society, or human and non-human, is a modern phenomenon that ignores the mutual interconnectedness of both.[24] In Wales and the UK, as globally, many areas referred to as natural, wild or wilderness are national parks or areas of outstanding beauty which are the product of and maintained by human interactions.[25]

However, much early years' literature refers to 'nature' when considering children's experiences playing outdoors, which in my view is a useful catchall for the non-human environment. Moss and lichen growing on a wall, a small

patch of trees, a grassy lawn, a puddle, falling rain, sunlight on the school yard
–all are part of the non-human world. They are the everyday opportunities
children in Euro-American cultures have to interact with the non-human world
and to understand our interconnectedness with it. Even landscapes perceived
as 'wild' or 'wilderness' are, in the context of the UK, a product of centuries
of human-environment interactions. Understanding these 'fuzzy borders' and
interconnections come from children having a diversity of opportunities to
interact with the non-human world in all its contexts.[26]

However, despite the acknowledgment of outdoor learning and play within
early years' literature this does not necessarily correlate with respecting or
empathising with the non-human world. Hillevi Lenz-Taguchi discusses that
early years' theory and practice takes an anthropocentric view of the world.[27]
The emphasis is on the child in terms her wellbeing, learning and rights,
whether supporting the constructivist approaches to early years pedagogy with
an emphasis on learning in real environments, 'young scientists' experimenting
in and learning from their environment, or exploring socio-constructivist or
socio-cultural approaches which consider the role of a child's peers and adult
community in supporting learning.[28]

The discourse in early years is often a dualism around the role of the adult-
child relationship, with debates around the view of children as independent and
competent learners on one hand as opposed to being dependent or led by the adult
on the other hand. As Lenz-Taguchi notes, until recently early years' discourse
reflects that '… only humans are granted agency and power to act, to learn, to
transform'.[29] On the other hand, the Reggio Emilia approach recognises, 'the
environment as the child's third teacher' alongside the parent and educational
community.[30] However, the Reggio Emilia philosophy does not specifically
highlight the outdoor environment and the focus remains human-centric in terms
of a focus on the benefits for the child rather than acknowledging the child-
environment interaction and how they can influence each other. Sustainable
development discourse also takes a very anthropocentric, technocentric and
accommodationist view.[31] Humans recycle, lower carbon emissions, develop walk
to school schemes to save themselves as a species into the future, as opposed to
valuing the non-human world intrinsically. However, ecocentric philosophies and
deep ecology champion a much more nature-centred stance.[32] According to these
philosophies, non-human entities have an intrinsic value and the human species
is part of this as opposed to being of a higher value or more significant. Authors
such as Gray suggest that traditional hunter-gatherer or indigenous communities
appear to understand this interconnection and thus their cultural behaviours and
lifestyles are more in tune with the interactions of their ecosystem.[33]

In comparison, industrialised cultures have damaged and significantly altered much of their own ecosystem and that of ecosystems far beyond their own homes due to their separation from the non-human world. However, Milton suggests that this is not wholly accurate as any indigenous 'oneness' with nature is an environmentalist myth.[34] Nevertheless, significantly, Euro-American communities were hunter-gathers at some point in history and have embraced an increasingly anthropocentric stance during the course of their development. Practicing a deep ecology in the reality of an industrial society would be difficult without revolutionary changes to social, political and economic systems. In such a context it may be pertinent to consider if, for young children reengaging with daisy, dandelion, acorn, spider, pebble, stick as significant 'non-human others '– equivalent to Vygotsky's 'more knowledgeable others' – can practically support the valuing of the non-human parts of the world.[35] This of course is difficult to qualify. Anecdotally, the publication of books such as the *The Lost Words* and updates to children's dictionaries that omit the names of historically more familiar plants and animals suggest children could be losing this direct connection with aspects of the non-human world that comes from exploring it directly in their play.[36] There is also an acknowledgment in early years' philosophy that learning first-hand may provide insights that for young children cannot be gained from books and other media. However, whether this learning would lead to an understanding that could support the sustainability discourse into the future and engagement in the patterns and flows significant within the principles of Harmony is unclear. Much of my own early play experiences were with the non-human world, as was the case for many of my contemporaries, and despite this, my generation has contributed much to the sustainability crisis.

In terms of experiences for young children, one area that is gathering momentum in the outdoor play literature, especially in relation to physical development, is affordance.[37] James Gibson suggested that 'The world is perceived not only in terms of object shapes and spatial relationships but also in terms of object possibilities for action (affordances) — perception drives action'.[38] In the context of early childhood, children in any environment will use different objects in different ways. For example, in manufactured play parks children may use slides to slide, swings to swing, monkey bars to hang from. They may also choose to use these objects in creative ways, if they are allowed or encouraged to do so by adults and practitioners, such as climbing up slides, making dens under climbing frames, or playing superhero games between playground structures. However, such affordance is often not observed where specific rules are enforced on how the environment should be used. In environments devoid of manufactured toys, children may see a slope as somewhere to roll, slide, or run down, and they may perceive trees as climbable, huggable, or a resource for bark rubbings among other things. Daisies can be picked, smelled, mixed in potions, drawn or made into daisy chains. In their play, children will therefore have interactions with the non-human that depend on their perceptions of those particular environments and the boundaries provided by adults.

However, affordance is only one part of the complexities of our behaviour and may have no influence beyond the present activity. It is instead long-term opportunities for free play with the non-human world that allows children time for trial and error individually or with peers and adults which can develop initial perceptions of objects into deeper learning. To illustrate, for several weeks I was a participating observer with one seven-year -old child who was practising his tree climbing skills during his outdoor play. He tried to climb several trees but however was disappointed that he was unable to climb very high. The trees he found were not very climbable with very few branches and long slender trunks. Together we discussed the frustration and tried different ways of climbing and supporting him up the tree. We also discussed that these trees may be quite young with less time to develop sturdy branches. A few weeks later on a visit to a local wooded area the child discovered a tree that he was able to climb to a higher point. Having returned to the floor he enthused that, 'That tree was a lot older and had far more branches and that's why I went so high'. This episode revealed that this young child had gained much from the long-term opportunities to practice tree climbing, including confidence and physical development linked to balance and gross motor skills.[39] However, I was interested in this episode in terms of the child's perceptions of climbing the tree. He identified that the tree, due its characteristics of being older and having a more complex architecture, had allowed him to climb. The other trees he encountered were younger and less complex; the child had tried to climb and hang on to these trees to no avail. Their structure and current physical stature did not allow for this. The child showed he experienced much happiness from climbing this particular tree and demonstrated a positive disposition towards this particular tree. For the child this tree had a higher status, a tree which was climbable. Alongside other trees in the same woodland this tree has been transformed into a climbable tree which reflects its special material and physical properties. In subsequent play the child has purposefully looked for similar trees in terms of architecture and complexity which would allow him to climb rather than focusing as previously on his own perceived lack of climbing skills.

Such moments of play also suggest to me opportunities for engaging with concepts such as biodiversity. The child recognised trees as living, complex and with diverse structures. This brief tree climbing experience resonates with my own childhood and experiences I have observed with other children. Finding woodlice, ladybirds, an oil slick rainbow in a puddle, or a rainbow in the sky; these experiences have the possibility to transform their understanding or perception of the non-human world, and in turn these interactions may have implications for these children's feelings towards their non-human world. These learning experiences are part of the child's wider learning in the formal classroom and from structured outdoor play and digital media. My own experience observing early years' practice suggests that the time provided children within the formal curriculum and in every day play to engage with the non-human environment has depleted, and thus this opportunity for learning has been reduced and replaced by adult-led or adult-controlled experiences. Work by Chawla, Jickling and Froebel would however suggest that the need to include these experiences is significant for children's holistic development.[40] Outdoor play, unlike more structured classroom activities, can also support many aspects of learning in a way that many more formal learning activities may not. For example, the boy climbing the tree developed emotionally (confidence, self-esteem), physically (gross and fine motor skills, balance), linguistically (discussion why he was able to climb and using new words), and socially (climbing with others, sharing the experience) by being outdoors playing and climbing, which sitting reading a book, drawing a picture, or filling in a worksheet could not provide in isolation. He also gained several curriculum insights linked to science, mathematics, language, literacy, and physical and creative development.

When reflecting on the climbing tree experience, I maintain that in some ways the child had not climbed a tree himself, but this specific tree had let him become a climber. In recent social studies' discourse the 'material turn' and 'new materialism' have been considered as a post-humanist move away from viewing society from an anthropocentric paradigm and instead recognising the relationships between the human and non-human world.[41] Barad discusses 'intra-action' in the relationships between the human-non human world, suggesting that intra-activity allows a 'way of understanding the world from within and as a part of it'.[42] Although Barad is discussing the quantum level, the focus on understanding the non-human world resonates with my own interest in opportunities for children to interact with the non-human world. Furthermore, in the context of early years practice and research, Lenz-Taguchi has developed new materialism as an alternative paradigm.[43] For example, when discussing a child playing in a sand pit she highlights 'the materiality of the sand can equally transform the notions, conceptions and emotions of the child as much as the child can transform the sand'.[44] The sand is an active player in the child's play and not simply a material which the child alone plays with. In the example of the child climbing the tree and, as Lenz-Taguchi notes for the sand, 'The humans and non-humans are to be understood as performative agents that have power to act and transform each other and themselves'.[45]

However, in practice, different materials are given a different status, depending on the social-cultural context of a given society or time in history. For me there is therefore a danger in over-romanticising the status of the outdoors and concepts of 'nature', especially in a Euro-American context. As noted earlier, 'nature' is a contested construct and the notion of 'wild areas' which are devoid of any human impact in an era of climate change and plastic pollution is problematic. Therefore, it is necessary for us to shift our gaze, thus discovering and valuing the non-human environment as the result of our everyday interactions with it. It then becomes visible in the school yard, pavement cracks, cloud formations, rainfall and everyday interactions. In terms of the education for sustainability context, digital devices and plastic toys are also materials that children and adults interact with. Therefore, if children have less opportunities to engage with the 'non-human' world directly, these become the dominant materials in engendering their sense of place. This can also be compounded because using the outdoor environment in early years' settings requires a risk assessment.[46] Many events linked to supporting practitioners to go outdoors with children, such as Forest School, involve training on risk assessing the environment, reflecting Health and Safety legislation, and setting policy.[47] However, my own reflections on risk assessments that lead to discussions on the dangers of a conker, the implications of stinging nettles, or the myriad of poisonous plants and physical features that could have negative consequences for a child and practitioner leans towards the 'ecophobia' (fear or hatred of non-human living things) discussed by Sobel.[48]

This may explain why, in recent years, there has been a move towards risk-benefit assessments where the risks and benefits of outdoor experiences are recorded.[49] Therefore a slope offers the risk of slipping, but it also offers the benefits of developing balance, body-sense and gross motor skills, further supporting the interaction between human and non-human.[50] Ironically, a short-term anthropocentric view of the world means plastic toys could be perceived as less risky than acorns and conkers, despite the global risks and consequences of plastic pollution which have been made visible in recent years. Driving to a weekly Forest School experience has become one way of engaging with the outdoors, despite the economic and carbon cost. In a sense we have created an environment where play has moved from the woodland, beach, field, wasteground spaces once easily available to children to the perceived safer, indoor, or manicured outdoor spaces. Or where the non-human world is part a 'special' visit or event. Yet in my own childhood the non-human world was in the less 'special' areas, including the cracks in walls, the puddles and ditches. These environments for me resonate with Olds who suggested that 'Some environments encourage children "to pause, play, and stay awhile", while others do not'.[51] Some environments foster a "sense of place" in young children; others do not'.[52] Several early years' authors suggest children require extended periods of time outdoors every day and opportunities to engage with 'nature'.[53] This will be difficult if we depend on special weekly Forest School events or visits to areas that are perceived to be 'wild' or pristine. I suggest that the everyday experience of the non-human world should therefore not be undervalued and can take place in the backyards, local parks, school and nursery yards and other local environments which underpin our sense of place. I would argue that children need to have these unstructured opportunities alongside the indoor, digital and structured outdoor play experiences that currently form their play and learning context.

There is also a growing commercialisation of outdoor learning in early years, with training to support practitioners taking children to learn outdoors and catalogues allowing 'loose parts' materials, such as pebbles, pinecones and pieces of wood, to be purchased to supplement outdoor play.[54] There is however a danger that this approach to outdoor learning hides the real links to Harmony principles and sustainability. Making natural materials durable – such as laminating leaves, providing pre-painted pebbles, or collecting pinecones so they can be brought outdoors at all times of year – can mask the natural cycles and interaction of the child and material. It can also lessen the preciousness and uniqueness of the resources. Real leaves rot, smell, crunch. Pebbles are only painted if we paint them, pinecones grow and fall from real trees at certain times of the year. In another context, early childhood settings often use plastic cups and plates for snacks and lunch times. I have however, on a few occasions, visited settings that use glass or china crockery. Dropping a plastic cup does not destroy the cup, only spills the content. However, children who drink from breakable materials tend to use these as precious commodities. They are transformed by the vessels' material and thus the material becomes significant. During another outdoor experience one young child's engagement during an encounter with a butterfly also suggested this focus on the precious. Other children were chasing the butterfly, whereas his focus was as protector, ensuring that the butterfly was not hurt, spending much of the time making sure that when the butterfly landed it was not caught or squashed. As an observer, this appeared to me to be the initiation of a transformative moment and was inextricably linked to the precious and uniqueness of the butterfly.

In the reality of 21st century living I do not suggest a move back to childhoods of the past that can be perceived as idyllic. In many ways current thinking in Wales in terms of children's rights, inclusive practice and the creativity offered by modern technology provides a positive context missing from own childhood. Furthermore, the digital world also encourages children to 'pause and play' which may promote a significantly different way to engage with nature. One could argue that, only recently, many of us walked across littered streets and beaches obliviously, and that only after viewing programmes such as the *Blue Planet* documentary with images of plastic pollution on a global scale did we wake up to the interconnectedness with the non-human world, the need for a significant discourse on sustainability and the principles of Harmony.[55] However, with regards education specifically, I would support the work of Lenz-Taguchi and others who note that education should avoid reductionism and instead embrace complexity.[56] Young children need many places to develop many relationships with the variety of the living and non-living non-human world. In fact, this may be something which was missing in my own childhood. My own childhood interactions with frog, ditches and ponds may have been in a cocoon that failed until now to see the wider implications of my own plastic use, production of carbon dioxide pollution, and impact on biodiversity. Systems thinking considers these complexities and acknowledges how different issues interact and impact on each other.[57] Such a holistic approach may also resonate with the Wellbeing of Future of Generations Act which, in a Welsh context, implies that wellbeing is an interconnection of social, environmental, cultural and economic issues.[58] Latour argues that the separation of nature and society does not reflect the complexity of the real world and that separating the human and non-human world is simplistic.[59] On a practical level therefore a diversity of play experiences could provide this interconnectedness.

Right thinking

This chapter considers the 'material turn', affordance, and systems thinking as ways of considering our wider understanding of the cycles and interactions that create a sense of place. Children interacting with a diverse range of unstructured play opportunities indoors and outdoors over longer periods provides a basis to learn beyond the formal curriculum and to consolidate learning within the early years' curriculum. If, as a child, my interaction with plastic had allowed me to understand its lack of degradability and if, as a child, I had observed the rotting of leaves and the invertebrates, bacteria and fungi which underpins the carbon cycle, I may have had a holistic view of the implications of the materials we were increasingly becoming dependent on. When risk assessing a site for my own students to use, one of the pointers is to litter pick before the students arrive.

However, I often reflect if this is an artificial construct and if it is the litter that we need children and practitioners to acknowledge, so it allows us to confront the real context of unsustainable practice, and provide another learning experience. Such discussion can also be framed as part of 'junk modelling' activities where recycled 'rubbish' materials are the focus of the play.[60]

In early years practice there is an opportunity to engage with the complex interactions between humans and the non-human world and note the relationships Lenz-Taguchi explores in her work.[61] I have observed bug hunts where plastic bugs are hidden in bushes and hedges, which prompts the question: 'if we go bug hunting should it not be for real bugs'? From the 'material turn' perspective, plastic bugs are different materials and provide a different experience, perhaps more a tune to finding a plastic crisp packet or Lego block than a moving, fluttering, buzzing animal. If the plastic ladybird is left outside, how long will it be there for? Why does it not breakdown? What about the laminated leaf or real leaf? The outdoors should allow for ladybirds, acorns, conkers, dandelions and stinging nettles to be found.

However, there is a cultural (rather than simply environmental) component to consider here too. My own child berated me recently for picking a dandelion, having heard that picking wildflowers was illegal. However, dandelions are often perceived as weeds which are routinely killed with weed killer. Again, the complexity struck me. Picking a dandelion, using it to make a dandelion tea, or as part of a 'what's the time game?' are staples of our historic cultural and play context, as are weaving daisy chains or playing daisy 'she loves me, she loves me not' games. Picking all dandelions or daisies would be harmful, if very difficult to achieve for annual, early successional plants. Being outside, not picking any flowers is not reflective of sustainability. All animals have to eat and use resources. However, the discussion regarding picking or not picking dandelions allows us to develop a systems' thinking approach to one's relationship with the landscape. I would not have picked wild orchids or bluebells, because I have cultural knowledge about these plants, but I would have supported children to pick dandelions, within limits. Again, this is the discussion that allows us to understand how the patterns and cycles of life are entwined with the cultural notions of the wider world. In a world where we have over harvested several natural areas, if we wish to understand more sustainable approaches we should also allow children to engage with what these mean and the types of behaviour that can lead to unsustainable practices. For very young children, I maintain that being allowed to play in non-human environments is a significant first step. To be transformed by the non-human environment requires children and adults to engage with it in ways that allow the environment to teach us, and not the other way around.

Notes

1.   David Cadman, 'Harmony', The Harmony Institute, at https://www.uwtsd.ac.uk/harmony-institute [accessed 16 May 2019].

2.   John Siraj-Blatchford and Valerie Huggins, 'Sustainable development in early childhood care and education (SDECCE)', *Early Education Journal* 76 (Summer, 2015): pp. 3–5; Amy Cutter-Mackenzie, Susan Edwards, Deborah Moore and Wendy Boyd, *Young Children's Play and Environmental Education in Early Childhood Education* (Heidelberg: Springer, 2014); Ingrid Pramling-Samuelsson and Yoshie Kaga, eds, 'The contribution of early child-hood education to sustainable society' (Paris: UNESCO, 2008), at https://unesdoc.unesco.org/ark:/48223/pf0000159355 [accessed 21 April 2020].

3.   Graham Donaldson, *Successful Futures Independent Review of Curriculum and Assessment Arrangements in Wales* (Crown Copyright Limited, 2015).

4.   HRH Prince of Wales, Tony Juniper and Ian Skelly, *Harmony, 'A new way of looking at the world'*, (London: Blue Door, Harper Collins Publishers, 2010).

5.   Louise Chawla, 'Significant life experiences revisited: A review of research on sources of environmental sensitivity', *Environmental Education Research* 4 (1998): pp. 369–383.

6.   Bob Jickling, 'Education Revisited: Creating Educational Experiences That Are Held, Felt, and Disruptive', in Robert Jickling and Stephen Sterling, eds, *Post Sustainability and Environmental education: Remaking Education for the Future* (London: Palgrave Macmillan, 2017) pp. 15–30.

7.   Sarah Whatmore, 'Materialist returns: practising cultural geography in and for a more-than-human world', *Cultural Geographies* 13, no. 4 (2006): pp. 600–609.

8.   Robert Michael Pyle, *The Thunder Tree: lessons from an urban wildland* (New York: The Lyons Press, 1998), pp. xvii.

9.   Karen Barad, 'Posthumanist Performativity: Toward an Understanding of How Matter Comes to Matter', *Signs: Journal of Women in Culture and Society* 28, no. 3 (Spring, 2003): pp. 801–831.

10.   Fredrick Froebel, *The Education of Man* (1826; repr. New York: Dover, 2005).

11.   DCELLS, *Framework for Children's Learning for 3 to 7-year-olds in Wales* (Cardiff: Welsh Assembly Government, 2008); Welsh Government, *Curriculum for Wales. Foundation Phase Framework* (Cardiff: Welsh Government, 2015); Amanda Thomas and Alyson Lewis, *An Introduction to the Foundation Phase: early years curriculum in Wales* (London: Bloomsbury Academic, 2016).

12.   M. D. Derby, *Place, being, resonance: A critical ecohermeneutic approach to education* (New York: Peter Lang, 2015), as quoted in Jickling, 'Education Revisited: Creating Educational Experiences That Are Held, Felt, and Disruptive'.

13.   Samuel Waldron, Mirain Rhys, Chris Taylor, *Evaluating the Foundation Phase Key Findings on Pedagogy and Understanding* (Welsh Government, 2014), at https://gov.wales/sites/default/files/statistics-and-research/2019-07/140506-evaluating-foundation-phase-pedagogy-understanding-en.pdf [accessed 21 April 2020].

14.   Project Dirt, 'The impact of outdoor learning and playtime at school and beyond: a summary of the survey findings conducted for outdoor classroom day 2018' (Project Dirt, 2018), at https://outdoorclassroomday.org.uk/wp-content/uploads/sites/2/2018/05/FINAL-Project-Dirt-Survey-Outdoor-Play-and-Learning-at-School-2018-15.05.18.pdf [accessed 10 September 2019].

15.   Richard Louv, *Last child in the woods: saving children from nature-deficit disorder* (Chapel Hill, NC: Algonquin Books, 2008); Peter Gray, *Free to Learn* (New York: Basic Books, 2013).

16.   Gray, *Free to Learn*.

17. Sue Palmer, *Toxic childhood: how the modern world is damaging our children and what we can do about it* (London: Orion Books Limited, 2006); Tim Gill, *No Fear: Growing Up in a Risk Averse Society* (London: Calouste Gulbenkian Foundation, 2007); Sarah L. Hollaway and Helen Pimlott-Wilson, 'Reconceptualising play: Balancing childcare, extra-curricular activities and free play in contemporary childhoods', *Transactions of the Institute of British Geographers* 43 (2018): pp. 420–434.

18. Vidar Ulset, Frank Vitaro, Mara Brendgen, Mona Bekkhus and Anne I. H. Borge, 'Time spent outdoors during preschool: Links with children's cognitive and behavioral development', *Journal of Environmental Psychology* 52 (2017): pp. 69–80, at https://doi. org/10.1016/j.jenvp.2017.05.007; Vinathe Sharma-Brymer and Derek Bland, 'Bringing Nature to Schools to Promote Children's Physical Activity', *Sports Medicine* 46, no. 7 (July 2016): pp. 955–962, at https://doi.org/10.1007/s40279-016-0487-227; Tim Gill, 'The Benefits of Children's Engagement with Nature: A Systematic Literature Review', *Children, Youth and Environments* 24 (2014): pp. 10–34 (p. 24); Allen Cooper, 'Nature and the Outdoor Learning Environment: The Forgotten Resource in Early Childhood Education', *International Journal of Early Childhood Environmental Education* 3, no. 1 (Winter, 2015): pp. 85, at https://files.eric.ed.gov/fulltext/EJ1108430.pdf [accessed 20 September 2019]; Ruth Davies and Paula Hamilton 'Assessing learning in the early years' outdoor classroom: examining challenges in practice', *Education 3-13* 46, no. 1 (2018): pp. 117–129, at DOI: 10.1080/03004279.2016.1194448 [accessed 20 September 2019].

19. Katherine Bates, 'Bringing the Inside Out and the Outside In: Place-Based Learning Rendering Classroom Walls Invisible', in Tonia Gray and Denise Mitten, eds, *The Palgrave International Handbook of Women and Outdoor Learning* (London: Palgrave, 2017), pp. 731–751; Froebel, *The Education of Man*; Friedrich Froebel, *The Education of Man* (1826; repr. New York: Dover, 2005).

20. Glenda Tinney, 'A all plant ifanc newid y byd? Addysg ar gyfer datblygu cynalidawy a'r Cyfnod Sylfaen', in S.W. Siencyn, ed., *Y Cyfnod Sylfaen 3-7 oed. Athroniaeth, Ymchwil ac Ymarfer* (Caerfyrddin: Cyhoeddiadau Prifysgol Cymru Y Drindod Dewi Sant, 2010); E. Pearson and S. Degotardi, 'Education for Sustainable Development in Early Childhood A Global Solution to Local Concerns', *International Journal of Early Childhood* 41, no. 2 (2009): pp. 97–111; Amy Cutter-MacKenzie and Susan Edwards, 'Environmentalising early childhood education curriculum through pedagogies of play', *Australasian Journal of Early Childhood* 36, no. 1 (2011): pp. 51–59; Julia Davis and Sue Elliott, *Research in Early Childhood Education for Sustainability: International Perspectives and Provocations* (London: Taylor and Francis, 2014); Alice Warwick and Paul Warwick, 'Towards a pedagogy of love: sustainability education in the early years', *Early Education Journal* 76 (Summer, 2015): pp. 6–8; Glynne Mackey, 'To know, to decide, to act: the young child's right to participate in action for the environment', *Environmental Education Research* 18, no. 4 (2012): pp. 473–484.

21. DCELLS, *Education for Sustainable Development and Global Citizenship: A Strategy for Action (Updates)* (Cardiff: Welch Assembly Government, January, 2008).

22. Jickling, 'Education Revisited: Creating Educational Experiences That Are Held, Felt, and Disruptive', pp. 15–30.

23. Roy Haines-Young, 'Nature: An Environmental Perspective' in Nicholas J. Clifford, Sarah L. Holloway, Stephen P. Price and Gill Valentine, eds, *Key Concepts in Geography* (London: Sage Publications Ltd., 2009), pp. 312–330.

24. Bruno Latour, *We have never been modern*, trans. Catherine Porter (Cambridge, MA: Harvard University Press, 1993).

25. George Perkins Marsh, *Man and Nature: or, physical geography as modified by human action* (Seattle, WA: University of Washington Press, 2003).

26. Marsh, *Man and Nature: or, physical geography as modified by human action;* Pyle, *The Thunder Tree: lessons from an urban wildland.*

27. Hillevi Lenz-Taguchi, 'New Materialisms and Play', in Elizabeth Brooker, Mindy Blaise and Susan Edwards, eds, *The Sage Handbook of Play and Learning in Early Childhood* (London: Sage Publications Ltd., 2014), pp. 79–90.

28. Jean Piaget and Barbel Inhelder, *The Psychology of the Child* (USA: Basic Books, 1972); John Dewey, *Experiences and Education, The 60th Anniversary Edition Indiana* (1939; repr. USA: Kappa Delta Pi, 1998); Lev Vygotsky, *Mind in Society: Development of Higher Psychological Processes* (Boston, MA: Harvard University Press, 1978); Barbara Rogoff, *The Cultural Nature of Human Development* (New York: Oxford University Press, 2003); Jerome Bruner, *Acts of Meaning* (Boston, MA: Harvard University Press, 1990).

29. Lenz-Taguchi, 'New Materialisms and Play', p. 80.

30. Teresa Strong-Wilson and Julia Ellis, 'Reggio Emilia's Environment as Third Person', *Theory in Practice* 46, no. 1 (2015): pp. 40–47.

31. Tim O'Riordan, *Environmentalism* (London: Pion, 1981).

32. Haydn Washington, Bron Taylor, Helen Kopnina, Paul Cryer and John J. Piccolo, 'Why ecocentrism is the key pathway to sustainability', *The Ecological Citizen* 1, no. 1 (2017): pp. Y–Z. at https://openaccess.leidenuniv.nl/bitstream/handle/1887/50284/WashingtonetalWhyecocentrismisthekeypathwaytosustainability2017.pdf?sequence=1 [accessed 19 September 2019]; Arne Naess, 'The shallow and the deep, long-range ecology movement: a summary', *Inquiry* 16 (1973): pp. 95–100.

33. Gray, *Free to Learn.*

34. Kay Milton, 'Nature and environment in indigenous and traditional cultures', in David E. Cooper and Joy E. Palmer, *Spirit of the Environment: religion, value and environmental concern* (London: Routledge, 2005), pp. 81–94.

35. Vygotsky, *Mind in Society: Development of Higher Psychological Processes.*

36. Robert Macfarlane and Jackie Morris, *The Lost Words* (UK: Hamish Hamilton/Penguin Random House, 2017).

37. Jane Waters, 'Affordance Theory in Outdoor Play', in Tim Waller, Eva Ärlemalm-Hagsér, Ellen Beate Hansen Sandseter, Libby Lee-Hammond, Kristi Lekies and Shirley Wyver, eds, *The SAGE Handbook of Outdoor Play and Learning* (London: Sage Publications Ltd., 2017), pp. 40–54.

38. James Jerome Gibson. *The ecological approach to visual perception* (London: Lawrence Erlbaum Associates, 1979).

39. Jan White, *Playing and Learning Outdoors: making provision for high quality experiences in the outdoor environment with children 3-7* (London: Routledge, 2014).

40. Fredrick Froebel, *The Education of Man* (1826; repr. New York: Dover, 2005); Jickling, 'Education Revisited: Creating Educational Experiences That Are Held, Felt, and Disruptive'; Chawla, 'Significant life experiences revisited: A review of research on sources of environmental sensitivity'.

41. Karen Barad, 'Posthumanist Performativity: Toward an Understanding of How Matter Comes to Matter', *Signs: Journal of Women in Culture and Society* 28, no. 3 (Spring, 2003): pp. 801–831.

42. Barad, 'Posthumanist Performativity: Toward an Understanding of How Matter Comes to Matter'.

43. Lenz-Taguchi, 'New Materialisms and Play'.

44. Lenz-Taguchi, 'New Materialisms and Play', p. 80.

45. Lenz-Taguchi, 'New Materialisms and Play', p. 80.

46. Sara Knight, ed., *International Perspectives on Forest School Natural Spaces to Play and Learn* (London: Sage Publications Ltd., 2013).

47. David Sobel, *Beyond Ecophobia: Reclaiming the Heart in Nature Education* (Great Barrington, MA: The Orion Society, 1996).

48. Sobel, *Beyond Ecophobia: Reclaiming the Heart in Nature Education.*

49. Tim Gill, *Balancing Risks and Benefits in Outdoor Learning and Play. A briefing for teachers and practitioners working with children,* at https://outdoorclassroomday.org.uk/wp-content/uploads/sites/2/2016/06/160606_PROJECTDIRT_ECD_BOOK7_A4-1.pdf [accessed 19 September 2019].

50. White, *Playing and Learning Outdoors: making provision for high quality experiences in the outdoor environment with children 3-7.*

51. A. R. Olds, Nature as healer. *Children's Environments Quarterly* 6, no. 1 (1989): pp. 27–32, as quoted in Ruth Wilson, 'A sense of place', *Early Childhood Education Journal* 24, no. 3 (1997): pp. 191–194 (p. 191), at https://link.springer.com/article/10.1007/BF02353278 [accessed 21 April 2020].

52. Wilson, 'A sense of place'.

53. White, *Playing and Learning Outdoors: making provision for high quality experiences in the outdoor environment with children 3-7;* Helen Bilton, *Outdoor Learning in the Early Years. Management and Innovation. 3rd edition (*London: Routledge, 2010); Sue Waite, ed., *Children Learning Outside the Classroom: from birth to seven,* 2nd edition (London: Sage Publications Ltd., 2017).

54. Gill, *Balancing Risks and Benefits in Outdoor Learning and Play. A briefing for teachers and practitioners working with children.*

55. *Blue Planet,* at https://www.bbc.co.uk/programmes/b008044n [accessed 19 September 2019].

56. Lenz-Taguchi, 'New Materialisms and Play'.

57. Davis, 'Early childhood education for sustainability: why it matters, what it is, and how whole centre action research and systems thinking can help'.

58. Well-being of Future Generations (Wales) Act 2015, at http://www.legislation.gov.uk/anaw/2015/2/contents/enacted [accessed 19 September 2019].

59. Latour, *We have never been modern.*

60. Jackie Neill, 'Loose Parts Play Creating Opportunities for Outdoor Education and Sustainability in Early Childhood', in Tonia Gray and Denise Mitten, eds, *The Palgrave International Handbook of Women and Outdoor Learning* (London: Palgrave, 2017), pp. 623–635.

61. Lenz-Taguchi, 'New Materialisms and Play'.

4

SYNTAX AND DESIRE
IN EARLY LANDSCAPE PHOTOGRAPHY

Susanne Klein and Lilith Goldschmidt

Introduction

The invention of photography was a breakthrough in technology and changed human consciousness for ever. For the first time, accurate visual communication was possible; that is, the observer could be sure that the image presented a true likeliness of the object without manipulation for artistic or political reasons. 'One advantage of the discovery of the Photographic act will be, that it will enable us to introduce into our pictures a multitude of minute details which add to the truth and the reality of the representation, but which no artist would take the trouble to copy faithfully from nature'.[1] By trusting the process, credible visual experience became possible beyond the confines of direct verification. Photographing a giraffe is depicting it without a human filter, without a human interface trying to make sense of a description. The photographer was not seen as part of the process. The person just operated the camera, the rest was done by nature. William Henry Fox Talbot (1800–1877) therefore called photography 'The Pencil of Nature'.

Photography, therefore, played a significant part in creating believable visual memories. As Fox Talbot wrote, 'What would not be the value to our English Nobility of such a record of their ancestors who lived a century ago? On how small a portion of their family picture galleries can they really rely with confidence?'[1] Not only could nobility finally record the true likeliness of bride and groom on their wedding day (and keep it for their children who would be amazed that their parents were once young), but the relatively low cost of photography also allowed a much wider audience to record important events for posterity.

In addition, photography allows time to be frozen. The moment in time when the image is taken is unaffected by the past and the future, and the instantaneousness of photographic imaging also allows motion, too fast for the human eye, to be visible, as seen in the work of Etienne-Jules Marey (1830–1904).

Using this ability, Marey used the method of multiple exposure to record most phases of an action in motion. To reduce confusion, his moving objects, like a marching soldier for example, were dressed in black, their joints marked with shiny buttons and they were then connected with metal bands.[2] The resulting image depicts a graphic diagram of the movement only.

Today everyone can take a photograph. Not even task-specific equipment is needed anymore. A modern smart phone is equipped with a camera with additional features such as motion stabilization, colour correction and face recognition. The image data recorded by the device can be distributed worldwide by sending the digital data to a platform of choice. Creation and distribution are more or less instantaneous. Most images will now never be printed, i.e., never be translated into an image on a physical substrate. The situation in the nineteenth century was different. The aim of the photographer then was not only to catch the light, but to make the image a permanent physical object.

In contrast to today, every single photograph in the nineteenth century was carefully planned and composed, whether it was in the studio or in open landscape. A multitude of photographic processes were invented, all variations on the theme of recording an image and making it permanent. Roger Fenton (1819–1869) and Timothy H. O'Sullivan (1840–1882) used the wet collodion process, William H. Bell (1830–1910) the dry collodion process. In both cases the glass negatives had to be prepared 'on the go'. Collodion is the name for nitro-cellulose dissolved in ethyl ether and ethyl alcohol, a substance originally used to cover wounds.[3] In 1851 Frederick Scott Archer (1813–1857) published the collodion process in 'The Chemist'.[4] Potassium iodide and potassium bromide were added to a collodion solution. A glass plate was then coated with the solution and, when the coating had set, it was immersed into a silver nitrate bath. The interaction between silver nitrate and potassium iodide resulted in light sensitive silver iodide in the collodion layer. Before the collodion layer was dry, it was put into a lightproof container and transferred into the camera. After an exposure of five to thirty seconds, the plate had to be returned quickly to the darkroom and had to be developed while still wet. The plates were washed and dried and needed to be stored carefully until the photographer had returned home and would print the positives.

The dry collodion process was not really dry. A hygroscopic ingredient was added to the light sensitive layer which kept it moist for several hours and made it possible to prepare the glass plate in advance and allowed a delay between exposure and development. A travelling photographer had to take a supply of glass plates, a complete dark room, water and all the chemicals necessary for preparing and developing the plates. Travelling light was not an option, as Figure 1 demonstrates. The image shows Marcus Sparling, Roger Fenton's (1819–1869) assistant and a photographer himself, on the photographic van they used to document the Crimean war in 1855. The glass plates and the equipment were heavy, and only a limited amount of plates and chemicals could be taken. The subjects of the images were therefore chosen carefully and the weather and lighting conditions had to be right, so setting up could take several hours. If the weather had changed or the light was not right anymore, the photographer had to wait. A quick snapshot was simply not an option.

Figure 1. Marcus Sparling, Roger Fenton's assistant and a photographer himself, on their photographic van they used to document the Crimean war in 1855, Library of Congress Online Catalogue, LC-USZC4-9240, public domain.

The syntax of landscape photography

Landscape photography is defined as everything which is not portrait (including groups of people), still life, or sport. It includes architecture and the urban landscape. The syntax of photography, or the composition of the picture, is determined by technology – the camera, lens system, detector technology, sensitivity of film or plate, filters, and printing or distribution methods. Today, in contrast, the accessibility of a recording device, for example a mobile phone, the speed of recording and minimal cost for storage and distribution of the image content, leads to images with much less composed content than when an analogue film camera is used. When using analogue film, the photographer will be aware that each picture costs a substantial amount of money, independent of whether the image is pleasing or not. Moreover, using this method, mistakes are not easily corrected, since there is a time delay between recording and viewing the photographic result. By the time any errors might be noted, the photographer in no longer in the location where the picture was taken and time has moved on – a flower has withered, the rain has stopped, the race is over.

Regardless of method, all photographic processes are restricted by the technology which translates light into an image and, depending on the technology, there are certain colours that cannot be recorded accurately. Early photographic processes were most sensitive to the short wavelengths, specifically the blue end of the spectrum. As a result, the sky in early landscape photography was often overexposed and had to be remedied when the positive print was taken.[5] This influenced the composition of the image. In addition, the length of the recording process made the photographer choose slow moving or motionless subjects. The snapshot was not yet possible. Even a smile in a portrait could be risky since the exposure time was so long that is was hard work to keep the face in a smiling expression. Trees moving in high winds or high, crashing waves could only be depicted as a blur. Additionally, each photographer wanted to communicate content by arranging their images so that they would tell a specific story.

In the nineteenth century, four themes in landscape photography were prevalent and used to articulate the following narratives:

- Landscape as the manifestation of the divine
- Paradise lost
- Humanity tames nature
- Wilderness and national identity

The hobby photographer did not yet exist, and the topics were chosen on a commercial, and with that, a political basis.

Landscape as the manifestation of the divine

In the nineteenth century, religious symbolism was part of everyday communication. Images then would have been interpreted in a very different way to that of a modern observer. Mike Weaver, in collaboration with Anne Hammond and Chris Titterington, has compiled a list with of symbols which would have been familiar to a nineteenth century viewer, but may be lost to a modern audience.[6]

- The Tree: stump, intertwining trees, three trees (Sacrifice/Redemption)
- The Rock: boulder, stone, mountain (Vengeance/Foundation)
- The Cliff: cave, sandy bank, crag (Entombment/Virginal Conception)
- The Arch: vault, clearing (Hell/Heaven)
- The Stairway: ladder, pathway, road (Descent into Hell/Ascension)
- The Mill: granary, threshing-floor (Judgment/Resurrection)
- The Waterfall: well, pool, sluice (Deluge/Salvation)
- The Bridge: aqueduct, canal-lock (Flight/Conversion)
- The Sanctuary: church, castle, cottage, vehicle (Destruction/Forgiveness)
- The Cloud: banner, sail, linen (Devine Wrath/Ministry)

Figure 2. Roger Fenton: Tintern Abbey (1854), Museum of Fine Arts, Huston, Accession number 84.353, public domain.

Figure 2, Roger Fenton's Tintern Abbey, may be seen as a romantic picture of a day out at Tintern Abbey by a modern observer. However, according to Weaver, a nineteenth century observer could have interpreted the image as the passion of Christ. The tree in the photograph could have been read as the crucifixion, the archway to the left with building rubble in front of it as the open tomb indicating the resurrection of Christ, and the big window to the right as the gate to heaven, referencing Christ's ascent to heaven.

In the nineteenth century, folklore and paganism became fashionable.[7] Druids were reintroduced to British society and the forests and meadows were populated again by fairies, little people and other magical creatures. Using that mindset, the same image of Tintern Abbey offers an alternative set of symbols. For example, the tree could have been a fairy tree, the archway to the left the entrance to the world of dwarves, and the ruin of Tintern Abbey itself a place where magical creatures met in the moonlight. Both interpretations may be unfamiliar today but, according to Weaver, would have been well understood 150 years ago.

Paradise lost

In the second half of the eighteenth century Europe began to change from an agricultural to an industrial society. The British Isles were in the vanguard with respect to technological innovation and the creation of a capitalist economic system, and rapid expansion of machine powered manufacturing shifted the population from rural villages to towns expanding around factories. This migration brought huge social changes and a new organization of work with it, which was itself soon criticized. John Ruskin (1819–1900) voiced his disdain for technological advancement and mourned how rural England was disappearing in *Fors Clavigera*. His comment on photography combines his grieving for lost landscapes and his disdain for modern technology.

> You think it a great triumph to make the sun draw brown landscapes for you. That was also a discovery, and some day may be useful. But the sun had drawn landscapes before for you, not in brown, but in green, and blue, and all imaginable colours, here in England. Not one of you ever looked at them then; not one of you cares for the loss of them now, when you have shut the sun out with smoke, so that he can draw nothing more, except brown blots through a hole in a box.[8]

In the tradition of the romantic movement, landscape photographers tried to document the rural idyll before it disappeared.[9] It is safe to assume that the houses in Figure 3 had no sanitation or running water and that the only heating was provided by a fire in the kitchen. In all likelihood food became scarce towards the end of the winter and, in consequence, child mortality was high. Nevertheless, the arrangement of the photograph shows that the photographer's intention was not to document harsh living conditions but a rural landscape which represented an idealized life style of harmony between human beings and nature based on craftmanship and agriculture.

Figure 3. Benjamin Brecknell Turner (1815 – 1894): At Compton, Surrey, 1852 – 1854, V&A collection, museum number PH.33-1982, public domain.

Humanity tames nature

Figure 4. Thomas H. Johnson (born about 1821) : Waymart, 1863 - 1865, open access image National Gallery of Art.

Figure 4 shows the other extreme of nineteenth century sentiment towards nature. Maybe it was an early recording of an environmental disaster; however, it is more likely that it demonstrated the power that humanity exerted over nature. Nature, especially when untamed, was seen as a threat to human survival. 'There was now a distinct manifestation of morning in the air, and presently the bleared white visage of a sunless winter day emerged like a dead-born child'.[10] With this sentence, Thomas Hardy (1840–1928) evokes the hostility of nature and conjures up nature as a merciless child killer. The three men in Figure 4 have their backs turned to the camera and guide the viewer's gaze towards the tidy and modern settlement in the background, suggesting that here is a bright future – that a battle has been won, that the wildness of unmanaged forest had been tamed, and life threatening animals and evil spirits had been removed.

In the US, photographers celebrated America as the land of the future by documenting human progress and urban landscape, as Diane Waggoner demonstrates:

> Picturing railroads, river and canal transportation, infrastructure such as bridges and waterworks, factories and mills, mining and logging, shipyards and docks, urban and domestic architecture, and other subjects capturing American innovation, progress, and consumption, photographers in the East (of the US) created works of astonishing beauty that aestheticized the technological alterations that fundamentally transformed the landscape and created the conditions of modernity.[11]

The embodiment of progress was the railroad. The railway connected energy sources to towns, made whole areas of the US accessible to settlers, and provided a new and pleasing way to view touristic attractions. Railway companies were early adopters of photography as a means of publicity. The Baltimore & Ohio Railroad company was the first to use photographs as a tool for advertising, commissioning photographers to produce promotional material for shareholders, publicize their scenic routes and attract potential passengers.[12] The photographs were a mixture of breath-taking landscapes and a celebration of the engineering feats of the railroad, suggesting technology's ability to control nature.

Wilderness and national identity

European nations have been able to define themselves by remnants of the past such as the Colosseum in Rome or Stonehenge. The US, on the other hand, has defined itself by the landscape.[13] Early on, Niagara Falls, for example, became a national attraction and was one of the first landscapes photographed, daguerreotypes by Hugh Lee Pattinson being the earliest photographic images of the falls.[14]

By the end of the American Civil War in 1865, photography had developed into an industry, producing millions of prints every year. Landscape photography was presented to the public in the form of stereographic cards, creating the illusion of three-dimensionality. Vast parts of the western regions of the US were still unknown and unexplored, even though thousands of settlers and the railroads were pushing west. In 1867 the first survey expedition took place, led by Clarence King (1842–1901) and financed by the American government. Three other fully funded expeditions followed between 1869 and 1871, led by Ferdinand Vandeveer Hayden (1829–1887), John Wesley Powell (1834–1902) and Lt. George M. Wheeler (1842–1905).[15] All expeditions had field photographers. Timothy H. O'Sullivan (1840–1882) was the photographer on the US Geological Exploration of the Fortieth Parallel, led by King, and the photographer of Wheeler's survey of the 100th meridian west, replaced by William H. Bell (1830–1910) in 1872. William Henry Jackson (1843–1942)

Figure 5. William H Jackson: Lone Star Geyser, Yellowstone's Photo Collection, Yellowstone National Park Service, image 14863, public domain.

accompanied Hayden. The goals of the expeditions ranged from generating maps for military and transport purposes and recording the locations of ore rich mines to purely scientific studies of botany, petrography, palaeontology, ethnography, archaeology, and ornithology.[16] Why photographers were taken is not clear. The investment was substantial, but most of the photographs reached only a specialist audience of stakeholders in the expeditions. O'Sullivan, Bell and Jackson were the first to record pure wilderness, untamed by human intervention. Perhaps King took O'Sullivan along in order to document the hand of God in the western landscape.[17] Jackson's photographs of Yellowstone taken during Hayden's survey expedition helped to convince the US Congress to declare Yellowstone the first national park in the US (Figure 5 shows the Lone Star Geyser). Creating the first national park in the world, the US Congress declared American natural monuments as national monuments, equal, if not surpassing, the architectural monuments of the old world.

Conclusion

The slowness of the photographic process in the nineteenth century and its time- and material-consuming procedures meant that landscape photography was an arduous art. As a result, subjects had to be chosen carefully and only those conforming to the photographer's intention were frozen in time. In contrast to our present-day snapshot culture, as represented by Instagram and other similar programmes, in the nineteenth century all photographs were carefully choreographed. The 'I was there' picture that has become ubiquitous today did not exist. Landscape photography of the past carried carefully composed messages from divine manifestation to national monument. It brought nature back into urban homes, and in the US it helped to define what it means to be American.

Notes

1.   William Henry Fox Talbot, *The Pencil of Nature* (London: Longman, Brown, Green and Longmans, 1844).

2.   Marta Braun, *Picturing Time, The work of Etienne-Jules Marey (1830 – 1904)* (Chicago, IL: The University of Chicago Press, 1992), p. 81.

3.   William Crawford, *The Keepers of Light* (New York: Morgan & Morgan, 1979).

4.   Frederick Scott Archer, 'On the use of collodion in photography', *The Chemist* 2 (1851): pp. 257–8.

5.   Joel Snyder and Josh Ellenbogen, *One/Many, Western American Survey Photographs by Bell and O'Sullivan* (Chicago, IL: The David and Alfred Smart Museum of Art, The University of Chicago, 2006), p. 78.

6.   Mike Weaver, 'Roger Fenton: Landscape and Still Life', in Mike Weaver, ed., *British Photography in the nineteenth century: The Fine Art Tradition* (Cambridge: Cambridge University Press, 1989), p. 106.

7.   Michael F. Strmiska   'Modern Paganism in World Cultures: Comparative Perspectives', in Michael F. Strmiska, ed., *Modern Paganism in World Cultures* (Santa Barbara, CA, Denver, CO, and Oxford: ABC-Clio), pp. 1–53.

8.   John Ruskin, *Fors Clavigera* (London: George Allen, 1907), p. 86.

9.   Carl Woodring 'Nature and Art in the Nineteenth Century', *Publications of the Modern Language Association of America* 92, no. 2 (1977): pp. 193–202.

10.   Thomas Hardy, *The Woodlanders* (1887; Gutenberg EBook #482, 2008), Chapt. IV, at http://www.gutenberg.org/files/482/482-h/482-h.htm [accessed 5 June 2020].

11.   Diane Waggoner, '"A Nation Announcing Itself" Photographing the Eastern Landscape, 1839 – 1900', in Jennifer Raab, *East of the Mississippi, Nineteenth-Century American Landscape Photography* (New Haven, CT, and London: Yale University Press, 2017), p. 23.

12.   Waggoner, *East of the Mississippi,* p. 158.

13.   Jennifer Raab, 'Landscape across media', in Jennifer Raab, *East of the Mississippi, Nineteenth-Century American Landscape Photography* (New Haven and London: Yale University Press, 2017), p. 2.

14.   Waggoner, *East of the Mississippi,* p. 19.

15.   Joel Snyder, 'Photograph on the Western Surveys', in Joel Snyder and Josh Ellenbogen, *One/Many, Western American Survey Photographs by Bell and O'Sullivan* (Chicago, IL: The David and Alfred Smart Museum of Art, The University of Chicago, 2006), p. 18.

16.   Snyder, *One/Many,* p. 19.

17.   Josh Ellenbogen, 'Inhuman Sight: Photographs and Panoramas in the Nineteenth Century', in Joel Snyder and Josh Ellenbogen, *One/Many, Western American Survey Photographs by Bell and O'Sullivan* (Chicago, IL: The David and Alfred Smart Museum of Art, The University of Chicago, 2006), p. 68.

5

WHAT GOES DOWN MUST COME UP: EZUAMAS AND THE NON-MATERIAL CONNECTIONS OF MOUNTAINS, RIVERS AND SEA IN A SOUTH AMERICAN INDIGENOUS LANDSCAPE

Alan Ereira

The title of this volume, on *Rivers, Mountains, Sky and Sea*, presents us with four apparently distinct landscape elements, and implicitly invites us to consider ways in which they relate to each other and to humans. It assumes that they are distinct and separate things. My concern here is to present some new knowledge on the environmental practice of the Kogi, or Kaggaba, a relatively isolated, non-literate indigenous highland culture in northern Colombia.[1] To do that, it is necessary to move away from the construction of their landscape as composed of separable things. They relate to it as a living organism, and I will suggest that, if we were to look for them, we might find similar practices in other societies that revere mountains. I propose that their methods can be viewed as a form of earth acupuncture. I am not trying to explain how they know what they appear to know, and I want to avoid suggesting a theoretical framework for their system of interrogating the non-human world. It is not my purpose to interpret what they know or perceive, beyond striving to place it in a simple classical understanding of the natural world.

In order to make sense of this, I need to establish a context in which mountain, river, sky and sea are recognised as not being 'things'. Martin Heidegger began his book *What is a Thing* by pointing out that the question is as old as what he calls 'Western' philosophy, and made a significant contribution to reinforcing intellectual structures associated with an understanding and perception of the world based exclusively on the separateness of things.[2] The Kogi have a different perception, and with that comes a different way of knowing and acting in the world which corresponds more closely to the reality of landscape.

A recent essay on reading the world as an assembly of separate things was presented in 2017 by the influential American philosopher Edward Casey, who builds on the phenomenological approach associated with Heidegger.[3] In

The World on Edge, Casey stresses the importance of edges in our construction of understanding. 'Edges... are essential to being a thing or a thought... Nothing distinct or finite can emerge except as edged'.⁴ His first 'thing' is a Californian coastal outcrop, whose edges 'open themselves out to sea and sky' and 'draw back into the earth from which they have emerged'.⁵ He recognises obvious problems with this way of perceiving waterscapes and landscapes, but pleads that without the imposition of bounding 'they would be all over the place'.⁶ They are. The cliff has no edges at the sea and in the earth. The sky's edges belong only to the observer's visual field, not to the sky itself.⁷ So what is this 'thing'?

Casey's example crystallises the problem of separating one thing from another, and so of knowing what is meant by 'mountain'. The peak of the Matterhorn is a study in edginess for any mountaineer – it claims an average of twelve lives a year.⁸ But where does the mountain end and the rest of the world begin? Where are the natural edges that split the Matterhorn from the other mountains of the Alps? There is a Matterhorn circuit trek, but it does not actually circumscribe the mountain. That would be pretty well impossible. The *Complete two-way trekking guide* insists that there is no mountain to walk around, not even a massif, just a mountain range. It is only the range that can be said to have defined edges, which are traced through seven valleys.⁹

Of course, we know that the sky and the sea are boundless. By 'sea' here I am using the word in the sense of Ὠκεανός, *Oceanus*, who personified the world-encompassing river, the sea that circled the world, known today as the World-Ocean. I distinguish it from the more-or-less enclosed seas such as the Mediterranean. That separated sea was the realm of Poseidon, which is why he carried a fisherman's trident and whose name – 'in the middle of the earth' – indicates that this sea does indeed have edges. It is less obvious, but equally true to say that rivers don't have edges either. We can define a summit by the distance it stands above the sea and approaches the sky, but mountains, like sea, like sky, like rivers, are constructions bounded only in our imagination. Thought and language give these words meaning, but they do not exist as distinct 'things'. None of them can be measured or separated. Using Casey's logic, we can understand that mountains, rivers, sky and the ocean sea are not things at all but ways of seeing what presents itself to us. People, us, make sense of them. We shape them, and so shape ourselves. Landscape is alive with us.

Mountain, river, sea and sky make an entity which demands a form of understanding that transcends the ideas of separation inherent in the words we use. In this context, by 'we' I mean the people spread around the world who read newspapers, use the internet, watch TV and have been trained to pass an internationally recognised public exam. 'We' share a way of knowing and understanding the world which is defined by, but not limited to, the European-American cultural hegemony. Our language simply doesn't have a word that embraces this wholeness, but I will be talking about another culture, with another language, that does. This is the Kogi culture, in the Sierra Nevada de Santa Marta. There I have learned something that I really did not know about this complex entity that is made up of people and the elements we call mountains, rivers, sky and sea.

The Sierra is an isolated 80-mile equilateral triangular massif in northern Colombia. On the north side, it rises steeply from some 600m below the surface of the Caribbean. On the east it is sharply bounded by the plains of the Magdalena river valley and on the west by the narrow valley of the Cesar river and by the Guajira desert. It is a small distinct tectonic plate at a collision point between the Caribbean and South American plates, which was forced upwards and rotated clockwise through 30 degrees to produce this extraordinary structure, quite unconnected to the Andes.[10] It rises 5,700m from the tropical sea to twin snow-peaks in just 42 km, the world's highest coastal summit.

It is inhabited by four indigenous peoples, each with their own language and dress: Kogi (Kággaba), Arhuaco (Ika), Wiwa (Sanka, Asario) and Kanguamo – the names in brackets are traditional. The Kogi are the least acculturated, the most hidden of these four peoples. They are said to be the last indigenous theocratic chiefdom on the American continent.[11] They belong to the massif, and they speak of it as *Gonavindua*.

I understand that, thanks largely to the work of Tim Ingold, anthropologists have learned to think of hunter-gatherer societies as ones which 'dwell' in the landscape rather than using it as makers and builders.[12] The Kogi, a settled agricultural people, see themselves as living within *Gonavindua*, 'the seed of existence from which everything germinated and has developed through time', and the buildings they erect as expressions of its form and nature.[13]

The word *Gonavindua* is not a noun, representing a thing. It is true that in our perception, this Sierra does have edges, natural geographical boundaries. But their perception is of an unbounded multidimensional entity that lives both within and outside space and time. '*Gonavindua*' is a narrative, rather like a storyboard. It begins *Go*, which says that this is about the moment of birth. Then comes *na*, anticipation, a word to describe astronomical dawn, the faint growing light that precedes dawn itself. It is followed by *vin*, quickening, the first fluttering sense a mother has of new life in her womb. Finally comes the eruption of life into the world that is *dua*, the birth of all life: *dua* means all living things, especially the tiny seeds of life, tiny sea creatures, sperm and the spectacular spray of ejaculation that fills the sky, and that we call the Milky Way.

Gonavindua is not a thing. It has no edges. It is a manifestation of the story of the quickening of the world.

When the Kogi speak of injury to *Gonavindua*, their language is literally visceral. Here is the womb of creation, and non-indigenous people who do not understand 'would only ever tear out the guts of the Mother, without compassion, without feeling pain'.[14] This language is not metaphorical. They regard *Gonavindua* as a biological entity, equivalent to a living body containing the internal and surface organs that sustain it. It has, by my count, forty-six rivers; many of which descend from glacial lakes to coastal mangrove lagoons, and their flow is regarded as serving similar functions to blood, urine, bile and other liquids within the human body. Its forests and plants are necessary covering for its skin-surface and are sometimes referred to as hair. Each individual part of the structure has its own life – cutting down a tree is equated with taking a life – but that is within the larger context of the living mountain.

But the way in which they believe this body functions, and their way of working with it, has come as a surprise to me, after knowing them for over 25 years. I believe it has considerable significance for understanding the way many other societies have worked with the landscapes that support them, and which they support.

The Kogi are primarily concerned with fertility. The best conquest-era account we have of the Sierra, by Juan de Castellanos, speaks of priestly figures, *los alunos*, fasting as they work for the fertility of people and the land.[15] *Aluna* is the is the cosmic mind, and *los alunos* appears to be his word for people who work in *aluna*, the space of cosmic consciousness at the heart of the Kogis' belief. Today, they perform just the same work and believe that the very purpose of their existence is to care for the life-bearing properties of *Gonavindua*.

> We have forgotten nothing.
> We know how to call the rain.
> If it rains too hard we know how to stop it.
> We call the summer.
> We know how to bless the world and make it flourish.[16]

Ancestrally, they were remarkably successful at this. Estimates of the population of the Sierra in the early sixteenth century, when the Spanish first arrived, have recently risen to over 500,000.[17]

The pre-conquest occupants lived at every level of the mountain, exchanging materials, seafood, resources, crops and fruits from the different vertically structured ecological zones, using well-crafted stone paths and stairways. The

Spanish invaders of the sixteenth century found substantial stone-based cities in the lower parts of the north face. They called the inhabitants Tairona, and described a social structure of warrior chieftains and quasi-shamanic authorities called *naomas*. These cities and their inhabitants were wiped out in a genocidal campaign early in the seventeenth century.[18]

The Kogi remember these inhabitants as *Nañi*, a distinct but closely associated lowland culture. Its remnants were absorbed into the culture of their conquerors.[19] The indigenous people that lived above 600m survived. Originally calling themselves *Askwínkala*, they now form four distinct identities sharing a common cultural framework and oral history. The communities we know today eventually formed under the guidance of a priesthood, who the Kogi call Mamas. These took over the duty of managing their communities in the absence of chiefs.

These people did not have, and still lack, a written language. Mamas, many of whom are trained from infancy in virtual darkness for up to 18 years, are the repository and guardians of oral history, communal knowledge and technical practice. They believe that it is their function to maintain the health of this ecosystem and that we, their 'younger brothers', are recklessly damaging it.

The evidence is all around them. Many of the river valleys down to the coast had been forested at their lowest levels until the 1970s, when a coastal road was completed from Santa Marta to Venezuela, all the way along the north shore of the massif. Many were then stripped bare by the arrival of cattle and marijuana farmers. Today, this territory supports less than a tenth of the original population and requires a UN food assistance programme. The Mamas are also very well aware of a decline in large animals, migrating birds, cloud cover, precipitation and glaciers.

The Kogi had always been famously secretive and withdrawn. That has been their survival strategy for many generations. Their mission, as they now put it, is to care for *Gonavindua*, and in so doing to care for the whole world. That is why they avoided acculturation and stayed out of the reach of Younger Brother. They believed that being hidden was essential to avoid the fate, as they saw it, of all other indigenous people – cultural annihilation, which would not just be fatal for their society, but fatal for their mission, and so for the world. But in the 1980s they made a conscious decision that this policy of silence had run its course, and they needed to reveal themselves in order to startle and warn us. They trained a half-Kogi Wiwa, Ramon Gil, in history, culture and the theory of translation to work with the outside world. That decision resulted in the BBC documentary 'From the Heart of the World; The Elder Brothers' Warning', which I helped them make and which was broadcast in December 1990, in time for the Rio Summit. Ramon gave the clearest statement of the warning:

Humans need water, they have to have water to live. The earth is the
same. It was made perfect by Serankua.[20] But now it is weak and
diseased, The animals die, the trees dry up. People become ill, many
new illnesses will appear, there will be no cure for them And the
reason is that Younger Brother is violating fundamental principles,
continually and totally. Drilling, mining, extracting petrol, minerals.
Stripping away the world.[21]

It had some impact, but of course little if anything actually changed. Their
communication was generally seen as being ethical rather than practical, insisting
on the obligation of humans to care for the world as a living and feeling being,
and esoteric, suggesting that they have a mystical or spiritual connection with
the natural world that may be valuable but has no testable validity. Although
the Kogis' presentation had a powerful emotional appeal, and many people felt
strongly that they needed to take it seriously, it had little to add to scientific
and pragmatic understanding of environmental issues, or to distinguish it from
the general perspective presented by indigenous people globally. Their message's
weight lay in the Kogis' presentation of themselves.

They had thought that we did not know how much damage is being caused
and their warning would inform us and change things. They chose not to have
the film translated into Spanish, apparently because they were wary of being
seen to criticise the power from which they had been hiding for so long. They
did not understand that we know and think about nature in a completely
different way, and they never addressed the question of whether they have any
concrete understanding of ecological systems that is different from, and perhaps
supplementary to, our own.

The Kogi have now learned that we see the world as made up of distinct
edged 'things' which may be individually assessed, manipulated, or destroyed,
some of which are not seen as being alive at all. They understand *Gonavindua*
as an indivisible organism; earth and water, sky and sea, plants, humans, stones
and creatures are fully interconnected. The Mamas feel confident acting within
this infinite complexity because of an orally transmitted specialised education
(one Mama learning about birds, another about trees and so on) checked on
a daily basis by 'consultation' with *Aluna*. This frequently involves the careful
study of minute variations in apparently random phenomena, most particularly
the movement of bubbles from a quartz bead in a small bowl of water.

Every Mama has been trained in this. To get a little closer to this baffling
behaviour, it may help to be aware of the complex multiple meanings of ñi,
water. It has an uncreated state, ñi-baksu, which may be translated as the Greek

λόγος (logos) in the sense of a primordial principle of order and knowledge. It is also the ocean (ñi-buñi) and precipitation (ñi-kalda), and has extensive further connections which include a certain kind of village (ñi-kuna), the physical sun (ñi-uwi) and gold (ñi-uba). So when they say the water 'speaks' through the bubbles, it is not water as we understand it.

They compare the knowledge they glean with that provided by commercial environmental assessments made when industrial enterprises begin development projects. Those assessments, based on individual studies of isolated and separated phenomena, seem to them catastrophically and sometimes childishly flawed – especially when they relate to interfering with water. ('If you dry up the lagoon on the shore why do you think that has no effect everywhere else? If I cut off your foot do you think the rest of your body will be fine?', asked Mama Manuel).

The most obvious example was the catastrophic destruction of Colombia's largest coastal lagoon, Cienega Grande, with its vast mangrove forest at the foot of the Sierra. This resulted from a number of environmentally approved 'improvements', in particular the construction of a road between the lagoon and the sea. A huge effort is now being made to undo some of the harm that flowed from the failure to understand the interactions of salt and fresh waters which the Kogi made every effort to explain.[22] The repair procedures now being undertaken are still derived from the same model of a landscape of separated things. Indigenous people are ignored as ever larger coastal 'megaprojects' are approved and the world continues to heat up.

I had stayed in touch, and visited from time to time, to meet Mamas in lowland locations. But in 2005 I was surprised to receive a summons from Santos Sauna, the new Cabildo or Governor of the Kogis' political organisation, Gonawindua Tairona, to leave London immediately and accompany him on part of his inaugural journey. We were going to a meeting at a high location that had always been forbidden to me. I doubted my ability to make such a tough walk, but he placed me on one of his mules and up we went. On the way, he said that the time for secrecy was now over. The Kogi needed to be more explicit about the world and about themselves.

They want to place their advice on what we would see as a more scientific basis, and open a dialogue with 'Younger Brother' scientists. They proposed a new educational documentary, which I would help them make. It would take seven years. The meeting was at around 3000 metres at a nodal point on the neural network of *Gonavindua*. It's called an *Ezuama*.[23] The gathering was entirely of Mamas and their female equivalents, Sagas. They were addressed by a passionate speaker, who I knew as Mama Pedro Juan. But the words he spoke were not his own. He was echoing what was being said in unison by the Sagas, the women sitting before him.

They felt their words flowed into them from the earth. The world itself is the Mother. In its uncreated state, as past and future, as memory and possibility, it is called *Haba Aluna*, which can be translated as the Great Mother Mind. *Gonavindua* emerges from *Haba Aluna* as a physical trace in the present, a material manifestation in the Now consciously aware of its past and fearful for its future, here given voice by women and magnified for my ears by a man. This was *Gonavindua* calling.

'We have not spoken clearly enough to the Younger Brother. The situation doesn't only affect us but everyone in the world, even the English on the far side of the sea. What is happening is a massacre of the sites!'[24] I was told that an *Ezuama* is a site with authority. *Ezua* means 'One', *ma* means 'hot'; the same word means political authority, but it is part of nature. It is a place where humans connect with the living world, embedded in nature but in dialogue with it. This was all new to me, even though I had been working with the Kogi for such a long time. Of course I was never there as an anthropologist but as a film-maker helping them say what they wanted. This term, *Ezuama*, which I did not hear in my first fifteen years of engagement with the Kogi, does not seem to appear in the literature before 1997, when it was thought to signify a mid-highland region rather than a specific site.[25] But my journey was apparently intended to start a new process of communication, which included a new open-ness. That is why they had brought me to these few large boulders, unremarkable to the passing tourist or soldier, in the clouds around two miles above my hotel.

> *Ezuama*s are located in the higher zones and are of central importance. They were established to fix in place the principles that order the Universe. There we find all the principles, norms and procedures of the Law of Origin to legislate and direct the administration of our ancestral territory and every aspect of the cultural life of our people. They are, in a manner of speaking, the cultural universities of our people. They have jurisdiction over part of the ancestral territory in which there is specific territorial jurisdiction of the Mamas, Sagas and authorities who are responsible for maintaining and working with the Law of Origin and the original ordering of the territory. *Ezuama*s are political spaces that exercise the power of government. Each of them has functions and a mandate coming from original principles which define its specific territorial competence and jurisdiction.[26]

In this translation, their words describe the cosmos as a place of law, justice and jurisdictions, but they have no legal structures and do not have a word for 'justice'. Instead they speak of *seshgowi* (*siaghawi*), 'organising'. The laws which determine the nature of each living thing, what we might consider its DNA, are accessed at *Ezuamas*. Each *Ezuama* is a spot where the ordering of that part of the world is to be checked and, where necessary, restored. This knowledge is pure thought, and can only be accessed in these very particular places. Here there is a fissure in material reality, a dangerous hot-spot giving access to primordial blackness.

Black is a term with special significance to the Kogi. It is not a colour but a state of matter, and that state can be described as 'uncreated'. Blackness is the condition of the world before it had been brought into material existence, when it had only been conceived in the mind that is *Haba Aluna*. The act of creation was a separation or withdrawal of *Haba Aluna*. Ramon Gil told me to imagine there was a flat cloth. The cloth is uncreated, black, an unrealised field of thought. The cloth itself is *Aluna*, memory and possibility, doubled over as past and future. Then a corner of the cloth was lifted, separating the cloth below from the cloth above, separating memory and the past from possibility and the future.

The newly opened space between is the Now, material reality, the physical world we inhabit, the present. On either side was and will be blackness, but here, suddenly, there is light. The birth of material reality begins with the thought that allows all *Haba Aluna*'s other thoughts to become manifest, a thought quite familiar to us – 'Let there be light'. Illuminated space is not part of the cloth, it is not the Mother's thought but manifests its trace.

Each *Ezuama* is located on a crack in reality, a radial Black Line that runs from the summit to the coast. The word for these lines is *Séishizha*. Like *Gonavindua*, it signifies a boundless concept. *Sé* is the void, the nothingness where *Aluna* thinks, the place of natural law that precedes any concept. *Shi* is a thread, a line of thought which can become manifest on a spindle, in a fabric, or traced on the ground – or within it. *Zha* is an expression of finality. This line of thought emerges from before time into the created world and dynamically joins it to the end of time.

> *Séishizha* signifies the circadian rhythm of rest and wakefulness, visible and invisible, including everything that makes the Universe work, such as the infinite night singing of the crickets, or the daytime songs of the snakes.[27]

These threads are necessary because somehow *Haba Aluna*'s thought still has to be accessed in the Now, this space from which it was withdrawn. That is how the Mamas use *Séishizha*. They are understood as fissures in space and time. 'Everything to do with coal, oil, underground water, is in the invisible line, all the inner layers of the earth, the buried gold and the idea-beings below are contained, connected or are part of the *Sezhizha*.' *Ezuama*s are nodal points on these 'black lines', where the Mother may be directly accessed. That is why I had been taken to an *Ezuama*.

Each *Ezuama* is the responsibility of a particular lineage and where the Kogi have territorial security a resident Mama devotes his life to its care. Its authority extends through an invisible natural network, analogous to a political administrative network, and each connects the peaks to a specific place on the coast.

Mama Shibulata explained that

> *Ezuama*s connect with the shore. They connect with the sea and they have authority over everything. It's a hot spot, a meeting point. Its power reaches over the sea and the mountains. It has always been this way. We visit *Ezuama*s to make offerings to the Mother in the mountains and along the coast.

Those offerings, represented by fragments of leaf, of cotton, of shell, held between thumb and forefinger, are the focus of a tremendous concentration. They are brought from places at other elevations on the line, creating a material connection, and sometimes soaked in sexual fluid. The job of the Mama is to strive to comprehend, by concentration and observation, his place in the laws that shape reality and to participate.[28]

They decided to place their narrative in this new film within the framework of another kind of 'Black Line', a modern construct with a political purpose.[29] In 1973 the four peoples of the Sierra defined it as the boundary of their traditional territory. This is an act of communication, giving *Gonavindua* edges, so that we can see it as an entity.[30] Of course this Black Line is cartographic, only embracing two of this living being's dimensions. In reality, *Gonavindua* reaches up into the sky and down below the ground, including air and winds and precipitation, as well as subterranean water, the life of the sea, and the mountain below the waves. It also has a transcendental presence which would need to be somehow circumscribed to turn *Gonavindua* into some-thing. But in a political context, this circumscribing Black Line serves its purpose well.

The indigenous peoples have defined a sequence of so-called 'sacred sites' that are linked like beads on a necklace. For our new film, the Mamas joined nineteen of these sites on the Caribbean coast with a gold thread, walking this circumferential Black Line on the northern face of the Sierra.

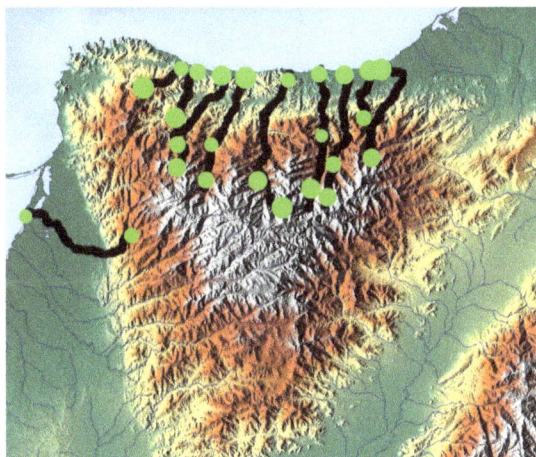

Figure 1. Some of the Black Line linkages between ezuamas and the shore of the SNSM. (The Tairona Heritage Trust)

Each of these coastal sites is directly and invisibly linked by a radial black line, a thread, to an *Ezuama*. On this very incomplete diagram, *Ezuama*s are shown as green points in the highlands, directly connected on black lines to corresponding points on the coast.

The coastal sites with which *Ezuama*s connect are all identified as *Haba*, Mother, or *Haté*, Father of a creature or activity – places of origin. For their new film, to illustrate the significance of *Ezuama*s in relation to the frontier Black Line, the Kogi began their site-connecting walk in the east, at *Haba Shikaka*, on the outlet of the Rancheria river by the town of Riohacha. *Haba Shikaka* means the mother of the thread from which the cloth of the world was spun. It is directly connected by a radial black line to an *Ezuama* called Mamarongo, at least two days travel up the river valley.

Some of the connections that pass through an *Ezuama* are more visible than others. They include underground flows, air currents, the movements of birds and animals and so on. For their new film, called *Aluna*, their specific illustration of the connection was the *Ezuama* of Sezhua, where the environment shows signs of serious damage attributable, in their view, to damage done at the

corresponding location on the coast. The lower site had been used to construct
a coastal power station, Thermoguajira, commissioned in the 1980's.

The operation of the plant had resulted in the drying out of the mangrove
swamp around it. It is by the estuary of the River Ancho, which comes down
from the Sierra. and is now, quite simply, dead. The Kogi say it is the Mother of
animal life. They speak of the original law which defined the form and nature of
each species. The Kogi connect this with specific parts of the earth-body, and say
that there are – or were – three lagoons here at which offerings must be made
when damage is observed to the structure of an animal species.

The power station has drained the Rio Ancho. Much further up, at about
2000 metres, they took me to the associated *Ezuama*, Sezhua, next to the river.
They wanted to show how damage below had caused damage above. The effect
of the power station had been to accelerate the river flow, causing torrents
and landslides and draining the source lakes of the river in the high tundra at
about 4,500 m. The flow then fell away greatly, and significant changes are now
occurring to the vegetation around Sezhua, including the death of an ancient
huge coca bush which they regard as central to their culture. Damage below
had caused damage above.

Professor Germán Galvis of the National University of Colombia, an
authority on river drainages, told them that was impossible. 'Nothing ever moves
upwards. The downward flow has obvious effects. Erosion and deforestation
higher up affect the coastal areas below. The other way round is not at all
evident'.[31] The reaction of Mama Shibolata was simple contempt:

> You say he is learned. I don't believe it. We have studied the mother
> well. She shows what must be protected. This man has learned nothing
> at all. You don't teach each other not to damage the mother. You dig.
> You exploit the earth. If you knew she can feel, you'd stop. But you
> plunder her. All the estuaries are like this. You block the lagoons. How
> would you feel if someone stuck a cork up your ass?[32]

He was not being scatological but medical. Professor Galvis complained that
the Mamas had not described any mechanism that would convey an effect from
the estuary of a river to its source, and Mama Manuel despaired of this inability
to see the obvious.

> If we explain this step by step they still won't understand. How can
> we put this? The rain that falls in the highlands has its home down
> here. You just see the water coming down the mountain but first it has

to ascend from here. The home of the rain that falls up there is down here. The lagoons down here supply lakes up there. Imagine going for a walk and returning to find your home knocked down. You wouldn't feel too good about it.[33]

Most people would agree that rivers depend on evaporation, clouds and precipitation. Less commonplace is the Kogis' contention that the water in that cycle has 'homes' in specific localities. They say the estuarine clouds travel directly inland. That is why the drying up of a river's source is explained by the disappearance of water from the river's mouth, and when the evaporated water flows back from its 'walk' through the sky to the summit, it finds that its home has been destroyed. This poetic vision reflects the most modern work on creating a synthesised, holistic understanding in which rivers are not analysed as things in themselves.[34] Understanding riverine ecosystems and not pretending that they have edges has had direct practical results, such as removing dams and canals to rescue rivers.

As part of their commitment to the new policy of open-ness, in September 2018 the Kogi created a printed book to explain details of their thought. The authors include a panel of twenty-one Mamas. They have struggled to find a way of communicating within the conceptual framework of Spanish, and are fully conscious of the problem. They spent two years wrestling with it.

It is important to make clear that our knowledge is structured and expressed in the territory itself. Copying it to paper represents a problem and a risk because we must resort to a different language. In doing so, we are inevitably producing a 'mestizo' book because we seek to preserve the foundations of our culture using translations into Spanish. For example, for us, the territory is Jaba and its approximate translation into Spanish is 'Madre'. However, we are aware that each expression contains a concept whose content, meaning and dimension come from the worldview of its culture. So this book can be interpreted as a dialogue between Jaba and 'Madre'.[35]

Cautiously, they have controlled its availability and not yet published it publicly. It is called *Shikwakala*, which refers to the network of threads, lines of thought which hold the Sierra and the whole world together. *Ezuama*s, they explain, are the main connecting points between those lines and the created world. That means that the ideas which became manifest at the time of creation, ideas whose traces make up the physical living world, with its rocks and rivers, birds and animals, insects and fish, are all directly accessible at these apparently unremarkable spots. And each of them is a store of knowledge that is particularly relevant to its location. Each Mama and authority credited as an the author of *Shikwakala* is identified by name and by his *Ezuama*. The Mamas are responsible for their *Ezuamas*; the authorities are informed by their *Ezuamas*.

Figure 2. The resident Mama of Seizua (The Tairona Heritage Trust)

This Mama is a permanent part of his *Ezuama*, and can never leave.[36] His hat, rising to a conical point, is particular to Mamas. It is a representation of the snow peak; the Mama is not just on the surface of *Gonavindua*, but inside it. Lineages are attached to particular sites; so are creatures. The work that a Mama is required to do at an *Ezuama* is defined by the specific geographical, animal and vegetable information stored there. This is translated as its 'jurisdiction'. Jurisdictions are marked by hills, rivers and important sites.

> Within these limits are found the birds, animals, insects, plants, sands, hills, waters, stones, fruits, flowers and every other being that manifests the principles that were assigned to these places for their government. Everything is stored in the ancestral knowledge of each of these elements, their history, function and the structure of their lives. The traditional civil authorities and the Mamas of each Ezuama direct the management of all this, in the specific space of its jurisdiction in an appropriate form for the needs of the ancestral territory.

The complete map of the threads of the Sierra, the fabric of *shiwalaka*, is shown in their book with that name.

Figure 3. Some threads of the SNSM (The Organisacíon Gonawindue Tayrona)

These inter-connected threads or *shikwa*,

> help to sustain the Universe and, in the form of roads, cross the earth. They are the roads of the transcendental Mothers and Fathers. *Shikwa* can be observed physically as ancient roads, not made by humans but drawn by the Mother to show where the threads are passing and in this way, to allow payments to be made for the flow of energy.[37]

The Shikwa may also be understood as the thought-ancestors of each form of life. Making payments, offerings, involves transporting symbolic materials from one altitude to another along these ancient roads. They refer to these as spiritual food, payments for the use of nature's resources, to restore balance. They also carry goods to exchange. These ancestral paths seem to be river drainages. The Kogi all use ancient trackways between higher and lower. Families maintain farms at different levels and spend their lives walking up and down.

There is no market in the Sierra, and currency has only recently intruded. Instead, there is a morality of reciprocal exchange, called *zhingoneshi*. This corresponds to similar systems that have been described in Andean history.[38] But those are speculative reconstructions on the basis of archaeological evidence: the modern post-colonial societies there offer little insight into that vanished world.

Here we are taken right inside the way it works, and the way people understand it.

Zhingoneshi is not just a substitute for trade. It is perceived as the process by which life functions, with natural movements of birds, insects, animals and water keeping everything alive. Everything is done in accordance with what we would call laws of nature, and they call the Law of *Sé*, or the Law of Origin. Up and down the Sierra, they are walking, making deliveries in the social world and, if they are Mamas, 'in spirit'.

'In spirit' is an unhelpful term. In a cosmos created and suspended in consciousness, material existence is just a trace of an invisible larger presence, extending far beyond the present in a thought-space to which human consciousness can have access. hat space becomes, in Spanish, 'spirit'. The Kogi know that translating, which they describe as the dialogue between two world-systems, involves not just squeezing and chopping up the sensuous and boundless living cosmos into 'things' but also speaking in a theological mystical language that makes offerings even less comprehensible to us than just watching them being made.

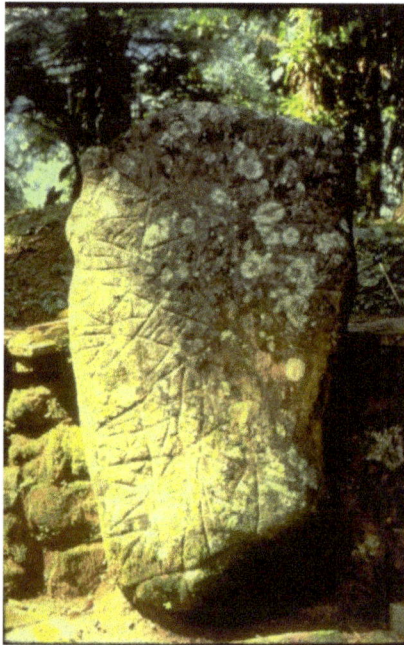

Figure 4. The 'mapstone' at Ciudad Perdida (The Tairona Heritage Trust).

The Kogi speak of *Pankatza*, 'stone maps which encode birds, snakes. tigers and everything that exists, ... They are maps of the order of the Universe and tell us how to fulfil our Mission to take care of the earth'.[39] This is a large stone at the entrance to the Tairona archaeological site Buritaca 2000, AKA 'Ciudad Perdida', which may be 1500 years old. It appears to map the network of *Shikwakala*, and so link the Kogi to Tairona practice. It suggests that the Tairona too believed that a small manipulation at the *Ezuama* can affect a lower site miles away.

The Kogi understand all life in terms of balance between masculine and feminine. Just as all beings have their origin in a Mother and a Father, all features of the world are gendered. Human actions create imbalance with immediate physical consequences. The ancient Chinese theory of acupuncture also has a philosophy of universal gendered complementarity, yin and yang, and claims that energy flows between them in the body along invisible channels.[40] The energy, called Qi, has to follow a specific pathway, and a small interference in its flow – by the insertion of a very fine needle – can correct an imbalance at its destination. Robin R. Wang proposes that *yinyang* is best understood as a paradigm that shapes the operations of rational thinking, it has equal reference to the cosmos and the body. This may help with understanding Kággaba, or Kogi, thinking. The Kogi management of nature using *Ezuama*s can be understood as 'earth acupuncture'. They make 'payments' at an *Ezuama* to affect the balance of nature at some point elsewhere on the living *Gonavindua*-body.

In *Shikwakala* they document their success in recovering and restoring the fertility of one river valley, 'the waterway and basin of the Rio Cañas between Kágueka and Dumingueka, having as its axis the town of Bunkwanguega (Bonga)', which had been lost to them for centuries – they say for 500 years; it is in the area from which the Tairona were driven in the early 17th century. This is of particular interest to me as I was responsible for channelling, at their request, the fee for our original filming into the purchase of the land on which Bonga was constructed. At the time I was told that it would be a meeting place for official visitors to meet Kogi. Mama Shibulata was given charge of the new site, to which they imported a small population. He is listed first among the author-Mamas and his *Ezuama* is directly thread-linked to Bonga. Their book provides evidence that their restoration of nature here was successful, but does not explain this system of work at a distance. What it does, though, is to spell out that the work is performed at linked *Ezuamas* at different altitudes in the river valley at Kángueka, Mamalúa and Guamanaka, which is actually in the neighbouring Rio Guaravita valley. The most powerful in this valley is Kángueka, where a stone is engraved with a form of map of the connections. They have also mapped, in a form we may grasp, the 'authority' and jurisdiction of the surrounding hills, which they have to work with at the *Ezuamas*.

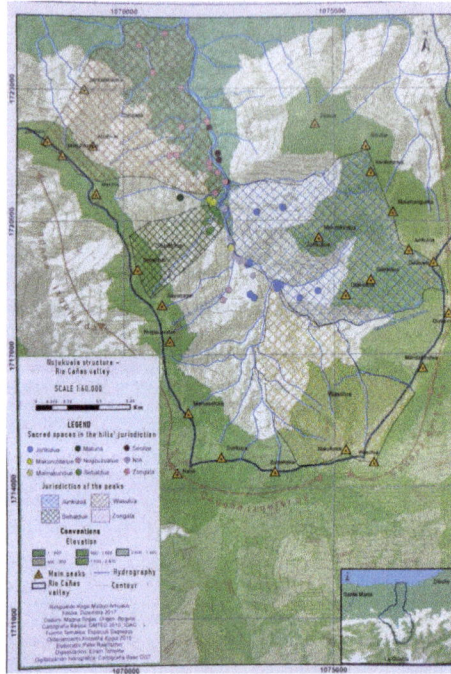

Figure 5. Authority exercised by the ezuama of Nujuakala in the Rio Cañas valley
(Organisación Gonawindua Tayrona)

Shibulata's restoration work began with the building of meeting houses for the inhabitants of the new town. Every meeting house – a *nuhue* for men, a *juitema* for women – is built with the architecture of the cosmos. The circular roofs have rings around the inside which are seen as the nine worlds, the nine planets, the nine months of gestation, all descending from the central cross on which the world stands. Each such world-house is also, of course, the mountain. Every *Ezuama* has an associated *nuhue*.

Being inside it is being inside *Gonavindua*, which contains life, landscape and law. It is the same place as the *nuhue* of the *Ezuama*. It connects rivers, sea and sky on a systematic basis. The idea of 'original law', the law that is inherent in the darkness, *Sé*, within which *Aluna* must function (as the law of gravity governed the creation of the earth) – that idea is fundamental to Kogi science and ethics. They understand all nature to be subject to *Sé*, and it is the job of humans to work and live according to this natural law. That includes an obligation to repair damage done by human action. The work begins in the world-house, the *nuhue*.

The Kogi speak of 'sacred sites' ('sitios sagrados') when communicating with Colombians.[41] In 2009 there was a mass indigenous protest to try to prevent the destruction of a hill at the mouth of the Rio Ancho.[42] It is called Jukulwa and is primarily concerned with childbirth. To them it was the equivalent of demolishing a defensive wall, but no-one believed that. 'Sacred' has no equivalent in Kogi, but they know it means 'untouchable' to us. So this protest was framed in our mystical language of the sacred.[43] They were talking about natural law, cause and effect, but know that we can't grasp what to them are obvious facts. So they say the land is full of sacred places. One Mama, Mama José, was to be heard complaining in despair, 'I wish we could speak Spanish so we could explain to the state and others that this destruction would cause fierce storms and landslides'.

Use of mystical language such as 'sitios sagrados' because we seem to understand it, obscures their central belief that there is a material connection between specific lower and upper sites, which is manifested in such things as underground water flow, evaporation and precipitation patterns and the sustenance of plants and animals, so that elimination of an estuarine lagoon can dry up a glacial lake (what goes down must come up). They tried to explain the wider devastation that would inevitably follow flattening this coastal hill, but were reduced to speaking about sacred places,[44] which gets no-where. Understanding the connections between *Ezuama*s and lower sites, and knowing that what comes down must go up was once an important part of sustaining over half a million people here. Refusing to despair, they decided to open a new avenue of communication and produced *Shikwakala*.

The Kogi extend the idea of black-line linkage within the Sierra Nevada de Santa Marta to all mountains. The top of the spindle, the snow peak represented in a Mamas' hat, is *Gwinendua*. That is where all mountains are connected, where threads linking all the mountains of the world come together. Because these are the threads that shape life, *Gwinendua* can be said to contain the blueprint of everything that exists everywhere. It is the source, they say, of the energy that sustains the world and makes it grow and develop. 'There is the ancient energy that shapes water, wind, earth, trees, animals, humanity. There is the non-material food that circulates throughout the earth'.[45]

Currently, one Mama, Mama Senchina, has been visiting surviving Muisca communities on the altiplano of the Colombian Andes, where he reports he has found the *Ezuama* system is still remembered and locations can be identified. I have been told by a Muisca spiritual leader that they believe their ancestral knowledge was secreted and guarded in the Sierra Nevada de Santa Marta when they were being overwhelmed by the conquest, and that they understand the

Kogi Mamas to be assisting them in a process of recovery. Mama Senchina is on a mission to work with the Muisca to restore the health of the land by restoring traditional land management.

Muisca culture, which flourished for millennia on the high Andean altiplano, depended for its sustenance on lower regions, and they made offerings as sites at different levels with what looks like the same idea of what I am calling earth acupuncture.

This may raise questions about the meaning and function of the artificial mountains that so many cultures have created around the world. The Mayan sites are obvious candidates for this interrogation. The pyramids of Tikal, which it is now thought were surrounded by an artificial lake, are possibly to be interpreted as sites which carefully link upper and lower to manage the land around.[46]

Mama Senchina Skyped me early in May 2021 to say that Mexican Maya had taken him to the great pyramid of Teotihuacan and shown him what they regard as an *Ezuama* – not on its top, but deep inside. A number of archaeologists, including Bill Sillars of the Institute of Archaeology at UCL, have suggested to me the similarity between these radial lines, and also the Inca system of forty two ritual lines radiating from Cuzco in Peru. Examined by Brian Bauer in 1992, and known as Ceques, these have some 328 shrines dotted along their length and are believed to have been walked as ritual paths. Some are still used that way.[47]

This is not just applicable to *Gonavindua*. For that reason, Arhouaco leaders, who were keen to be involved in the new film, urged that that it should be presented from the top of Everest. They wanted to show that their message was from the earth, not just the Sierra. They had already been in contact with Sherpas and exchanged ritually significant stones through an experienced mountaineer. The Kogi had no understanding of the physical issues, but they did know that there is an issue with going to a mountain top. Quite apart from the presentational and physical problems of indigenous Colombians speaking to the world from 5,650m above the top of *Gonavindua*, ascending any summit is traditionally forbidden. It is dangerous for the mountain, for the world. That has not stopped the summit of Everest from being overwhelmed by queues of climbers, who leave behind 50 tons of detritus a year. The concept 'throw away' is meaningless. You can throw things up, throw things down, but where is 'away'? These 'things' have no edges, and the rubbish bleeds into the mountain, recording the climbers' achievement by undermining the life of everything else there.

Obviously, the belief system of the Sherpas has been shaped by Buddhism and by their relatively recent migration to this part of the Himalayas, but conversations between some of them and the Mamas indicates that their *beyuls* or so-called 'sacred' valleys involve the use of apparently similar practices to sustain fertility.

In pre-Buddhist China, mountains were places for offerings to sustain harmony between material and non-material existence.[48] They were later considered sacred by association with particular deities, but a tradition of making offerings to mountains, waters and the earth of China, Tibet and Mongolia continued.[49] The Mongolians build miniature mountain shrines, on the vast steppe. They still regard digging into the earth as a forbidden act. In 2009 I was taken to visit the shaman who claimed to advise the President of Outer Mongolia. It was a suitably dramatic encounter in his large Ger, the felt equivalent of a nuhue, on a mound outside Ulaanbaatar. A violent thunderstorm was in progress, and I had to wade through knee-deep floodwater to climb the mound. He was holding audience with people seeking help, while lightening flashed and thunder exploded overhead. We discussed the Kogi view of nature, which he said he shares, and he said that to hold it in balance requires an understanding of how to relate to a greater consciousness through the mountain.[50]

Perhaps the black line concept of ecological harmonisation could even have included a society quite close to home. The Preseli mountains, now called, slightly dismissively, the Preseli Hills, were dense with ritual activity, of unknown meaning. This has now been confirmed as the source of the famous bluestones of Stonehenge. They were quarried around 5,300 years ago.[51]

Three hundred years later, they were taken from wherever they had been installed, to Stonehenge, 140 miles from their origin. This colossal expenditure of time and effort by what we suppose was a primitive society can have had just one primary purpose. To connect a place on Salisbury Plain to a mountain in Wales. A Kogi did come and explain it all to me. He felt quite at home. He believed that he was touching petrified ancestor figures, who understood that what comes down from the mountain always sends something back up. And who had been waiting too long for their food. Mountain, river sky and sea are not really four different things, and so long as we think of them in terms of their edges, we can have very little understanding of the life they share.

Notes

1.   Today's Kogi prefer officially to be called Kággaba, which they connect with Kágguba, the pre-creation idea of a human being. So Kággaba means 'material humans', and is related to Kaggi, meaning earth. Kogi, jaguar, is a lineage name.
2.   Martin Heidegger, *What is a Thing?*, W.B. Barton, Jr. and Eugene T. Gendlin, trans (Chicago, IL: Henry Regnery Company, 1967), p.2.
3.   Edward S. Casey, *The Fate of Place: A Philosophical History* (Berkeley and Los Angeles, CA, and London: University of California Press, 2014).
4.   Edward S. Casey, *The World on Edge* (Bloomington, IN: Indiana University Press, 2017).

5. Edward S. Casey, 'Place in landscape archaeology: a western philosophical prelude', in *Handbook of landscape archaeology* (London and NY: Routledge, 2016), pp.44–50.

6. Casey, *The World on Edge.* p.175.

7. Casey, *The World on Edge*, p.75.

8. Lee Black, *Mountaineering.*(Edina, MN: ABDO Publishing Company, 2014), p.29.

9. Kev Reynolds, Introduction, in *The Tour of Mont Blanc: Complete two-way trekking guide* (Kendal: Cicerone, 2015).

10. German Y. Ojeda and Augustín Cardona, 'Sierra Nevada de Santa Marta and Adjacent Basins', *Journal of South American Earth Sciences* 29, no. 4 (October 2010): pp.761–870.

11. Augusto Oyuela-Caycedo, 'Ritual Paraphernalia and the Foundation of Religious Temples: The Case of the Tairona-Kágaba/Kogi, Sierra Nevada de Santa Marta, Colombia', a paper presented at the Society of American Archaeology in San Juan de Puerto Rico (23–26 April 2006), *Baessler–Archiv, Band 54* (2006): p.145.

12. Pau Obrador, 'Dwelling', in I. Douglas, R. Huggett and C. Perkins, eds, *Companion Encyclopaedia of Geography: From Local to Global* (London: Routledge, 1995), pp.957–68.

13. Falk Xué Para Witte, 'Living the Law of Origin: The Cosmological, Ontological, Epistemological, and Ecological Framework of Kogi Environmental Politics',(PhD thesis, Downing College, Cambridge 2017), p.xxiii.

14. Alan Ereira, *The Elder Brothers' Warning* (London: Tairona Heritage Trust, 2008), p.70.

15.   tienen prolijísimos ayunos
              Por sus hijos o por su sementera;
              Y entoces solamente los alunos
              A cosas necesarias salne fuera,

Juan de Castellanos, *Elegías de Varones Ilustres de Indias* (Madrid: 1847), p.258. Castellanos was one of the earliest conquistadores.

16. Ereira, *The Elder Brothers' Warning*, p.108.

17. Santiago Giraldo, 'Lords of the Snowy Ranges: Politics, Place, and Landscape Transformation in two Tairona Towns in the Sierra Nevada de Santa Marta, Colombia' (PhD thesis, University of Chicago PhD thesis, 2010), p.57.

18. Ereira, *The Elder Brothers' Warning*, pp.234–38.

19. Witte, 'Living the Law of Origin', p.172.

20. Serankua is the personification of an aspect of the Mother. In the process of creation these aspects took the form of personalities – the Mother had sons. Serankua (Seizánkwa) is the active principle of world-shaping.

21. 'From the Heart of the World: The Elder Brothers' Warning', https://youtu.be/ HfSnTUc52C8 [accessed 8 March 2023].

22. L. Botero and M. Marshall, 'Biodiversity within the living, dying and dead mangrove forest of the Cienaga Grande de Santa Marta, Colombia, Final Report' (Sarasota, FL: Mote Marine Laboratory, 1994); PROCIENAGA, 'Plan de Manejo Ambiental de la subregión Ciénaga Grande de Santa Marta 1995–1998. Proyecto de Rehabilitación de la Ciénaga Grande de Santa Marta' *CORPAMAG, INVEMAR, CORPES-CA, GTZ* (1995); E. González, 'El manglar de la Ciénaga Grande de Santa Marta; Ecosistema en peligro de extinción', *Colombia sus gentes y sus regiones, IGAC* 21 (1991): pp.2–21; Mancera Pineda, Jose Ernesto and Luis Alfonso Vidal, 'Florecimiento de microalgas relacionado con mortandad masiva de peces en el complejo lagunar Cienaga Grande de Santa Marta, Caribe Colombiano, Colombia', *Revista De Investigaciones Marinas* 23 (1994):

pp.103–117; Hilary B. Moore, 'Aspects of stress in the tropical marine environment', *Advances in Marine Biology* 10 (1972): pp.217–69. Juan Restrepo Ángel, 'Los sedimentos del Río Magdalena: Reflejo de la crisis ambiental', *Fondo Editorial Universidad EAFIT* 267 (2005). Medellin Colombia. Repensando la ciénaga. 2010; Toro, 'Recurso suelo en el valle geográfico del río Cauca, Patrimonio y deterioro ambiental. Contraloría Departamental del Valle', *Impresora FERIVA* (1995).

23. Herinaldy Gómez Valencia & Pueblos Indígenas de Colombia, *Judicias indígenas de Colombia: reflexiones para un debate cultural, jurídico y político*, Bogota: Consejo Superior de la Judicatura, 2015), pp.526–34, reproduces the Kogis' 2010 declaration to protect *Ezuama*s but does not explain what they are. María Luisa Eschenhagen and Carlos Eduardo Maldonado, *Un viaje por las alternativas al desarrollo: Perspectivas y propuestas teóricas* (Editorial Universidad del Rosario, 2014), simply say they are connected to the Law of Origin.

24. *Aluna: An Ecological Warning by the Kogi People*, YouTube Channel *Aluna–The Movie*, https://www.youtube.com/watch?v=ftFbCwJfs1I [accessed 16 October 2022].

25. Carlos César Perafán, 'Economía tradicional kogui en processo de cambio: reporte de las cuencas del San Miguel y Garavito', in Antonio Colajanni , ed., *El pueblo de la montaña sagrada. Tradición y Cambio* (La Paz, Bolivia : Editorial Gente Común, 1997), pp.71–132

26. Perafán, 'Economía tradicional', p.113

27. Mama Luis Noevita, *Jaba Séshiza: The Black Line*, in Yanelia Mestre Pacheco and Peter Rawitscher Adams et al., *Shikwakala* (private publication of Organisación Gonawindua Tairona, Santa Marta, 2018), p.31

28. Guillermo E. Rodriguez-Navarro, 'Spiritual Significance and Environmental Effects of Offerings Amongst the Indigenous People of the Sierra Nevada of Santa Marta', in *Earth in Transition Conference Proceeding*, (Indigenous People's Restoration Network, 2005).

29. Matthew T. Evans, 'The Sacred: Differentiating, Clarifying and Extending Concepts', *Review of Religious Research* 45, no. 1 (2003): pp.32–47. doi:10.2307/3512498.

30. G.E. Rodriguez-Navarro, 'Traditional Knowledge: An Innovative Contribution to Landscape Management', in K. Taylor et al., eds, *Conserving Cultural Landscapes; Challenges and New Directions* (New York: Routledge, 2014), contains a summary identification of sites on the territorial boundary.

31. *Aluna: an Ecological Warning.*

32. *Aluna: an Ecological Warning*

33. *Aluna: an Ecological Warning.*

34. James H. Thorp, Martin C. Thoms, and Michael D. Delong, *The Riverine Ecosystem Synthesis: Toward Conceptual Cohesiveness in River Science* (London: Academic Press, 2008); Stefan Schmutz and Jan Sendzimir, *Riverine Ecosystem Management: Science for Governing Towards a Sustainable Future* (Vienna, Springer, 2018)

35. Yanelia Mestre Pacheco and Peter Rawitscher Adams et al., *Shikwakala* (private publication of Organisación Gonawindua Tairona, Santa Marta, 2018), p.19.

36. Astrid Ulloa, *The Ecological Native: Indigenous Peoples' Movements and Eco-Governmentality in Colombia* (London: Routledge, 2005).

37. Author's translation from Pacheco and Adams, *Shikwakala*, p.7.

38. Mary Van Buren, 'Rethinking the Vertical Archipelago: Ethnicity, Exchange, and History in the South Central Andes', *American Anthropologist* New Series 98, no. 2 (June 1996): pp.338–51.

39. Mama Luis Noevita, *Jaba Séshiza: The Black Line*, p.31.

40. Robin R. Wang, *Yinyang: The Way of Heaven and Earth in Chinese Thought and Culture* (Cambridge: Cambridge University Press, 2012).

41. G. Rodríguez, "Sacred natural sites in zones of armed conflicts: The Sierra Nevada de Santa Marta in Colombia,', in *Sacred Species and Sites: Advances in Biocultural Conservation*, G. Pungetti, G. Oviedo, and D. Hooke, eds (Cambridge: Cambridge University Press, 2012).

42. 'Policía impide protesta indígena contra Puerto Brisa en La Guajira', *El Espectador*, 14 April 2009, https://www.elespectador.com/colombia/mas-regiones/policia-impide-protesta-indigena-contra-puerto-brisa-en-la-guajira-article-135804/ .

43. Evans, 'The Sacred', pp.32–47.

44. Francisco Felipe Gelves Gómez, 'Learning and adaptation as conservation practices in resilient traditional socio-ecological systems: The Elder Brothers of Sierra Nevada de Santa Marta', *Revista de Tecnología: Journal Technology* 12, no. 1 (October 2015): pp.99–109. DOI10.18270/rt.v12i1.654.

45. Pacheco and Adams, *Shikwakala*, p.19.

46. W. Fash, 'Dynastic Architectural Programs: Intention and Design in Classic Maya Buildings at Copan and Other Sites', in Stephen D. Houston, *Function and Meaning in Classic Maya Architecture: A Symposium at Dumbarton Oaks, 7th and 8th October 1994* (Dumbarton Oaks:1998), p.250.

47. Brian S. Bauer, *The Sacred Landscape of the Inca: The Cusco Ceque System* (Austin, TX: University of Texas Press, 2010).

48. Wei-Cheng Lin, *Building a Sacred Mountain: The Buddhist Architecture of China's Mount Wutai* (Seattle, WA: University of Washington Press, 2014).

49. Johan Elverskog, *Our Great Qing: The Mongols, Buddhism, And the State in Late Imperial China* (University of Hawaii Press, 2006), p.138.

50. МӨНХ ТЭНГЭРИЙН ШАШИН, БӨӨ МӨРГӨЛ (Ulaanbaatar: 2008).

51. Mike Parker Pearson, Richard Bevins, Rob Ixer, Joshua Pollard, Colin Richards, Kate Welham, et al., 'Craig Rhos-y-felin: 'A Welsh bluestone megalith quarry for Stonehenge', *Antiquity* 89, no. 348 (2015): pp.1331–52.

6

SUN, SEA AND THE AFTERLIFE
IN THE BRONZE AGE AEGEAN

Ilaria Cristofaro

Introduction

This chapter explores the phenomenon by which the reflection of the sun on the sea at twilight casts a horizontal and elongated path of light, a phenomenon commonly known as the glitter path or glitter pillar.[1] The glitter path is formed by the light of the sun reflecting on the inclined surfaces of waves that point toward the observer.[2] The elongated reflection of sunlight on the sea is a very attractive and ordinary manifestation of nature. However, no effort has been made yet to contemplate the glitter path from an anthropological or archaeological perspective, by questioning how populations might have interpreted, used, or been culturally shaped by watching the reflections of sunlight in water.[3] My research aims to gain a deeper understanding of the intangible materiality of this marine light phenomenon, translating it into a set of identifiable qualities. I explored the glitter path through systematic observations of the phenomenon itself, and I looked for similar qualities, shapes, temporalities, and substances within the archaeological record, including iconographical analysis of the decoration of funerary pottery. I am also concerned with eschatology – literally the study of ends – in the form of beliefs about the afterlife, in view of the fact that my observations were of the setting Sun, together with its rising as an expression of life regeneration. I explore this with reference to a particular time and location, the period known as Late Bronze Age III, from around 1425/1400 BCE until 1050 BCE, on the Aegean islands and peninsulas, even though this argument might be expanded to later Greek eschatology[4].

Late Bronze Age III eschatology in the Aegean world

Context

The cultures which occupied the Aegean world in the Late Bronze Age III period reveal a uniformity of pottery production, although different local customs did remain.[5] Stuart Manning pointed out that Bronze Age Aegean pottery is conventionally named according to the provenance site: they are categorised as Minoan (LM), Cycladic (LC), or Helladic (LH), if recovered in Crete, in the Cycladic Isles, or in mainland Greece; however, Late Cycladic pottery is commonly named LM or LH according to the relevant influence from Crete and the mainland.[6] The pottery style that I analyse, the Octopus Style, was typical of these three provenance sites, so that it can be considered Aegean although Michimasa Doi argued that it has Cretan origins.[7] My decision to focus on the Late Bronze Age III period is due to the significant body of iconographic funerary evidence recovered in relation to previous periods, due to the introduction of decorated clay coffins and other funerary pottery, such as Octopus Style stirrup jars.

The sea and the octopus

Previous archaeological research, such as Chrysanthi Gallou's work in 2002, has stressed the fundamental role of the sea in ideas regarding the afterlife, more noticeable for the Minoan culture, with their gifts of boats for the burial (fig. 1.a), than for the Mycenaeans, who used to inter the dead with chariots symbols.[8] Due to the major presence of maritime elements in funerary art, Minoan scholars regard the sea as a fundamental part of the Minoan netherworld: in the words of Nanno Marinatos, the sea was 'meant to receive the death'.[9] The main theme depicted on coffins, or larnakes (small chests used to hold human remains), is the sea: on the 167 Minoan and Mycenaean LM/LH III larnakes identified by Emma Saunders, 125 have marine illustrations, such as ships, cuttlefish, other fish, and shells.[10] The octopus, in particular, is the most preferred motif depicted on larnakes (fig. 1.c-d).[11] For Lucia Alberti, this preference for the octopus is further emphasised by the production of a new form of burial pottery of much smaller size, known as the Octopus Style stirrup jar (fig. 1.e-f), manufactured in the Late Bronze Age IIIC in parallel with, and later substituting for, the production of larnakes.[12] The possible role of octopus images within Aegean cosmology was discussed since Ernst Grumach, who suggested that the motifs of sea creatures on larnakes, such as the octopus, might have acted as safeguards for the dead on their journey through the underworld-sea.[13] On the same line of thought, Doi concluded that the octopus was a symbolic representation of the sea, suggesting that it served as protector during seafaring journeys and, in funerary contexts, performed an apotropaic function for the dead in protecting against evil and securing 'their journey to the lands beyond the sea'.[14] Doi stated that 'the octopus-decorated vases from settlements are far fewer than those used as funerary gift', clearly emphasising the octopus's relevance for the world of the dead.[15]

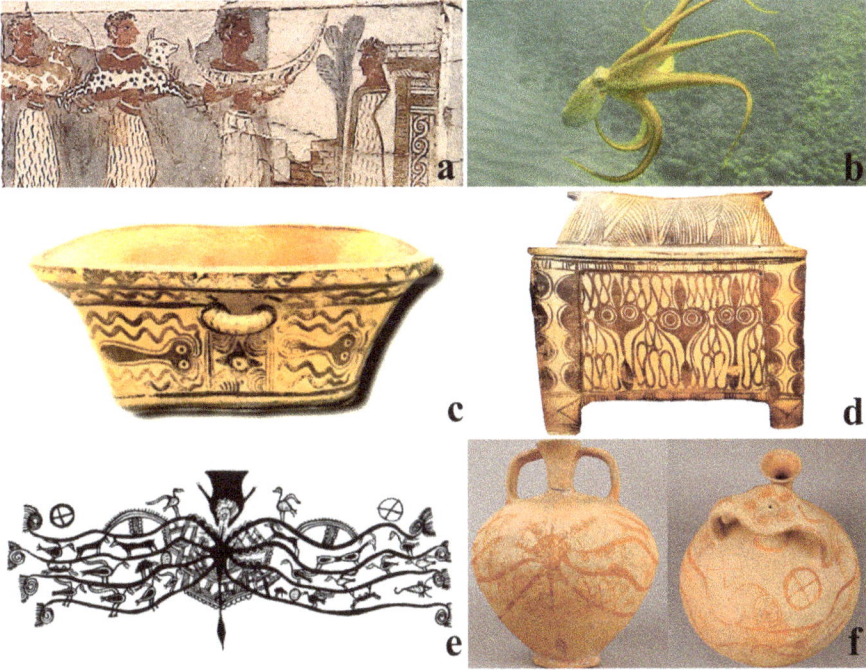

Figure 1. a) Funerary procession with a boat offered to the deceased. Aghia Triada sarcophagus. LM III. Archaeological Museum of Heraklion. b) An octopus in the Mediterranean Sea. Photo by Danilo Sacco. c) Bathtub larnax decorated with two stylised octopuses and a star-like motif. Episkopi cemetery. LM IIIA2/B1. Archaeological Museum of Heraklion. d) Chest larnax decorated with stylised octopuses. Armenoi cemetery. LM III. Archaeological Museum of Khania. e-f) Stirrup jar, LH IIIC, Kalymnos (Dodecanese). Octopus Style stirrup jar painted with orange-brown octopus and various animals within its tentacles, wheels above tentacles. The octopus is depicted as tree of life, hosting or carrying land creatures on its limbs. The British Museum, London. © The Trustees of the British Museum. On the right its decoration after Forsdyke 1925, p. 193. Where no stated, photos by author.

The sun

Although there is no clarity about the final destination place of departed souls
– below the sea, on a faraway land, or in the sky – the sea seems to have been
regarded as a fundamental liminal passage in the Minoan post-mortem journey.
The sun was also considered to have had an eschatological function: Lucy
Goodison, after having highlighted the close relationship between the sun and
the sea within Aegean funerary beliefs, proposed that the journey of the deceased
was connected with the movement of the sun across the chthonic – underworld
- sea.[16] Similarly, Nanno Marinatos, drawing on her work on templates from
Near East and Egyptian belief systems, stated that 'the ultimate journey of
the dead was the arrival at the land of the Sun', the afterlife destination, in
her interpretation symbolised by the double axe.[17] At the present time, there
is no strong agreement within the academic world on the eschatology of Late
Bronze Age Minoan and Mycenaean world views. However, both Goodison and
Marinatos have highlighted the relationship between the sun and the chthonic
sea, suggesting that the sun was regarded as an emblem of the soul's resurrection
in the afterlife. Finally, sun and sea symbolism were often combined in Minoan
and Mycenaean material culture (fig. 2).

Figure 2. Minoan gold cup, LM I c.1850-1550, Aegina (Attica). Gold cup with four
stamped spirals and a central rosette, combing sun and sea elements. Made on Crete, or
by immigrant Cretan craftsmen on Aegina (Attica). The British Museum, London.
© The Trustees of the British Museum

Methodology

Phenomenology

My research method consisted of two strands: first my personal qualitative responses to the sun's reflection (fig. 3), and second, analysis of LM/LH III funerary jars. This twofold approach is informed by Colin Renfrew's theory that the material culture produced by a society is a symbolic reflection of the local natural world.[18] Thus, my primary methodology was phenomenological, following Chris Tilley and Tim Ingold's phenomenology of landscape inspired by Maurice Merleau-Ponty's thought. It focuses on the perception of the environment through body experience, since 'the human body provides the fundamental mediation point between thought and the world'.[19] This is understood as an intentional regression of consciousness into the realm of naïve bodily perception in front of the periodic drama of nature: a sunrise, a sunset, the sea. I recorded my impressions gained from systematic observations of glitter paths over three months in Crete, recorded in written notes, photographic documentation, drawings, and paintings, and aiming to embrace an in-depth response to the sun's elongated reflection on the sea (fig. 4). I try to answer questions such as 'which is the agency of the sea? Which is the agency of the sun? Which is the agency of the sun's reflection on the sea?'. As an example, I can share an extract from my journal notes on my inner response to an early morning sunrise with a glitter path, written on 12th July 2017 at Milatos Paralia, near the Old Mill (fig. 3):

> It is a so powerful phenomenon
> like a serpent descending from the sky
> so blinking
> my skin shining as gold.
>
> Instable Sun across the waters
> performing its morning ritual
> reclaiming its ruling position
> in the Sky and in the Earth.
>
> Returning the world into colours
> the Moon quietly obeys,
> the stars since long have now gone.
>
> Growing into a fiery dragon
> with its eye in the sky
> and its body in the water;

There is nothing comparable:
all the rest stay still to look
and to receive the light,
the life
and the death.

Figure 3. A scanned page of the author's sky journal written on 12th July at Milatos
Paralia, Crete, at 6.47 local time in front of a glitter path. On the left side of the page, a
pen sketch of the sun rising over the sea drawn on site © I. Cristofaro, 2017.

Another journal extract, written in front of a sunrise glitter path at Milatos Paralia on 31st July 2017, reads:

This blinking light from the Sun

is bothering my sight
but reflected in the water I can still gazed at it

only for few seconds more
before it becomes a constant blue vision
painted on the retina,
making oneself sightless for too much light.

This reflection reveals a beaming sea,
alive and inflamed,
I hide my face to shade it.

In my inner landscape
light flows across my body
emanating from the central Sun
it pours from the head to the feet:
light is multiplied,
increased infinite times.

By adopting a phenomenological method, it is possible to gather knowledge of the natural world by documenting the somatic response of the bodily constitution of the observer (in this case, me) resonating with the materiality and temporality of the observed phenomenon, as I argued in my 2017 phenomenological exploration of water-skyscapes.[20] As Maurice Merleau-Ponty wrote, '… beings in depth, inaccessible to a subject that would survey them from above, open to him alone that, if it be possible, would coexist with them in the same world'.[21] Furthermore, I coded my fieldwork notes by highlighting the qualities of the glitter path in terms of its materiality and temporality, such as the sunlight's multiplication, sense of direction and connection, undulatory movement, and liminality – its existence as a boundary phenomenon. I then related my observations and responses to octopus imagery on funerary pots.

Figure 4. Photographing the setting sun over the sea from Khania, Crete, on 26th June 2017 at 19.28 local time. The resulting photo is compared with a drawing by the author. Photos by Marco Cristofaro (on the left) and by author (on the middle).

Imagery

My analysis of the iconography of the pottery is based primarily on the catalogue provided by Doi. I approached the imagery by embracing its potentially multivocal layers of significance, following Victor Turner's statement that 'a single symbol, in fact, represents many things at the same time: it is multivocal, not univocal'.[22] Alfred Gell avoided using the term 'symbolic meaning', but instead framed his iconographical theoretical discussion on 'agency, intention, causation, result, and transformation' by focusing on how the work of art acts as an active means of transformation within a society, thereby going beyond the mere interpretation of encoded signs.[23] Nevertheless, to understand the potentiality of action of an image, its qualitative value and its context of appearance should be decoded first. Gell's theory reflects Laura Preston's approach to Minoan coffins: she highlighted the function that larnakes have for communicating beliefs regarding death and the afterlife, as embodied in the choice of their decorations and shapes.[24] According to Marinatos, the decoration of Late Minoan larnakes represented a 'crude, childlike execution', in contrast to the detailed and realistic quality of the Palatial frescos.[25] This tendency to simplification of the style is interpreted by Marinatos as a hint to assign more value to the symbolic function, rather than to any decorative and aesthetic purpose.

The attempt to decode Minoan eschatology is a hard task: Christopher Hawkes's ladder of inference, as applied to prehistoric societies, demonstrates that, beginning with production techniques, moving on to subsistence of economies, then social/political institutions and, finally religious and spiritual belief systems, the latter is the most difficult aspect to unlock.[26] Indeed, any narrow analytical procedure of quantitative analysis would only circumvent the point. For this reason, the interpretation of octopus imagery is here approached as the expression of an intricate connection of relationships, ultimately arising from dwelling within the natural world. The iconographical material evidence is integrated with the phenomenological observations: one approach supports the other, and their interplay aims to give a thick interpretation, i.e., an understanding of the intricate web of stratification of meanings which made up Late Bronze Age eschatological beliefs.

Sunlight reflections in water and Octopus Style stirrup jars

Axial position

My question is whether the glitter path as a phenomenon is related to octopus imagery on LM/LH III funerary pots and eschatology? The first thing to notice is that, within Octopus Style stirrup jars, the main body of the octopus is always represented in a vertical symmetry on the front of the jar, as Alberti stated, with waving tentacles embracing the round shape of the vase all the way to the back, often joining together in a stylised plant or palm.[27] In other abstract versions, as shown in Figure 5, the octopus decoration merges with the stylised plant-pillar into a single element, thus further crystallising its verticality.[28] Therefore, it is possible to notice how the syntax of the octopus motif adheres to a vertical axial symmetry, a quality similarly evidenced within the phenomenological characteristics of elongated sunlight reflection on the sea. Indeed, the glitter path always follows a specific axial position, since, due to its ubiquity as a reflective phenomenon, it is always positioned in front of the observer and perpendicular to the horizon (fig. 4). In particular, Marcel G. J. Minnaert discussed that the perspective effect of painting or drawing the glitter path would '… project everything on to a vertical plane in front of me, and for this reason every patch of light is bound to run in a vertical direction'.[29] Indeed, although the light path extends on the horizontal plane of the water, in every two dimensional realistic depiction it would be represented as vertical to the horizon (fig. 4), matching the decorative choice of the axial position of the LM/LH IIIC octopus.

Undulating forms

In his seminal textbook on Mycenaean and Minoan pottery, Arne Furumark developed the idea of the octopus-plant as a hybrid form of the flower motif combined with the octopus motif (fig. 5), mainly basing the association on the visual resemblance between octopuses' eyes and plants' volutes (decorative images).[30] The octopus-plant hybrid can be found in several Octopus Style jars with distinctive abstract connotations as opposed to previous Marine Style vases.[31] If we focus on the central feature of the octopus-plant hybrid, its pillar shape is at times filled with wavy lines, such as in Figure 7, and in other cases with lozenge, chequer, net, chevron, or zigzag motifs.[32] Even if such filling decorations are difficult to categorise, the inclusion of wavy lines may suggest the intention of representing water, clearly in line with the marine nature of the octopus and the undulating shape of its limbs. In parallel, the glitter path can be regarded as a water pillar, made up of sunlight. As the wind moves the waves, the glitter path can follow undulatory movements. By observing the sun's watery reflection during different weather conditions and from different perspectives, it becomes obvious that a calm body of water would cast a fixed and straight path of light, while a wavy sea would reflect sunlight in a scattered way depending on the height and direction of the waves, so as to make this path more dynamic or, at times, invisible.

The island of Crete can host very powerful winds, as Oliver Rackham and Jennifer Moody pointed out.[33] In environments characterized by a calm body of water, such as the River Nile in Egypt, the reflection of sunlight might have been associated with a glitter pillar, but in the windy sea of Crete, it seems more appropriate to speak about a glitter path. Depending on the waves, the path of light moves as a flexible entity, so that fluidity is one of its inherent qualities. John A. Adam described it as 'liquid gold'.[34] The glitter path is recounted in the author's fieldwork notes as being similar to a serpent, due to its undulating dance: evocative of a fluid movement, the glitter path vision suggests a state of transformation. Thus, pillar shapes within octopus hybrid motifs can be compared to glitter paths in a decorative style which evokes undulatory forms.

Golden sunlight

'How to see a beam of light? How to make it visible?' (24th July 2017). The sun appears as a circular form in the sky, whereas the reflection on a sea at twilight appears as a long band of sunlight. The glitter path is sunlight made visible: unless mediated by water or darkness (for instance within a dense forest or architectures), it is not possible to see properly a defined sun beam in diffuse light. Water and darkness share the same response to light, by isolating it, by making it tangible and

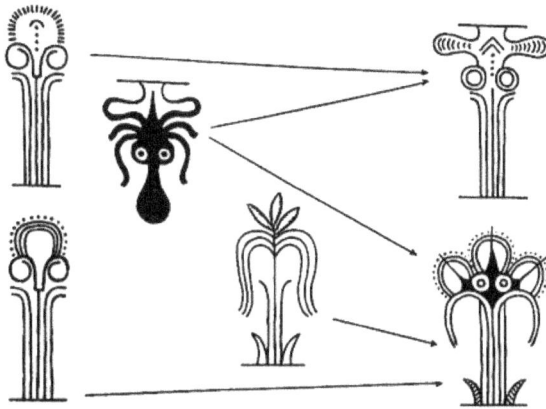

Figure 5. Process of plant-octopus hybridisation. Reproduced and adapted from
Furumark, The Mycenaean Pottery, p. 289.

near: a sunray is a defined path, a stable connection with the source of light, an
epiphany of the god. Thus, the sea channels the sun into glitter paths. Moreover,
when the sun reflects its light onto the sea, the water surface acts as a multitude of
mirrors giving back to the observer a certain amount of light. Joachim Schlichting
pointed out that 'the painters often need more paint for the light path than for
the light source from which it originates': sunlight is multiplied when reflected on
the sea.[35] During daytime the glitter path can appear blinking to the naked eye,
shining like gold on the surface of the sea. Twilight is the most enjoyable time to
look at the reflection, as the glitter path acquires a similar bronze luminescence
of the sun, as shown in Figure 4. Every object on the land – trees, stones, and
mountains – is illuminated in a similar bronze or golden light, so that modern
photographers call this moment 'the golden hour'.[36]

   The golden colour of the sun is very present in funerary context. Evidence
of the repeated use of solar symbols and sunlight colours can be attested in the
archaeology of funerary offerings. Robert Laffineur stated that golden plates with
octopuses and other motifs were common in Mycenaean shaft graves (fig. 6).[37]
Gold rings were found in Cretan tombs, such as the one with rosettes worn by a
woman from a tomb at Palaikastro. For Laffineur, the golden material in funerary
contexts is related to the durability of the magical virtues embodied by the tokens
and is a guarantee of immortality for the deceased.[38] The funerary role of gold
was also discussed by János György Szilágyi, who concluded that it related to the
sun's radiance, since gold '… consecrates the deceased as the inhabitant of the
realm of the Sun'.[39] The fact that tombs have been characterised by golden objects

such as jewellery, plates, and masks, may be evidence of a strong solar element in their eschatology.

More evidence suggests that the octopus may resemble an underwater sun (fig. 1.b). First, solar motifs are common in Octopus Style pottery, with rosettes often occupying a big portion of the decorative space.[40] For example, in the decoration on a jar from Sissi, the whole body of the octopus is replaced by a rosette.[41] Similar stirrup jars with decorations of rosettes along with tentacles were recovered at Armenoi and Episkopi cemeteries, as discussed by Athanasia Kanta.[42] This may indicate that the octopus had a solar trait, possibly because of the resemblance between the tentacles and the sun's rays. Second, the fact that Octopus Style stirrup jars contained oil is another element supporting the solar character of the octopus. Indeed, William Cavanagh and Christopher Mee suggested that stirrup jars were used as unguent – ointment – vessels filled with perfumed oil for offerings or for anointing the deceased.[43] The strong association between oil and the sun is revealed by the fact that oil was mainly used to produce light, thus replacing the role of the sun in dark places. Furthermore, the modern Greek word for oil, ἔλαιον, is etymologically close to ἥλιος, the sun. To follow this logic, the power of the Sun might have been transferred in gold burial offerings in Minoan and Mycenaean tombs, as well as in rosettes motifs and in the golden oil contained within Octopus Style pottery.

Figure 6. Octopus golden disc, LH I c. 1600BC-1500BC, Mycenae (Argolis).
Electrotype of a gold disc from Bronze Age Mycenae decorated with an octopus.
Replica: the original is in the National Archaeological Museum of Athens. Diameter:
6.10 centimetres. The British Museum, London. © The Trustees of the British Museum.

A liminal eschatological pathway?

This material evidence, with special attention to the jars where the octopus's body is replaced by a rosette, is consistent with Goodison's statement, that boats and marine animal motifs are interchangeable with depictions of the sun, all being vehicles used to reach the underworld.[44] For Franz Cumont, sunlight was believed to transport the dead, the sun being the psychopomp god.[45] Although Cumont's theories have been mostly superseded in the academic world, this idea of sunlight as a vehicle to reach the afterlife can be further understood by considering that the vision of the sun's reflection on sea looks like a pathway connecting the land to the beyond. Its condition of immateriality suggests that this path might be related to the journey of the souls to the afterlife beyond the physical world. Although it is not possible to deduce Minoan and Mycenaean eschatology from Cumont's theory, it is possible to embrace in-depth the natural environment in which these world views arose. From my observations, the glitter path reveals itself to have qualities of connection and directionality: it is indeed an intangible track of sunlight which, in its maximum extension at twilight, it appears to join the horizon to the seashore. My responses included a sense of being drawn towards the Sun and the experience of walking on the water, as if the glitter path wants to indicate a way within the sea's vastness. I am reminded of James B. Kaler's statement that the reflection phenomenon looks 'as if you could walk into space'.[46] In my fieldwork notes, I described the glitter path as 'a bridge of light', a 'road' or a 'channel' toward the sun. It acts as a means of communication and orientation, and naturally stands in the middle liminal point between sky and water. Since water is a flexible entity, it is subjected to the influences from the sky. 'It is a question of power', and I was asking myself , 'how to access the power from the sky?'. Water, being flexible and receptive, is easily influenced by external agency. It follows that water appears as a transmitter of energy: 'the water transports the light, the sun towards me, it is connecting', I wrote (9th July 2017). The glitter path also appears persistent and stable: being a relational phenomenon existing only between the sun and the observer, the light path follows the location of the observer along the shore. Finally, as a temporal phenomenon, the glitter path manifests itself at the turning between day and night, evokes the transition between life and death. As Turner stated, a '… coincidence of opposite processes and notions in a single representation characterizes the peculiar unity of the liminal: that which is neither this nor that, and yet is both': the glitter path can represent synchronically death and life, by embracing what Turner called a transitional state between them.[47] In a world view where the sea was considered the after-death passage, the glitter path can be culturally interpreted as an eschatological pathway, as inspired by its intangible materiality and liminal temporality.

Thus, the fieldwork findings brought to the fore the liminal character of the sun's reflection on the sea, reinforced by its time of manifestation around sunrise and sunset. A similar quality is evinced by the liminal position of a floral motif from the krater decoration (fig. 7.a), found in a tomb at Rhodes by Amedeo Maiuri.[48] The krater, described by Emily Vermeule and Vassos Karageorghis, depicts a narrative where 'the chariot wheel rolls along the rippling stem of an oblique flower caught under it, as along a river bed'.[49] On the reverse side of the krater, a flora landscape is combined with a similar oblique flower, which differs in style from the nearby floral composition and seems floating. Due to this dissimilarity and their position on both sides of the vase, the oblique flower may be interpreted as a liminal cosmological symbol, or a gateway. This argument is supported by the belief that the chariot was considered a possible means to reach the afterlife, which is evinced by the custom of depositing models of chariot or boat within tombs, as reported by Gallou.[50] The oblique flower is also related to the previous discussed Minoan and Mycenaean plant motifs before the hybridisation with the octopus. In this specific case, the oblique flower echoes the shape of a glitter path seascape, due to the wavy lines which fill up the flower, whereas the dots around its top part may indicate a luminous glow. Moreover, the double presence of the oblique flower may be indicative of the west and east horizons and of the liminal character of sunset and sunrise, suggesting a circular story of the journey to the afterlife around the vase, with a cosmography similarly decodable on the globular form of Octopus style stirrup jars (octopus/west on the front and regeneration symbols/east on the back). This particular krater, although unique in its decoration, provides a further evidence to support the idea of the cosmological liminality of the octopus-plant symbol in analogy with the phenomenology of the glitter path, sun and sea.

Regeneration of life

The idea that the octopus might have been attributed the role of directing souls toward the hereafter by acting as psychopomp or as mediator for the seafaring passage into the netherworld was put forward by Grumach.[51] Thus, it is possible that solar-octopus imagery was intended to cause regeneration, which itself is also represented by flowers and hunting scenes in funerary art. For Marinatos, 'solar deities are responsible for life, plant growth, and all regeneration and blessings that the Sun can bestow'.[52] Moreover, as Laffineur pointed out, the octopus is able to regrow its own limbs, thus it inherently embodies the power of self-regeneration, and for this reason was chosen among other marine creatures.[53] To sum up, following Gell's emphasis on 'agency, intention, causation, result, and transformation', the after-life regeneration might have been considered the

Figure 7. a) Krater from cemetery at Ialysos, Rhodes, Greece. LM III. The narrative depicted may be interpreted as the journey towards the afterlife. The two oblique flowers appear as liminal entities and may resemble the glitter path. Archaeological Museum of Rhodes. Reproduced and adapted from Vermeule and Karageorghis, Mycenean Pictorial Vase Painting, fig. XII.6. b) Designs from Mycenaean goblets, examples of the octopus-plant hybrid. From Evans, The Palace of Minos at Knossos, Vol. IV, 1, p. 350. c) Naxian Octopus Style stirrup jar, with sun-like shape from Doi, 'The Octopus Style', plate 201. d) The rising sun and glitter path from Milatos, 13th July 2017 at 05:28 local time. Photo by author.

result of a 'system of action intended to change the world' and the ultimate destiny and transformation of the deceased, by using the combination of the agency of sun, octopus, and plant imagery 'in the practical mediatory role of art objects in the social process'.[54] As shaped into artistic motifs on funerary vessels, it is possible to argue that the sun, by reflecting on the sea, might have been provided the perfect natural seascape for their eschatological beliefs, providing the intangible way towards the resurrection and cyclical regeneration of life.

Conclusion

Drawing together the different strands in my research, it is clear that the glitter path is a powerful phenomenon, creating a personal link between the Sun and the observer at a potent time of day – in my research I focussed on Sunset, when the Sun descends to the underworld, and Sunrise, time of life regeneration. The qualities of the luminous glitter path seem to have been translated into the octopus imagery. If we accept previous research that portrays the octopus as a psychopomp symbol, then it makes sense to consider it as an emblem of Bronze Age Aegean eschatology. First, we have the evidence of the axial perspective and the tendency to abstraction in hybrid pillar forms; second, the presence of solar elements includes its interchangeability with rosettes and the function of Octopus Style stirrup jar as unguent vessels; third, in the coastal context peculiar to the Aegean world, the Sunset over the sea produces the physical conditions of immateriality and liminality perfect for an eschatological path, a semiotic sign of a route to another location beyond reach, where the view of the sea's infinite horizon invites one to ponder on the ultimate destiny of life. Finally, I suggest that the octopus, a marine animal able to regrow its own limbs, with its hybrid plant or flower form, might have been chosen in order to represent after-death regeneration. With its tentacles resembling sun rays, the octopus, considered in its psychopomp role, seems have been shaped in LM/ LH IIIC funerary decorations in accordance to the experience of marine solar phenomena.

Fostered by my vision of the local seascape, I suggest that the Aegean journey to the hereafter was impressed as a standardised narrative within Octopus Style iconography. It can be read as a journey across the western dark sea by following the light of the octopus-sun cycle. Indeed, the vision of the path of sunlight on sea might have influenced the way in which Bronze Age III Aegean people decided to decorate their funerary Octopus style pottery. Following Gell's social art theory, the body of LM/LH IIIC iconography seems to have acted to cause a post-mortem vital and eastern solar regeneration of the soul beyond the sea, as evoked by the sun's daily course with its rising after darkness, the octopus's power to re-grow its own limbs, and the plants and flowers seasonal blossoming.[55] In particular, the conversion of naturalistic representations of the octopus into abstract shapes seems to have been intended as a way to represent the many layers of meaning which this animal embodied, in line with Turner's multivocality approach.[56] The prevalence of the octopus on funerary pots then draws together a complete multivocal symbol thread combining Sun, water, light, death, the octopus itself, the descent to the underworld and hoped-for regeneration in a remarkable union of sky, sea, human and animal.

Notes

1.   H. Joachim Schlichting, 'The Glitter Path: An Everyday Life Phenomenon Relating Physics to Other Disciplines' (paper presented in a poster session in the International Physics Education Conference in Durban, South Africa, 5–8 July 2004), p. 9.

2.   David K. Lynch and William Charles Livingston, *Color and Light in Nature* (Cambridge: Cambridge University Press, 2001), p. 83.

3.   John McKim Malville, 'Machu Picchu', in Clive Ruggles, ed., *Handbook of Archaeoastronomy and Ethnoastronomy*, (New York: Springer, 2015), pp. 879–891.

4.   Ilaria Cristofaro, 'When the Sun Meets Okeanos: The Glitter Path as an Eschatological Route, from the Late Bronze Age to Archaic Greece', *Journal of Skyscape Archaeology*, 6, no. 1 (2020): pp. 30-52.

5.   Erik Hallager, 'Crete', in Eric H. Cline, ed., *The Oxford Handbook of the Bronze Age Aegean (ca. 3000-1000 BC)* (Oxford: Oxford University Press, 2010), pp. 149–159, p. 156.

6.   Stuart W. Manning, 'Chronology and Terminology', in Eric H. Cline, ed., *The Oxford Handbook of the Bronze Age Aegean (ca. 3000-1000 BC)* (Oxford: Oxford University Press, 2010), pp. 11–28; Robin L. N. Barber, 'Cyclades', in Eric H. Cline, ed., *The Oxford Handbook of the Bronze Age Aegean (ca. 3000-1000 BC)* (Oxford: Oxford University Press, 2010), pp. 160–170, p. 160.

7.   Michimasa Doi, 'The Octopus Style: A study of octopus-painted Aegean pottery of 12th-11th centuries B.C.E., its regional styles, development and social significance', 2 vols, (PhD dissertation, University College of London, 2006), 1:239–242.

8.   Chrysanthi Gallou, 'The Mycenaean cult of the dead in central Greece' (PhD dissertation, University of Nottingham, 2002), pp. 123–142.

9.   Nanno Marinatos, *Minoan Religion and Ritual* (Columbia, SC: University of South Carolina Press, 1993), p. 231.

10.   Emma Saunders, 'Pictures from the sea: The role of marine imagery and artefacts in the Bronze Age Aegean' (PhD dissertation, Trinity College Dublin, 2008), n.p., as quoted in Ina Berg, 'Marine Creatures and the Sea in Bronze Age Greece: Ambiguities of Meaning', *Journal Maritime Archaeology* 8, no. 1 (2013): pp. 1–27, p. 15.

11.   Saunders, 'Pictures from the sea', n.p.

12.   Lucia Alberti, 'The Funerary Meaning of the Octopus in LMIIIC Crete', in Giampaolo Graziadio, Riccardo Guglielmino, Valeria Lenuzza, and Salvatore Vitale, eds, *Studies in Mediterranean Archaeology for Mario Benzi*, British Archaeological Reports International Series, Vol. 2460 (Oxford: Archaeopress, 2013), pp. 69–77, p. 72.

13.   Ernst Grumach, 'The Minoan Libation Formula-Again' (paper presented at the conference on Minoan and Mycenaean writing, University of Edinburgh, United Kingdom, 29th October 1966), pp. 7–26, pp. 24–25.

14.   Doi, 'The Octopus Style', 1:244.

15.   Doi, 'The Octopus Style', 1:225.

16.   Lucy Goodison, *Death, women, and the Sun: Symbolism of Regeneration in Early Aegean Religion*, British Institute Classical Studies, Supplement 53 (London: Institute of Classical Studies, 1989), pp. 33-49; Lucy Goodison, 'Horizon and Body: Some Aspects of Cycladic Symbolism', in Neil Brodie, Jenny Doole, Giorgios Gavalas and Colin Renfrew, eds, *Horizon: A colloquium on the prehistory of the Cyclades* (Cambridge: McDonald Institute for Archaeological Research, 2008), pp. 417–431.

17.   Nanno Marinatos, *Minoan Kingship and the Solar Goddess: A Near Eastern Koine* (Chicago, IL: University of Illinois Press, 2010), p. 148.

18.   Colin Renfrew, *The Emergence of Civilisation: The Cyclades and the Aegean in the Third Millennium BC* (1972; repr. Oxford: Oxbow Books, 2011), p. 405.

19. Christopher Tilley, *A Phenomenology of Landscape: Places, Paths and Monuments* (Oxford: Berg 1994), p. 14.

20. Ilaria Cristofaro, 'Reflecting the Sky in Water: A Phenomenological Exploration of Water-skyscapes', *Journal of Skyscape Archaeology* 3, no. 1 (2017): pp. 112–126.

21. Maurice Merleau-Ponty, *The Visible and the Invisible: Followed by Working Notes* (Evanston, IL: Northwestern University Press, 1968), p. 136.

22. Doi, 'The Octopus Style', 1:285-436, 2:456–863; Victor W. Turner, *The Ritual Process: Structure and Anti-Structure* (London: Routledge & Kean Paul, 1969), p. 52.

23. Alfred Gell, *Art and Agency: An Anthropological Theory* (Oxford: Clarendon Press, 1998), p. 6.

24. Laura Preston, 'Contextualising the Larnax: Tradition, Innovation and Regionalism in Coffin Use On Late Minoan II-IIIB Crete', *Oxford Journal of Archaeology* 23, no. 2 (2004): pp. 177–197, p. 178.

25. Marinatos, *Minoan Religion and Ritual*, p. 229.

26. Christopher Hawkes, 'Archaeological Theory and Method: Some Suggestions from the Old World', *American Anthropologist* 56 (1954): pp. 155–168, p. 162.

27. Alberti, 'The Funerary Meaning of the Octopus in LMIIIC Crete', p. 72.

28. Arne Furumark, *The Mycenaean Pottery: Analysis and Classification* (Stockholm: Victor Pettersons, 1941), pp. 288–292.

29. Marcel Gilles Jozef Minnaert, *The Nature of Light & Colour in the Open Air* (1954; repr. New York: Dover Publication, 2013), p. 21.

30. Furumark, *The Mycenaean Pottery*, pp. 288–292.

31. Doi, 'The Octopus Style, 2:figs. 83–85; Arthur Evans, *The Palace of Minos at Knossos: a comparative account of the successive stages of the early Cretan civilization as illustrated by the discoveries at Knossos*, Vol. IV, 1 (London: Macmillan, 1935), p. 312.

32. Doi, 'The Octopus Style', 2:figs 94, 96, 110, 114.

33. Oliver Rackham and Jennifer Moody, *The making of the Cretan Landscape* (Manchester: Manchester University Press, 1996), pp. 36–37.

34. John A. Adam, *Mathematics in Nature: Modelling Patterns in the Natural World* (Princeton, NJ: Princeton University Press, 2003), p. 63.

35. Schlichting, 'The Glitter Path', p. 2.

36. Ross Hoddinott and Mark Bauer, *Art of Landscape Photography* (Lewes: AE Publications, 2014), p. 112.

37. Robert Laffineur, 'Iconographie minoenne et iconographie mycénienne à l'époque des tombes à fosse', *Bulletin de Corrispondence Hellenique* 11 (1985): pp. 245–266, pp. 258–260.

38. Robert Laffineur, 'Fécondité et pratiques funéraires en Égée à l'âge du Bronze,' in Anthony Bonanno, ed., *Archaeology and Fertility Cult in the Ancient Mediterranean: Papers presented at the first International conference on archaeology of the ancient mediterranean, Malta 1985* (Amsterdam: Gruner Publishing, 1986), pp. 79–96, p. 87; Laffineur, 'Iconographie minoenne et iconographie mycénienne à l'époque des tombes à fosse', p. 260.

39. János György Szilágyi, 'Some problems of Greek Gold Diadems', *Acta Antiqua Academiae Scientiarum Hungaricae* 5 (1957): pp. 45–93, p. 74.

40. Doi, 'The Octopus Style', 2:figs 76–78.

41. Charlotte Langohr, 'Observations on some Late Minoan Pottery from Sissi', in Jan Driessen, ed., *Excavations at Sissi III: Preliminary Report on the 2011 Campaign* (Louvain-la-Neuve: Presses universitaires de Louvain, 2012), pp. 155–167, p. 159.

42. Langohr, 'Observations on some Late Minoan Pottery from Sissi', p. 159; Athanasia Kanta, *The Late Minoan III Period in Crete: A Survey of sites, pottery and their distribution*, Studies in Mediterranean Archaeology, Vol. 58 (Göteborg: Paul Aströms

Förlag, 1980), pp. 155, 253.

43. William Cavanagh and Christopher Mee, *A Private Place: Death in Prehistoric Greece*, Studies in Mediterranean Archaeology, Vol. 125 (Jonsered: Paul Åström Förlag, 1998), p. 119.

44. Goodison, *Death, women, and the sun*, pp. 36–39, p. 144.

45. Franz Cumont, *After Life in Roman Paganism: Lectures Delivered at Yale University on the Silliman Foundation* (New Haven, CT: Yale University Press, 1922), pp. 94, 160–161; Franz Cumont, *Lux perpetua* (Paris: Librairie orientaliste Paul Geuthner, 1949), pp. 301, 364, 379; Franz Cumont, 'La théologie solaire du paganisme romain', *Mémoires présentés par divers savants à l'Académie des inscriptions et belles-lettres de l'Institut de France* 12, no. 2 (1913): pp. 447–479, p. 464.

46. James B. Kaler, *From the Sun to the Stars* (New Jersey: World Scientific, 2017), p. 11.

47. Victor Turner, *In The forest of symbols: aspects of Ndembu ritual* (Ithaca, NY: Cornell University Press, 1967), p. 99.

48. Amedeo Maiuri, 'Jalisos -Scavi della Missione Archeologica Italiana a Rodi (Parte I e II)', in *Annuario della Scuola Archeologica di Atene e delle Missioni Italiane in Oriente 1923-1924*, Vol. 6-7 (1926), 83-340, pp. 151-152.

49. Emily Vermeule and Vassos Karageorghis, *Mycenean Pictorial Vase Painting* (Cambridge, MA: Harvard University Press, 1982), p.152.

50. Gallou, 'The Mycenaean cult of the dead', p. 124.

51. Grumach, 'The Minoan Libation Formula-Again', pp. 24–25.

52. Marinatos, *Minoan Kingship and the Solar Goddess*, p. 65.

53. Laffineur, 'Iconographie minoenne et iconographie mycénienne à l'époque des tombes à fosse', p. 259.

54. Gell, *Art and Agency*, p. 6.

55. Gell, *Art and Agency*, p. 6.

56. Turner, *In The forest of symbols*, p. 99.

7

THE AFON CYNFAEL – A RIVER'S PART
IN THE COSMOLOGY OF THE MABINOGI

Bernadette Brady

The Afon Cynfael

The Afon Cynfael is a small wandering river in North Wales which begins near Llyn Morwynion, the Lake of the Maidens. It then flows in a northerly direction for about five kilometres through a steep and narrow rocky path that winds around small hills. As it works its way through its stony route, it produces three small waterfalls. Eventually, at its end, it flows into the Ffestiniog Valley where, for a few hundred yards, it winds between two grassy meadows, finally joining the much larger Afon Dwyryd which dominates the valley. The Ffestiniog Valley itself is a long wide valley that runs for about 12 miles from the coast at its western end to deep into the Snowdonia Mountains towards the east. It therefore offers easy walking access to inland North Wales and provides good farming and places for communities along the broad base of the valley floor. This small mountain river is like many others in the area; however, this river holds a special place in the Welsh mythological stories known as the Mabinogi.

The Mabinogi

The stories of the Mabinogi appear in either or both of two medieval Welsh manuscripts: *White Book of Rhydderch* or *Llyfr Gwyn Rhydderch*, written c. 1350, and the *Red Book of Hergest*or or *Llyfr Coch Hergest*, written c. 1382– 1410. The tales are thought to be much older than the existing manuscripts, but there is no agreement concerning their age. Sioned Davies wrote,

> Their roots lie in oral tradition, and they evolved over centuries before reaching their final written form: as such, they reflect a collaboration between the oral and the literary culture and give us an intriguing insight into the world of the traditional storyteller.[1]

117

Davies pointed out that all the stories are set in a pre-Christian period and in the distinct geographical landscape of Wales.[2] Supporting this claim is the nature of the society described in the stories. The archaeological record indicates that in Europe around 600–300 BCE, the iron plough caused an agricultural revolution. Barry Cunliffe commented that in the west of Britain this produced regionalisation in the way of a proliferation of hill forts in the landscape.[3] He argued that these forts provided the living space for a 'larger community, comprising a group of lineages, designed to express its social cohesion and its ownership of a territory'.[4] Culturally, socially, and physically, this is the landscape of the Mabinogi, a culture embedded in regionalism, which used hill-forts, was involved in territorial conflicts, and subscribed to clan lineages and the use of the clan to maintain social cohesion. Based on this evidence, the narrative of the Mabinogi, at least in its origins, reflects the material evidence of the nature of the society that existed in Wales from around 600–300 BCE up to the century before the Roman conquest.

There are eleven stories that make up the Mabinogi and four of them fall into a group that is known as *The Four Branches of the Mabinogi*, so called because each of these stories end with the line 'and so ends this branch of the Mabinogi'.[5] The four branches are: *Pwyll Pendefig Dyfed* ('Pwyll, Prince of Dyfed'), *Branwen ferch Llŷr* ('Branwen, Daughter of Llŷr'), *Manawydan uab Llŷr* ('Manawydan, Son of Llŷr'), and *Math fab Mathonwy* ('Math, Son of Mathonwy'). Of these, the Fourth Branch, *Math uab Mathonwy*, contains what Karen Bek-Pedersen argued are 'intriguing details potentially pertaining to ancient cosmological ideas'.[6] The Fourth Branch is set around the area of the Llŷn Peninsula in North Wales and is a story of lust, rape, murder, magic, species morphology, shape changing, revenge, and trickery. The complexity is summed up by Sarah Sheehan, who remarked that throughout the story, 'Instability haunts bodies in the Fourth Branch' as they can be transformed with 'a wave of a magic wand or the thrust of a spear'.[7] All of these varying elements are held together with a thread of cyclic time, repetition of events, annual returns that must be measured to the exact day, and the story of a non-human hero whose role is to return balance to the world by his 'death' and then his retribution on the banks of the Afon Cynfael.

Sky stories in mythology

Arguing that any myth has sky origins can be problematic. In discussing folklore, Alan Garner pointed out that the times within a story of greatest confusion or absurdities, where characters take unexpected or non-logical actions, are the times when there is a hidden necessity at work.[8] He described this as the story being forced to fit the material facts which, for him, were to do with landscape and locations. Garner's arguments can be extended to the necessity produced by the sky, the inevitability of its regular clock-work motion. If a story describes naked-eye astronomy, then the characters will be forced to comply with celestial mechanics and any absurdities in the story will therefore have a sky-logic. Indicators of such a logic are the presence of an exacting string of details which sweep up the characters into a proscriptive and inevitable cyclic pattern reflecting some or all of the sky's regularity.

Extending Garner's thinking, such absurdities can be characters that are fixed in relationship to each other or fixed to a place, which implies that the story may refer to constellations, as the stars do not change their relationship to each other. Alternatively, if a story contains shifts, comings, and goings in a repeating cyclic pattern between characters, it could potentially represent the movement of the sun and the moon. If, however, characters in the myth take a fixed, unswerving path, regardless of its outcome, the story could be speaking of a comet. Stories of death, the underworld, and eventual rebirth can be motifs describing the phases of the stars or planets. Finally, stories of a person's soul soaring to the heavens as a great bird or on a ladder suggest that the a description of the movement of stars.[9] Thus, absurdities in a story can be interpreted as important markers, showing the workings of a hidden necessity. If this hidden necessity is caused by the sky, then the absurdities will conform to a sky-logic and the potential cultural relevance of the myth can be linked to calendar, seasons, lunar phases, or extraordinary sky events.

The story of the Fourth Branch

There are different story threads within the Fourth Branch. All are interwoven and held together by complex characters, which suggests many layers of meanings. However, the focus of this chapter is the thread which involves the Afon Cynfael and it is as follows. The setting is the kingdom of Gwynedd in North Wales where Lleû, one of the central characters, was born from a divine woman as a tiny light. He was not human but took human form. He was raised by Gwydion, a druid sorcerer. As the story develops, the teenage Lleû was cursed by his mother and not allowed to marry a human woman. To resolve this problem, Gwydion and the king, Math, created a woman from flowers. Her name was Blodeuedd and she became Lleû's flower bride. Blodeuedd, however, was unfaithful with the hunter, Gronw, who had just killed a stag on the banks of the Afon Cynfael.

As lovers Gronw and Blodeuedd plotted to murder Lleû. Blodeuedd used her charms as Lleû's wife to ask him if there is any way that he could be killed. With no concern for his safety, Lleû described the requirements:

By making a bath for me on a river bank, and making a vaulted frame over the tub, and thatching it well and snugly too thereafter, and bringing a he-goat', he said, 'and setting it beside the tub, and myself placing one foot on the back of the he-goat and the other on the edge of the tub.'[10]

It was by being in such a position, Lleû stated, that he could be killed by a magical spear.[11] The story then imposes an element of time and annual cycles, for the spear must be made over the course of an entire year and could only be worked on a Sunday, when people were at Mass. The inclusion of Mass is possibly a Christian overlay placed into the oral tradition. So Gronw worked one day a week for the whole year and finally completed the spear. The two lovers then went to the 'shadow of the hill on the banks of the Afon Cynfael'.[12] Blodeuedd prepared a bath and brought a collection of he-goats and ask Lleû to show her exactly what he meant by standing on the edge of the bath and on the back of a he-goat. Lleû obligingly balanced between the bath and the goat and Gronw hurled the magical spear, hoping to strike Lleû dead. Lleû, however, having been struck by the spear, screamed and transformed into an eagle that flew high in the sky and disappeared. Gronw and Blodeuedd considered that Lleû had been killed and Gronw took over as ruler of Lleû's lands.

Nevertheless, Gwydion, the druid sorcerer, knew that Lleû was not dead. Sometime later, Gwydion went looking for him in the dawn light and found him high in a magic Oak Tree, a tree that had no need for water or sunlight and existed in a place beyond the seasons. Gwydion sang to the eagle to call it back to earth. After each verse of his song the eagle dropped down a level in the tree until finally it landed on Gwydion's knee and transformed into a very weak and faltering Lleû. Later that year Lleû was restored to his adult strength and sought retribution against Gronw. He asked Math, the king, that he be allowed to do to Gronw exactly what had been done to him. On the king's command Lleû and Gronw returned to the banks of the Afon Cynfael and now the events were reversed. It was Gronw who balanced between tub and he-goat, while Lleû stood in the place first occupied by Gronw and hurled the magical spear that took a year to make. Gronw, being mortal, was killed by Lleû's spear. The story ends with 'Lleû Llaw Gyffes subdued the land a second time and ruled over it prosperously. And as the tale tells, he was lord thereafter over Gwynedd'.[13] Order is restored to the land and the reader is told 'and so ends this branch of the Mabinogi'.[14]

Approaching the Fourth Branch

The different threads of story contained in the Fourth Branch have been approached using different methodologies to reveal their cultural meaning. Sheehan pointed out that medieval Celtic studies have, in the past, tended to focus on language and issues of translation, but in recent times the Fourth Branch has been approached using methods from gender studies, the critical tools of psychoanalysis, and even queer theory. Sheehan herself looked for meaning in the story of the Fourth Branch using feminist literary scholarship.[15] Emily Lyle, however, suggested a different approach. She argued that such 'stories can, and should, be studied in the light of the periods in which they were set down' while also suggesting that such studies, if employing a 'ground-up' methodology, could prove fruitful for making connections to other Indo-European sources.[16] It is a 'ground-up' methodology that this work adopts by employing a cultural astronomy approach. Cultural astronomy is the study of the role of the sky in a culture and its methodologies, by definition, must be sensitive to the beliefs of the people who created the story or structure being studied.

Approaching the text of the Fourth Branch employing a cultural astronomical methodology means that the text is examined for signs of naked-eye astronomy, but any findings need to be relevant to how the creators of the story would have actually used the sky. Furthermore, with the cultural environment of the story being one of pre-Christian Celts, Jones and Jones argued that the Celts were a decentralised culture and embedded their gods and stories into 'specific natural features such as a mound or a stream' which reinforced their own as well as their god's local character.[17] The Afon Cynfael is such a stream and its geographical location thus needs to be a part of the sky, land, mythic picture.

The balance of light and dark: a brief journey into naked-eye astronomy

If the sky is observed from the same place for a year, one of the first things to be noticed is that the location of the rising or setting sun shifts along the horizon. For the northern hemisphere, as the winter approaches, the sun will keep rising further south until at the winter solstice it will rise at a place on the horizon at its extreme south east position (Fig. 1). Six months later it will rise in the north east at the summer solstice. When it rises halfway between these two extreme horizon points it will mark the time of the equinox, when day and night are equal, either at spring or at autumn. By watching the sun's rising or setting location on the horizon moving from south to north and then returning north to south, it becomes apparent that a horizon calendar can be created, with points along the horizon marking the individual days of the year. Many megalithic sites exemplify this type of sun-watching. Stonehenge, for example, has markers which point to the place on the horizon where the summer solstice sun will rise, while Newgrange in Ireland has a light box which captures the rising sun's light at the winter solstice by allowing a beam of sunlight to penetrate the centre of the structure and shine on a carefully placed carved stone. In contrast, at the equinox, the main cairn at a Neolithic cemetery at Loughcrew in County Meath in Ireland, captures the light of the rising sun, which shines on a carved stone deep inside the tomb.

This method of using the horizon to measure the key times of the year naturally divides the local horizon into zones: the north west/east is the part of the horizon marking the summer solstice rise and set positions, and can be thought of as the 'light' part of the horizon; the south west/east is then the 'dark' part as it marks the winter solstice rising and setting positions; and the midway point is linked to the balance of light and dark of the equinoxes. But these markers on the horizon are also linked to the moon. Both luminaries, the sun and the moon, are of equal size in the sky and share the role of producing light; in the summer, the sun is high in the sky while the full moons are low and spend little time above the horizon. The situation is reversed in the winter. When the sun is low and spends only a short time above the horizon the full moons are higher in the sky. This natural balance is further enriched by the local landscape, for the place on the horizon of the rising summer solstice sun is the same, with small variations, as that of the rising full moon at the winter solstice, and the position of winter solstice sunrise is the same as the rising full moon at the summer solstice (Fig. 1). The same applies to the setting position of the solstice sun and the opposite season's (six months later) full moon.

The landscape also pulls together the light and dark seasons. For a given location the position of the summer solstice sunset, to take one example, will be directly opposite the horizon place of the winter solstice sunrise (Fig. 2). Hence in any landscape there are two straight imaginary lines; indeed, they could be thought of as the magical spear which takes a year to be made, as these lines link the light and dark times of the year. The landscape, therefore, holds a calendar and the places of the greatest darkness and the greatest light are linked by straight axes.

This rhythm is embedded into any landscape, a rhythm which unites place and time with light and dark, sun and moon, all played out over the course of an exact year. Such landscape features, as evident by the orientations of earlier megalithic sites, were just as much part of the natural world as a stream, rock or mountain to the eyes of Iron Age people. Furthermore the night sky also held patterns of stars, and particular patterns held or marked the places where the sun or full moon were located at the time of the solstice. Thus these star patterns

Figure 1: Viewing the eastern horizon over the course of the year will show that the summer solstice sunrise location is also, with small variations, the winter solstice full moon rise location; similarly, in the south east the place of the winter solstice sunrise is the same horizon location, with small variations, of the summer solstice full moon rise. Image by author.

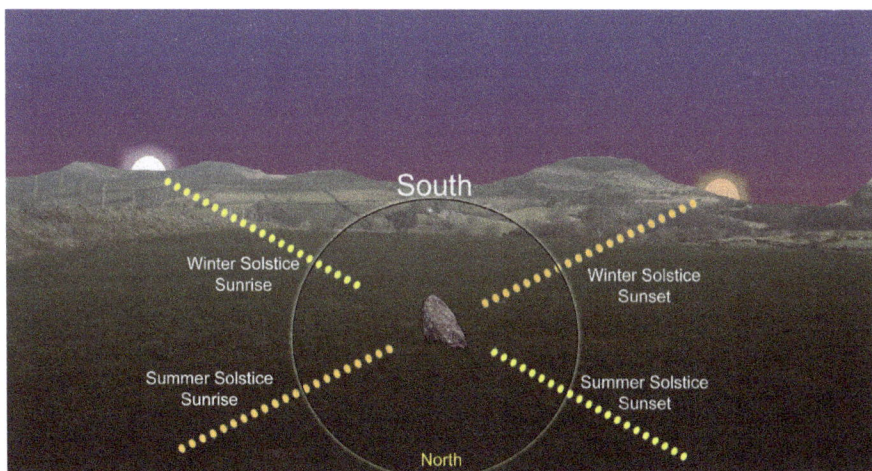

Figure 2: In an open landscape, the position of the sunrise and sunset at the winter solstice are opposite the horizon positions of the summer solstice sunrise and sunsets.

also touched the horizon at the same locations in the landscape calendar. Hence the sun, moon, stars, and landscape are all united in an exacting annual rhythm telling the story of a year.

The Greco-Roman constellations

Constellation imagery is remarkably consistent across time and across Western cultures. The classical images that populate the modern sky emerged partly from Greece and partly from Mesopotamia. For example, the Babylonians of the second millennium BCE had the sky deity, Pabilsag. He was a half human, half horse figure who stood holding his bow and arrow and who is, with few variations, our contemporary constellation of Sagittarius. Granted the constellation may have undergone name changes, but the actual imagery has been, at least in the west, carried across thousands of years by a wide variety of cultures.[18] These constellations consisted of the twelve zodiacal constellations and the thirty-six constellations described by the poet Aratus in his sky poem, *Phaenomena*, in the third century BCE.[19] By the first millennia BCE, as evident through the works of Homer and Hesiod, the classical constellations were embedded in the Mediterranean cultures.[20] The Celtic peoples, from the third to the late first millennia, would also have encountered these constellations, as they lived in areas stretching from the Mediterranean into western Northern Europe.[21] Some of these constellations are visible in the story of the Fourth Branch and begin to make sense of the absurdities of the bathtub and the he-goat.

Figure 3: The bathtub and the he-goat, the constellations of Aquarius and Capricorn, the markers of the winter solstice around 600–400 BCE. Image by author.

The constellation Aquarius is associated with measuring water; to the Romans he held a towel as he poured bath water.[22] He stands beside the he-goat, Capricorn (Fig.3). In the period of around 600 BCE, these two constellations were visible on the horizon just after sunset on the day of the winter solstice, the day of the greatest darkness. When the sun was with these constellations, it was on the 'edge' of a void, its extreme southerly horizon position. If these two constellations are the bathtub and the he-goat of the Fourth Branch it is not surprising then that the listener is explicitly told that Lleû can only die if he stands in *this* place.

South West   North East

Winter Solstice Sunset   Winter Solstice Full Moon Rise
Summer Solstice Full Moon set   Summer Solstice Sun Rise

Figure 4: The western horizon (an imaginary location) view for the day of the winter solstice for the latitude of North Wales (530 North), 600BCE. The full moon around the winter solstice would have risen in the north east, directly opposite the horizon place of the setting sun. Image by author.

The exact reverse of this situation is when the full moon sets between the he-goat and the bathtub, for then it was the time of the summer solstice – the longest day. If one considers that Lleû represents the light, then Lleû is threatened as he balances between the bathtub and the he-goat, but is at his strongest at the time of the reversal when the full moon stands in this *very* place. Furthermore, to restate, these points on the horizon are linked by an imaginary straight line as shown in Figure 2 – a spear throw.

Calendar as story

There is a cultural comparator to support this understanding of the Fourth Branch. The Coligny Calendar is an engraved bronze plate found in fragments in Coligny, France, in 1897 that represents a Celtic calendar from the pre-Roman conquest period. Although fashioned around the first-to-second centuries CE, it is generally agreed that it portrays the Celtic approach to calendar from an earlier period of the third to first centuries BCE.[23] The calendar that is revealed is one which seeks to harmonise the lunar calendar with the solar seasons.[24] There is a basic problem with a lunar year as it slips backwards against the solar year. In terms of whole days, the moon completes twelve lunar phases in 354/5 days, which is eleven days short of the length of the solar year. Therefore, after three years any particular lunar month would have slipped against the seasons by approximately thirty-three days. A lunar month which contained the summer festivals would thus quickly begin to occur in spring rather than summer, while the lunar months which held the festivals to mark the beginning of darkness would begin to occur in high summer. There are different methods of balancing the lunar calendar with the solar year, all of which involve the use of inserting leap months. The problem is to know when to insert a leap month. The Coligny calendar shows the Celtic approach to this problem and it reflects a culture that sought to maintain the balance of light and dark. The Celts injected their lunar leap months over a five-year cycle. One lunar leap month was added to the month before the lunar month of *Samon*, 'summery' (around the summer solstice) and the other was added to the dark part of the year before the lunar month of winter *Giamon*, 'wintery' (around the winter solstice).[25] Thus over a five-year cycle both the light and the dark were kept in balance with equal lunar months.

The evidence of the Coligny Celtic calendar's juggling of leap months fits into the narrative of the Fourth Branch. When the sun was between the 'bath tub and the he-goat' (Aquarius and Capricorn and thus around the winter solstice) it was a time when a lunar leap month could be added. Then thirty lunar months later (two and a half years later), when the full moon was seen between the 'bath tub and the he-goat' and which is the full moon closest to the summer solstice, another lunar leap month would need to be inserted. Granted the Fourth Branch does not refer to this thirty-month gap but it does focus strongly on the exact reversal between the sun and the moon and the timing of a year. This is the observation of the landscape calendar which is required to ensure that, over the course of the passing years, there is always a balance between the number of light and dark months of the cycle.

Hence the story of the Fourth Branch appears to be the same type of calendar portrayed in the Coligny calendar; however, instead of the calendar being hammered out in bronze, it is held in story. The two-and-a-half-year gap between the reversal of Gronw with Lleû is not in the narrative, but the fact that time has passed is clearly indicated. For Gwydion must first wait for Lleû's return and then he must recover to full strength; only then does Lleû ask for, and is granted, retribution. The spear, with its association to the notion of a year, is potentially a reference to the landscape positions of the solstice sun being opposite that of both the full moon at that time as well as the other solstice sun horizon position. The spear is an example of what Jones and Jones (cited earlier) referred to as the Celtic tendency to embed story into landscape.

An important aside, which lies beyond the scope of this work on the Afon Cynfael, is that the addition of leap months over a five-year period did not perfectly align the lunar calendar to the agricultural solar year. To avoid calendar drift, it was necessary to remove leap days at different times in the cycle. The judgment of those times is reflected in the Coligny calendar and required an experienced sky-watcher using either solar or stellar observations.[26] In that regard, the other main story lines in the Fourth Branch, which are beyond the scope of this paper, appear to describe how the sky-watcher, Gwydion, tests different ways to find the best method of keeping the solar agricultural calendar aligned to the lunar calendar.

The Ffestiniog Valley and the river

The question remains as to the role of the Afon Cynfael, and it is the wide and long Ffestiniog valley which offers an answer. If a person stands at the mouth of the Afon Cynfael, where it joins the Afon Dwyryd, then he or she is standing at a slight bend in the Ffestiniog valley. The observer's view is directed west and east by the path of the valley. Looking towards the western end there is a notch where the shape of two hills overlap. The orientation of this notch is such that the sun will set into it on 31 October, one of the cross quarter days in the Celtic year and the beginning of the season of darkness.[27] If one then turns to look up the line of the valley, towards the east, at the far end there is another notch between the hills. This notch directly captures the rising Summer Solstice sun (Fig. 5), and hence it will also capture the rising Winter Solstice full moon.[28]

Without doubt, if the banks of the Afon Cynfael had not been named by the story teller, this valley's orientation would remain a curiosity. However, the banks of Afon Cynfael are named and the Ffestiniog Valley is unique in North Wales for its size and roughly east/west orientation. There may be other locations along the 12 miles of the valley where one can see these two significant horizon calendar points highlighted by the topography. However, the mouth of the Afon Cynfael lies at a gentle bend in the Ffestiniog Valley and produces a clear view of these two key seasonal solar and lunar events.

Conclusion

As already noted, there are different threads of stories within the Fourth Branch and this work has only focused on one thread, that which is linked to the Afon Cynfael. Using the methods of cultural astronomy, the absurdities of the nature of Lleû's attempted murder and the description of his revenge are no longer absurd but are instead the necessity that the sky casts into story. The bathtub and the he-goat are direct statements about the constellations that are the

Figure 5: The solar events of the Ffestiniog Valley. TOP, left and right, views east and west generated by Google Earth, from the banks of the Afon Cynfael. BOTTOM left and right, photos by the author, 2012, of the same views. LEFT: The summer solstice sun will rise in the notch between two hills at the end of the valley. RIGHT: On 31 October the sun will set directly in the notch between the two hills. A tree in the centre of the image blocks a clear view of the notch in the western hills.

markers for the winter solstice, the spear (rather than Gronw using a sword or other weapon) is tagged with the theme of a year and is potentially a reference to the axes that the solstice and full moons make in any landscape.

The idea of the reversal is evident in both a horizon calendar of sun and moon and the approach to calendar evidenced in the Coligny Calendar. This bronze calendar showed that the pre-Roman Celtic people, over the course of a five-year interval, added leap months to their lunar calendar in a way that ensured the light part of the year was of equal length to the dark part over any five-year interval. Lleû's attempted murder is the insertion of one lunar leap month, with the exact reversal required some time later and portrayed as Lleû's retribution, which was the restoration of balance of the second lunar leap month in the other part of the year.

Finally, the role of the Afon Cynfael was to embed the story into the calendar, in order to act as a marker to its listeners. The wide Ffestiniog valley would have been a busy route from the coast to the middle of the Snowdonia Mountains, as well as a major farming area; thus the Iron Age Celts would have been aware of the horizon calendar features of the orientation of the valley, features which became visually marked by notches at each end at the valley when an observer stood at the mouth of the Afon Cynfael. These 'absurdities' within the Fourth Branch offer evidence of the role that the sky played in maintaining the Celtic calendar: a calendar that was placed into story to ensure that it passed from generation to generation amongst the Iron Age Celts of Wales.

Notes

1.   Sioned Davies, *The Mabinogion* (Oxford: Oxford University Press, 2007), p. ix.

2.   Davies,*The Mabinogion*, p. xxv.

3.   Barry W. Cunliffe, *Britain Begins* (Oxford: Oxford University Press, 2013), p. 247, pp. 51–8, p. 305.

4.   Cunliffe, *Britain Begins*, p. 305.

5.   Davies, *The Mabinogion*, p. x.

6.   Bek-Pedersen, 'Insular Celtic Religion', pp. 278–90 (p. 287).

7.   Sarah Sheehan, 'Matrilineal Subjects: Ambiguity, Bodies, and Metamorphosis in the Fourth Branch of the Mabinogi', *Signs* 34 (2009): p. 319.

8.   Alan Garner, 'Oral History and Applied Archeaology in East Cheshire', in *The Voice That Thunders: Essay and Lectures* (London: Harvill, 1997), pp. 65–79 (p. 71).

9.   Bernadette Brady, 'Star Phases: The Naked-Eye Astronomy of the Old Kingdom Pyramid Text', in Fabio Silva and Nick Campion, eds, *Skyscapes: The Role and Importance of the Sky in Archaeology* (Oxford: Oxbow, 2015), pp. 76–86, pp. 81–83.

10. Gwyn Jones and Thomas Jones, *The Mabinogion* (London: Everyman, 1949 [1993]), p. 60.

11. Gwyn Jones and Thomas Jones, *The Mabinogion* (London: Everyman, 1949 [1993]), p. 60.

12. Davies,*The Mabinogion*, p. 61.

13. Jones and Jones, *The Mabinogion*, p. 63.

14. Davies, *The Mabinogion*, p. 64.

15. Sheehan, 'Matrilineal Subjects: Ambiguity, Bodies, and Metamorphosis in the Fourth Branch of the Mabinogi', p. 320.

16. Emily B. Lyle, *Ten Gods: A New Approach to Defining the Mythological Structures of the Indo-Europeans* (Newcastle: Cambridge Scholars, 2012), p. 69.

17. Jones and Jones, *The Mabinogion*, p. 14.

18. Bernadette Brady, 'Images in the Heavens: A Cultural Landscape', *Journal for the Study of Religion, Nature and Culture* 7 (2013): p. 3.

19. Aratus, *Phaenomena* (Baltimore, MD: John Hopkins University Press, 2010).

20. Homer, *The Odyssey* (Penguin Books, 1986), p. 95; Hesiod, 'Shield of Heracles ', in Hugh G. Evelyn-White, ed., *The Homeric Hymns and Homerica* (Cambridge, MA: Harvard University Press, 1914), pp. 216–25.

21. Cunliffe, *Britain Begins*, pp. 242–43.

22. Richard Hinckley Allen, *Star Names Their Lore and Meaning* (New York: Dover Publications, Inc., 1963), p. 45.

23. Garrett Olmsted, *The Gaulish Calendar: A Reconstruction from the Bronze Fragments from Coligny with an Analysis of Its Function as a Highly Accurate Lunar/ Solar Predictor as Well as an Explanation of Its Terminology and Development* (Bonn: Habelt, 1992), pp. 73–75.

24. Adolfo Zavaroni, *On the Structure and Terminology of the Gaulish Calendar* (Oxford: Archaeopress, 2007), p. 18, p. 89.

25. Zavaroni, *On the Structure and Terminology of the Gaulish Calendar*, p. 18.

26. Zavaroni, *On the Structure and Terminology of the Gaulish Calendar*, p. 30.

27. This notch, measured from the mouth of the Afon Cynfael, has an azimuth of 249° and the notch is at 0° of elevation. For the latitude of that location (52.956064 north) this produces a declination of -12.5, the declination of the setting sun in last few days of October.

28. This notch in the hills is at an azimuth of 57° and an elevation of 5° which produces a declination of 23.4, which is the summer solstice sunrise.

8

WATCHING THE RIVER FLOW: WATER, MUSIC AND LIVERPOOL'S MATERIALITY OF PLACE

Alexander Scott

This chapter is an inquiry into the materiality of place of Liverpool. It focuses on two key aspects of Liverpool's history and culture: firstly, the city's relationship to water and waterways, particularly the River Mersey; and, secondly, representations of rivers and the sea in Liverpudlian culture, especially songs inspired by maritime travel. The aim is to investigate the complex ways in which places are constituted through intersecting sociocultural, spatiotemporal and psychophysiological matrices. More plainly, I want to explore how the 'things,' 'symbols' and 'ideas' that make up Liverpool and 'Liverpool-ness' mix together past and present, local and global, matter and myth, human and non-human, 'here' and 'there.' Without denying the specificities of Liverpudlian culture or the civic pride felt by current and past city-dwellers (this author included), my contention is that Liverpool's cultural imprint cannot be reduced to – or contained within – the political-geographical entity that sits beside the River Mersey. Summarised, 'a' place is always other places; anywhere is always a 'composite of elsewheres.' [1]

Issues of this sort are manifold with respect to the dense material and symbolic networks of the twenty-first-century city – but not uniquely so. Much of what follows could apply equally to, say, Lampeter as Liverpool. Focusing on rivers and waterways helps illustrate this. Water is neither exclusively urban nor rural, and its elusive, slippery, kinetic qualities – its lack of respect for boundaries – both offers relief from city/country binaries and exaggerates the 'hard-to-contain' quality of 'place.' Three particular characteristics of water equate to my hypotheses about place: water is pluralistic ('it' is not one 'thing' but both composed of and component of innumerable other 'things'), shapeshifting (variously changing from liquid to gas to solid and messy in-between states) and is characterised by constant state of mobility (both at a microscopic, molecular level and its observable capacity to move, be moved, and to move other things).[2] Music serves an analogous function in my analysis. Unlike the people, instruments and technologies that write, record, perform, produce and distribute it, or the bodily reactions that it stimulates in listeners, music *itself* does not have a clearly-identifiable physicality. This intangibility – while admittedly distinguishing it from water – gives music mobility and fluidity, allowing songs and tunes to move between (and transcend) particular historical and geographical settings.

The chapter is motivated by queries comparable to those posed by Felix Driver and Raphael Samuel about 'rethinking place':

> Can we understand the identity of places in less bounded, more open-ended ways? Can we write local histories which acknowledge that places are not so much singular points as constellations, the product of all sorts of social relations which cut across particular locations in a multiplicity of ways? What ways of telling the story of places might be appropriate to such a perspective?[3]

In attempting to 'tell a story of place' 'appropriate to' Liverpool, the chapter is informed by the ideas of anthropologist Tim Ingold. Like Ingold, I regard places as being 'like knots' possessing 'threads' that 'trail beyond' their immediate geographical locale. My discussion deploys the River Mersey and other waterways as motifs which help demonstrate that individual places are 'caught up with other places as are threads in other knots,' while also ascribing to Ingold's notion that places are 'delineated by movement, not the outer limits of movement'. The chapter thus emphasises mobility and the 'perambulatory' routes (both figurative and actual) traversed by Liverpudlian cultural artefacts – specifically maritime folksongs made in and about the city.[4]

My approach to place also engages with the philosophy Gilles Deleuze and Félix Guattari – a key influence on Ingold.[5] Deleuze and Guattari's *A Thousand Plateaus* (1980) used the phenomenon of rhizome – a term derived from botany to describe a subterranean system which connects plants' roots, branches and offshoots in a non-hierarchal manner – to understand language, knowledge and nature as systems of endlessly-multiplying interconnections. In this, Deleuze and Guattari emphasised the 'principles of connection and heterogeneity ... [that] any point of a rhizome can be connected to anything other,' mapping 'lines of flight' through and between things.[6] As will be elaborated below, Deleuze and Guattari accorded music (plus associated aquatic imagery) a critical position in their theorisation of rhizome. In particular, they stressed the importance of the 'refrain' – a repeated musical detail or remembered tune, rendered in French as *ritournelle* ('little return') – as a means of conceptualising linkages between different spatiotemporal territories. In doing so, they formulate a typology of musical refrains, including 'folk and popular refrains, themselves tied to an immense song of the people.'[7]

Taking these cues from Deleuze and Guattari, the chapter attempts to map 'folk and popular' refrains associated with songs about Liverpool, the Mersey and nautical culture more generally. It begins by appraising theories about the materiality of cities, place, space and water by scholars including Doreen Massey, Tim Edensor and Chris Otter.[8] The second section then uses Jacqueline Nassy Brown's ethnographic studies of Liverpool's African Caribbean communities to outline (and, in part, problematize) the extent to which Liverpudlian culture and identity are framed in relation to the River Mersey and other waterways.[9] The final section changes register somewhat, indulging in what Ingold might term 'trail-following' with respect to folksongs dating from the nineteenth century.[10] The most famous Liverpool musicians, the Beatles, are important here, as is another rock idol less obviously associated with the city: Bob Dylan. Having followed various routes traversed by Liverpudlian folksongs, I conclude with remarks about conceptual utility of water for theorising the material and affective qualities of place.

The materiality of place (and space) in urban studies

Contrary to first appearances, 'place' and its sometime correlate 'space' are 'complex words.'[11] Often used interchangeably in everyday speech, the two terms come freighted with baggage within the academy, eliciting perennial debate about their contiguousness to another. In broad brushstrokes, 'space' – especially when deployed as a means of understanding capitalism – tends to be conceptualised abstractly, whereas there is an inclination to perceive 'place' in more holistic, phenomenological terms. According to different political, philosophical and disciplinary traditions, this can lead to a divergent privileging of space over place – and vice versa. For example, David Harvey, a leading theoretician of the late-twentieth-century 'spatial turn' in the social sciences and humanities, deems 'place' sufficiently subordinate to 'space' that 'the only interesting question that can be asked is: by what social processes is place constructed?'[12] Contrastingly, Ingold values the 'groundedness of place,' and decries the very 'notion of space' as 'the most empty, most detached from the realities of life and experience … of all the terms we use to describe the world we inhabit.'[13]

Both of these stances are concerned with materiality – albeit in quite oppositional ways. Where Ingold is oriented towards the physical substances (matter) of which 'things' are composed, Harvey's materialism is that of the

Marxist tradition, centring on the workings of the economy and capital. The latter sense of materiality has been particularly influential amongst urban theorists. As Chris Otter has shown, a long line of thinkers (from Friedrich Engels, Georg Simmel and the Chicago School through to postmodernists such as Harvey and Edward Soja) have regarded cities' 'material form as little more than the outcome of the abstract force of capital,' leaving 'materiality itself – the forms, states and qualities of matter – analytically underexplored.'[14] This impacts upon how 'place' and 'the local' are theorised. A train of postmodernist thought in the 1980s–1990s argued that late capitalism had seen the triumph of space over place – and the global over the local. From this point-of-view, the distinctiveness of particular cities was being eroded and replaced by a uniform, worldwide urbanism of indistinguishable 'non-places.'[15] Postmodernist interpretations therefore extended a longstanding tendency to conflate 'place' and 'the local' with preindustrial society, and to contrastingly couple 'space' with 'the global' and modernity.[16]

The latter perspective can be reductive, though, glossing over 'the long history of connections between the local and the global.'[17] It also obscures the more dynamic conceptual potentialities of place. Doreen Massey, for example, has argued for a 'progressive ... outward-looking sense of place' which recognises that global connectedness does not automatically diminish local difference.[18] Instead, Massey insisted that 'local uniqueness is always already a product of wider contacts ... to the geographical beyond, the world beyond the place itself.'[19] Massey's point is, in fact, discernible in cities' material fabric. As Tim Edensor stresses, cities are products both of 'multiple and coinciding temporalities' and of 'entangled links with people, routes and materials from elsewhere.'[20] Edensor exemplifies this by examining the 'time-geography' of building stone in central Manchester.[21] Quarried in peripheral locations, and possessing a geological age long predating human history, samples of the same stone used to construct buildings such as St Ann's Church, the Arndale Centre and Manchester Central Library can be found as far away as New York and Tuscany.[22] Similar routes of connectedness characterise cities' aquatic infrastructure. Urban hydraulic systems are typically predicated on drawing water to the city from 'long-distance conduits' before expending it elsewhere. Additionally, the types of drinking water – 'purged of organic and mineral "impurities" and augmented with highly specific chemicals' – consumed by urban populations is not 'timeless' but the confluence of technological, scientific and governmental processes dating back to (at least) the mid-nineteenth century.[23]

Liverpool, the Mersey and the materiality of place

Liverpool is a paradigmatic example of a place which has *always* been constituted through connections to the wider world: its first royal charter was granted in 1207 as a base from which King John could mount naval raids to Ireland and Wales. In subsequent centuries, pancontinental trade emerged as Liverpool's *raison d'être*. Transatlantic slavery structured Liverpool's economy in the eighteenth and nineteenth centuries, transforming a small fishing village into a metropolis. The port remained a crucial centre-point of British imperial commerce into the twentieth century. Concomitantly, millions of New World migrants passed through Liverpool in the Victorian and Edwardian periods, with diaspora communities – Welsh, Irish, West African, Chinese and many more – also establishing permanent homes in the city. Liverpool's contemporary status too remains shaped by exigencies that are global in scale. Today, the city still feels the effects of the economic decline precipitated by the reorientation of international trade away from the port after the Second World War.[24]

Liverpool's internationalism and multiculturalism are central to Jacqueline Nassy Brown's ethnography *Dropping Anchor, Setting Sail: Geographies of Race in Black Liverpool* (2005). For Nassy Brown, Liverpool represents 'a decidedly local site … that is global by definition,' and she analyses ways that macrohistorical phenomena of 'race and empire have penetrated and helped form the present-day political subjectivities of Liverpool-born Blacks.'[25] This involves pinpointing ways individuals and communities 'make meaning out of the materiality of places'– both in terms of places' physicality (how locations 'look, feel, and where they are') and their 'effects on human consciousness and experience.' Brown argues the cityscape possesses *agency* to *act* upon city-dwellers, detailing the physiological, psychological and emotional impacts that Liverpool's topography and built environment – docks, warehouses, parks, streets, the River Mersey – have on those who encounter them.[26]

Brown also flags up instances where the discursive aspects of place are mobilised to 'explain' political issues.[27] Her main example is the manner in which physical blight was classified as a cause of major disturbances which occurred in July 1981 in Toxteth – a south Liverpool district historically home to the majority of the city's African Caribbean populace. Environmental explanations influenced policymakers' decision to plant trees in-and-around Toxteth as a prospective solution to the social problems highlighted by the riots/uprising.[28] The same logic underpinned the decision to stage the 1984 Liverpool International Garden Festival – a large-scale tourist event which acted as a lynchpin of the Thatcher Government's urban regeneration strategy for Merseyside.[29]

Discussions of Liverpool's materiality of place – including Brown's – invariably turn around one topographical feature above all else. 'Regarding Liverpool,' Brian Hatton has written, 'all must commence with the Mersey. On the primacy of the river, all are agreed.'[30] Colloquialisms give expression to this. In Liverpudlian dialect, the Mersey marks the city's westernmost frontier, and to venture 'over the water' to Birkenhead is to exit the metropolis and enter an inurbane netherland populated by 'woolybacks.'[31] The Mersey's cultural 'primacy' reflects its centrality to the region's port trade – yet it goes beyond mere economic factors. Writers frequently render Liverpool and the Mersey as coextensive, portraying the river as the city's defining *material* characteristic. An account of 'Liverpool-on-the-Mersey' from a 1907 guidebook by Walter Dixon Scott is exemplary:

> It is upon her River that the existence of this great, complex, modern organism unanimously depends. Rob her of her duties as port and harbour, and she becomes impossible. Let the river-estuary silt up, as this one is constantly endeavouring to do, and the whole elaborate structure instantly crumbles and subsides.

> ... This is the great fact of [Liverpool's] life. Its significance is chief, not merely because Liverpool owes her actual existence to the River, but also because the whole quality of that existence has been determined by the completeness of the dependency. It is not simply that it is upon this broadly curving estuary that Liverpool has rel[ied] in slashing her way to the position she now maintains; [the Mersey] ... has induced certain habits of poise, of outlook, of ideal, which are now [Liverpool's] most essential characteristics. The influence ... drenches the local atmospheres, private, social, civic, with a distinctive colour. It is revealed in the nature of the men in her streets, and the nature of the streets about the men. It is the deciding element in that inherent spirit of the place which those men and streets at once prefigure and evoke.[32]

Here, Dixon Scott invests the Mersey's materiality (its curves and propensity to silt up) with the capacity to shape, and explain, the physical and social characteristics of Liverpool – to the extent that 'dependency' on the river has the potential to bring down its 'elaborate structure.'

In this, Dixon Scott proved prescient. Overreliance on port trade – allied to failed attempts to diversify its industrial base – was the key cause of Liverpool's economic travails in the second half of the twentieth century. By 1981 the situation was so bad that the Chancellor of the Exchequer, Geoffrey Howe, infamously entertained subjecting the city to a 'managed decline.' Writing to Prime Minister Margaret Thatcher in the wake of the Toxteth disturbances, Howe counselled that 'concentrating cash into Liverpool' might be like 'trying to make water flow uphill,' adding: 'It would be regrettable if the brighter ideas for renewing economic activity were sown only on the stony ground on the banks of the Mersey.'[33] Howe was not unique in using aquatic symbolism to describe Liverpool's situation. A guidebook for the International Garden Festival, for example, likened changes in the local and global economy to tidal patterns: '"The Leaving of Liverpool" once referred to the embarkation of great ships but now indicates that the liners have left for ever. So have the jobs ... as large-scale industry drifts away in the wake of the ships.'[34] For his part, Michael Heseltine, Secretary of State for the Environment from 1979–1983, viewed the Mersey itself as the embodiment of Liverpool's socioeconomic difficulties. Once the 'life-spring of Liverpool,' the physical state of the river left a 'haunting ... impression' on Heseltine: filled with 'untreated sewage, pollutants [and] noxious discharge,' he deemed it 'an affront to the standards civilised society should demand of its environment.'[35] To try and rectify this, Heseltine helped found the Mersey Basin Campaign – a clean water initiative that has since encouraged fish species to repopulate the river.[36]

As influential as the Mersey doubtlessly is on Liverpool's economy and culture, synonymising the city and the river nevertheless relies on a sleight of hand. A simple truth is that the Mersey *is not* Liverpool – or at least not just Liverpool. Beginning at the confluence of the River Tame and River Goyt in Stockport, the river's course passes through several local authorities (Greater Manchester, Wirral, Halton and Cheshire) before emptying into the Irish Sea at Liverpool Bay. This lack of monopoly on the river's materiality actually bore negative consequences for Liverpool businessmen in the late nineteenth century. The Manchester Ship Canal, completed 1893, cut an inlet into the Mersey from Eastham to Ellesmere Port on the Wirral peninsula, allowing Mancunian merchants to redirect traffic away from Liverpool to the newly-established Port of Manchester.[37]

Furthermore, for all that Heseltine, Dixon Scott and others interpret the Mersey as the material basis of Liverpool's 'life,' the bodily sustenance of its citizens depends on water drawn from other sources. An 1847 Act of Parliament gave Liverpool Corporation municipal control over city's water supplies, with its first permanent reservoir being constructed at Rivington, Lancashire in 1857. As the city expanded, further water supplies were secured at Lake Vrynwy (built 1880–1888) and Llyn Celyn (1960–1965), both in Wales.[38] These two schemes drew controversy owing to them involving submerging the villages of Llanwddyn, Powys and Capel Celyn in the Tryweryn Valley. The latter especially became a cause celebre in Welsh culture, particularly amongst nationalists. The flooding of Capel Celyn is the subject of several pop songs (including 'Ready for Drowning' by Manic Street Preachers), and in 2005 Liverpool City Council formally apologised for the insensitive actions of previous municipal authorities. A protest memorial labelled 'Cofiwch Dryweryn' ('Remember Tryweryn') has stood at the entrance to Llanrhystud, a village in Ceredigion, since 1965.[39]

Liverpool folksongs and 'Scouse Atlantic' culture

I pass the 'Cofiwch Dryweryn' memorial every time I ride the bus from Lampeter to Aberystwyth. Liverpool has a habit of following me around like this – of cropping up on where I am not expecting it. This offers a reminder of Ingold's insight that 'lives are not led inside places, but through, around, to and from them, from and to places elsewhere.'[40] Conceptualising place in this open-ended manner has particular resonance with respect to Liverpool. Twenty-first-century Liverpudlians inherit a local culture which has traditionally regarded the sea, mobility and connections to the wider world as 'the premier signifier' of local distinctiveness.[41] Brown draws attention to the preponderance for motifs of arrival and departure in narratives about Liverpool, identifying a persistent Liverpudlian 'folk phenomenology' centring on 'men and ships dropping anchor and setting sail' – a gendered configuration that presumed husbands, sons, fathers and brothers crossed the oceans as seafarers while women remained domiciled in Liverpool.[42]

Such tropes are appreciable in Liverpool's musical heritage – particularly amongst folksongs derived from tunes sang by sailors at sea and in port. Music was an ever-present feature of maritime culture in the age of sail. Herman Melville's novel *Redburn* (1849) attests to this. Based on Melville's own experiences of passing through the port, *Redburn* chronicles the maiden voyage of a young sailor, Wellingborough Redburn, from New York to Liverpool. Setting sail across the Atlantic, Redburn quickly gets 'used to singing, for sailors never touch a rope without it,' discovering that seafarers possessing good singing voices earned 'a great name from officers and popularity among shipmates.'[43] Landing in Liverpool, Redburn encounters a 'singular spectacle' in which 'the songs of the seamen' mix with street musicians' 'hand-organs, fiddles and cymbals' and the 'noise of revelry and dancing' of dockland pubs.[44] Underlining the ubiquity of music and songs in nautical culture, Redburn even finds 'sailor-scrawls of … lovers' sonnets and ocean ditties' daubed on the walls of his Liverpool boarding house.[45] On the return voyage to the United States, Redburn likewise hears a nightly ritual of Jewish emigrants singing 'songs of Zion to the roll of the great ocean-organ ... as they hie to the land of the stranger.'[46]

Probably the best-known nineteenth-century Liverpool folksong is 'The Leaving of Liverpool' (a song alluded to in urban regeneration discourse above). In the 1950s, the folklorist William Main Doerflinger wrote that 'The Leaving of Liverpool' had been heard aboard Liverpool ships since the 1880s – although some estimates date it back to the Gold Rush of 1849.[47] Lyrical variations exist, but the basic conceit remains consistent, telling of a departing seaman lamenting lost love when embarking for California from Liverpool's Prince's Landing Stage. The chorus goes:

> So fare thee well, my own true love,
> And when I return, united we will be.
> It's not the leaving of Liverpool that grieves me
> But my darling, when I think on thee.[48]

Where movement and departure is integral to the drama of 'The Leaving of Liverpool,' the song itself has proved mobile and adaptable to different contexts. Most notably, it found renewed acclaim during the mid-twentieth century folk revival, with versions being recorded by the likes of Ewan MacColl, the Seekers and the Dubliners. Reflecting its status as a folk favourite, 'The Leaving of Liverpool' was part of the repertoire of a young Bob Dylan. Dylan modified the song's lines from 'The Leaving of Liverpool' for his 1963 track 'Farewell,' and the same year he aped its plot and subject when penning a song about a 'Liverpool Gal who lived in London Town.'[49] In 1967, Dylan also recorded a take on 'Johnny Todd' – a song thematically similar to 'The Leaving of Liverpool'. According to antiquarian Frank Kidson, who collected the song for an 1891 anthology, 'Johnny Todd' originated as 'a rhyme and game played by Liverpool children,' and it seems Dylan became familiar with the song via Captain Bob Roberts, an ex-sailor who found popularity as a singer and storyteller in the 1940s and 1950s.[50] Rehearsing familiar themes of lost love, migration and moving on, the song opens with this verse:

> Johnny Todd he took a notion
> For to go across the sea,
> And he left his love behind him,
> Weeping by the Liverpool sea.[51]

'The Leaving of Liverpool' and 'Johnny Todd' were amongst several such Liverpool seafaring songs that circulated on both sides of the Atlantic in the 1950s and 1960s. Local musicians too produced noteworthy work in the folk idiom during this period. The album *Liverpool Packet: Songs of the Great Seaport* appeared in 1958. Three years later Peter McGovern wrote 'In My Liverpool Home' – an updated take on a sea shanty that became one of the definitive Liverpool songs after being recorded by the Spinners, another Merseyside folk outfit.[52]

Folksongs also featured in the Beatles' discography. Liverpool-themed ditty 'Maggie Mae' was on the setlist when Paul McCartney first joined John Lennon onstage in 1957, and eventually a forty-second version of the song was included on *Let It Be* (1970). A narrative of sexual encounter and exile, 'Maggie Mae' bears thematic similarity to 'Johnny Todd' and 'The Leaving of Liverpool' – except that it involves a Liverpudlian woman travelling overseas (albeit involuntarily): it tells of a sailor who arrives in port from Sierra Leone before being led astray by a local sex worker, the eponymous Maggie, who is sent to Botany Bay penal colony for her supposed crimes.[53]

However, maybe the most lasting impact made by a traditional Liverpool tune in the 1960s was shorn of folk's sonic trappings. 'Johnny Todd' reached national prominence after being reworked for the theme tune of *Z Cars*, a BBC police procedural broadcast between 1962 and 1978. The *Z-Cars* version of 'Johnny Todd' was entirely instrumental based on an arrangement by Fritz Spiegl, of Liverpool Royal Philharmonic Orchestra.[54] Featuring flutes, drums and saxophones, Spiegl's jazzed-up 'Theme from Z Cars (Johnny Todd)' reached fifth in the UK singles chart when released by Johnny Keating in 1962. The success of Keating's recording led to it being embraced by an anthem by fans of Everton Football Club. It still plays before kick-off at home matches.

Everton's ongoing usage of 'Johnny Todd' bespeaks the subtle, often unnoticed, ways that maritime history continues to inflect Liverpool's culture long after the products and profits of docking have ceased to be a distinctive, visible feature of everyday life in the city. This is underscored by the output of Liverpudlian musicians. For instance, Robert Strachan discerns a 'surreal folk memory of seafaring and working-class labour' in the output of twenty-first-century Merseyside bands such as the Coral and The Zutons.[55] More tellingly, the Beatles' persuasive impact on popular music is partly a by-product of oceanic journeys 'to' and 'from' Liverpool. Access to American country, skiffle and blues records brought back to the city by Liverpudlian ship-workers (the so-called Cunard Yanks) was a formative influence on the 1960s Merseybeat scene; likewise, the Beatles' rock 'n' roll sound drew heavily on music made by African

Americans – music, that is to say, by descendants of enslaved peoples on whose backs Liverpool's initial notoriety and wealth was built.[56]

'Maggie Mae,' for one, bears echoes of such history. Thought to have originated in the early nineteenth century, its tune and plot were transplanted to the American slave states by a white evangelical pastor Benjamin R. Hanby for 'Darling Nelly Gray.' Composed in 1856, Hanby's version is sang from the viewpoint of an enslaved man mourning his lost partner Nelly, who was 'sold down the river' from Kentucky into the still harsher conditions of Georgia's cotton fields. 'Nelly Gray' became a popular abolitionist hymn during the American Civil War (1861–65), reflecting Hanby's role as a participant in the Underground Railroad, a network of safe houses which helped fugitives from slavery escape northwards into the free states or Canada. Muddying this legacy somewhat, renditions of 'Nelly Gray' became a commonplace of minstrel shows – including those starring white performers in blackface.[57]

Minstrel songs make a passing appearance in *A Thousand Plateaus*, when Deleuze and Guattari discuss the musical and linguistic techniques enslaved people used to adapt and translate African work songs to suit their experiences in the Americas, plus the parallel processes which saw plantation songs incorporated into blackface acts.[58] For Deleuze and Guattari, this is demonstrative of two key phenomena: 'deterritorialization' (which involves something moving from, or being shorn of, its original context) and 'reterritorialization' (which involves that same thing re-emerging, or being forcibly, transplanted elsewhere). In a similar manner, Deleuze and Guattari cited another, comparable musical example when explaining their concept of rhizome. Searching for an image to illustrate that 'a rhizome has no beginning or end; it is always in the middle, between things, interbeing, *intermezzo*,' they turned to the lyrics of an old show tune: 'As they say about old man river … he just keeps rollin' along.'[59]

Mention of 'Ol' Man River' returns me to earlier observations about water and the materiality of place. On one hand, personifying the Mississippi as 'Ol' Man River' captures the strong attachment many cultures share with waterways. On the other, the message of the lyrics – written by Oscar Hammerstein II in 1927 – impresses the river's *indifference* to humans: the Mississippi does not care about cotton or potatoes and those people who plant them are 'soon forgotten.'[60] The song, furthermore, has themes in common with Liverpudlian folksongs. As made iconic by Paul Robeson's performance in the film *Show Boat* (1936), 'Ol' Man River' is framed from the perspective of a black stevedore sitting aboard a ship who muses about sailors' harsh manual labour and their onshore antics (the protagonist gets drunk and ends up in jail).

Sufficiently stereotyped in its representation of African Americans that Robeson later refused to perform it without modified lyrics, 'Ol' Man River' nevertheless accentuates the importance of maritime travel in black history.[61] Paul Gilroy's seminal study *The Black Atlantic: Modernity and Double Consciousness* (1993) uses 'the image of ships' as its 'central organising symbol' for analysing the 'intercultural and transnational' experiences of the African diaspora.[62] In this, Gilroy is interested in the 'rhizomorphic, fractal' character of black Atlantic culture, concurring with Peter Linebaugh's verdict that 'the ship remained perhaps the most important conduit of Pan-African communication before the appearance of the long-playing record.'[63] Ships are also important for Gilroy because of their role in transatlantic slavery and 'the discontinuous histories of England's ports' ... interfaces with the wider world.'[64]

Gilroy's ideas have clear application to Liverpool history. For example, journalist Ed Vulliamy refers to 'the black/green/Scouse Atlantic' when discussing Liverpool band the Real Thing and their single 'Children of the Ghetto' (1977) – a song with a biography that offers another example of the transatlantic character of Liverpudlian music.[65] The singers Eddy and Chris Amoo wrote 'Children of the Ghetto' as an effort to emulate 'message songs' of the African American civil rights movement: sons of a Ghanaian seaman, they wanted to draw attention to the inequities and discrimination experienced by people of colour in Liverpool by a telling a narrative of inner-city life comparable to Marvin Gaye's 'What's Going On? (1971). 'Children of the Ghetto' subsequently became a standard amongst jazz and soul musicians in the United States, whilst back in Liverpool it acted as 'the anthem of, and soundtrack to the riots' of 1981.[66]

More broadly, 'Children of the Ghetto' testifies to the long, yet sometimes overlooked, role that African Caribbean musicians played in shaping Liverpool's musical heritage. Eddy Amoo's previous band the Chants, for instance, were veterans of Sixties Merseybeat – a musical genre and 'scene' which derived some of its vibrancy from proximity to concert venues catering to Liverpool's African and West Indian population (e.g. the Caribbean Centre, Jamaica House and the Sierra Leone, Ibo, Somali and Ghana Clubs).[67] In Paul McCartney's words:

> The big factor about Liverpool was it being a port. There were always sailors coming in with records from America, records from New Orleans. And you could get so many different ethnic sounds: African music, calypsos via the Caribbean community ... So with all these influences, from your home, the radio, the sailors, the immigrants, Liverpool was a huge melting pot of music.[68]

As McCartney implies, the different songs discussed in this chapter thus amplify broader cross-currents of that have congregated at, emanated from, or flowed through Liverpool over several centuries. Further explorations of reciprocities between Bob Dylan and the Beatles offer a coda to this.[69] Where Dylan pooled material from 'Johnny Todd' and 'The Leaving of Liverpool,' the Beatles drew inspiration from Dylan – as signalled by his presence on the sleeve of *Sgt Pepper's Lonely Hearts Club Band* (1967). Ringo Starr and George Harrison each collaborated with the American, and John Lennon admitted to undergoing a mid-Sixties 'Dylan period.' Becoming a fan in early 1964, Lennon took to sporting a Dylanesque 'Huck Finn' cap, confessing that 'You've Got to Hide Your Love Away' on 1965's *Help!* was an explicit attempt to imitate Dylan's song-writing and vocal mannerisms.[70] But musicologist Walter Everett has proposed another ancestry for the sound of 'Hide Your Love Away.' The song arrangement chosen by producer George Martin ends with a flute solo, encouraging Everett to speculate: 'Could Martin's idea be traced to the use of piccolos for a similarly arched tune in Johnny Keating's "Theme from Z Cars"?'[71]

Such creative back-and-forth stretched into the twenty-first century. In 2009, Dylan was spotted on a minibus of tour of John Lennon's childhood home, Mendips in Woolton, south Liverpool. Apparently, Dylan was moved by how much it 'recalled his own home in Hibbing,' declaring: 'This kitchen it's just like my mom's!'[72] The trip seems to have provided creative stimulus for Dylan. His 2013 album *Tempest* features 'Roll On John' – an elegy to Lennon filled with references to the Liverpool and Beatles. Amidst allusions to chained hands of enslaved Africans on the Middle Passage, the song finds Dylan imagining Lennon as a Johnny Todd-figure setting sail from the Mersey never to return.[73] The theme of departure echoes Lennon's own ruminations about Liverpool whilst exiled in London, New York and elsewhere. Famously, Lennon mined his childhood memories for 'Penny Lane' and 'Strawberry Fields Forever' (1967), and a similar sense of nostalgia may have informed the decision to include 'Maggie Mae' on *Let It Be* – the Beatles' swansong album. Recorded during the 'Get Back' sessions of January 1969, Jeremy Price interprets 'Maggie Mae' as 'marking the formation and the breakup of the group in a cycle of beginning and return to their Liverpool roots.'[74] Lennon, fot his part, kept returning to 'Maggie Mae,' recording solo versions of it in 1973 and 1980. He also had an uncanny autographical link to earlier iterations of the song: his grandfather Jack toured North America as a member of the Kentucky Minstrels in the 1890s.[75] Around the same time, Robert Zimmerman's maternal grandparents passed through from Liverpool when emigrating from Lithuania to the United States.[76]

Conclusion

The above excurses on the sonic and lyrical trajectories of Liverpool folksongs might seem quite detached from the dense theorising about the materiality of place elsewhere in this chapter. Here, though, it pays to remember the emphasis placed on music by Deleuze and Guattari, and the overlaps between their concepts of rhizome and the refrain. Popular music references recur throughout *A Thousand Plateaus*, as befitting Deleuze and Guattari's declaration that 'RHIZOMATICS = POP ANALYSIS.'[77] Deleuze and Guattari, moreover, were Dylan fans.[78] Indeed, Deleuze once stated that: 'As a teacher, I should like to give a course as Bob Dylan organises a song, as astonishing producer rather than author ... finding, encountering stealing, instead of regulating, recognising and judging.'[79]

This quote is as ambiguous as many of Dylan's lyrics. My guess is that Deleuze was gesturing towards Dylan's persona as an itinerant troubadour, and his ability to find, connect and refashion cultural artefacts accumulated during his travels. Along these lines, Richard Elliot has identified a 'poetics of place and displacement' running through Dylan's oeuvre – one 'steeped in [a] mythology of place and autobiography' which is characterised 'sometimes by moving on and restlessness, at other times by the projection of place from another, removed but stable place.'[80] Dylan's interest in Liverpool seafaring songs seems to complement Elliot's observations, while also embellishing a broader preoccupation with nautical themes: notably, Dylan's Nobel Prize acceptance speech featured lengthy meditations on two canonical maritime stories – Homer's *The Odyssey* and Melville's *Moby Dick* (1851).[81]

Collectively, Dylan's lateral connections with Liverpool, Lennon and the Beatles reinforce the entangled character of places and individuals' relationship with them. As Ingold puts it, 'people carry on their lives' along an 'entire meshwork of intertwined trails' – trails that interact with 'fellow humans ... skies, mountains, rivers, rocks, trees, houses ... [and] non-human animals.'[82] Ingold's thoughts give pause to reflect on the *agency* of water in the various meshworks enumerated in this paper. Paul McCartney is surely right that being a port is the 'big factor' in Liverpool history; but, on elemental level, water made the port. Being next to water – the Mersey, and by extension the Irish Sea and the Atlantic Ocean – gave Liverpool its original socioeconomic function, just as water carried the ships aboard which sailors sang the songs that helped mould Liverpool's musical culture. Viewed accordingly, Liverpool folksongs' transatlantic journeys enable us to appreciate that oceans *connect* landmasses, and that *water binds together* faraway places rather than *separating* them. Correspondingly, water helps destabilise the fixity of place, demonstrating that

Liverpool – or anywhere – is an amalgam of lines of flight that are global and endless in scale. Like my analysis in this chapter, water has a predisposition towards spirals and spherical movements and does not flow in straight lines. Even on flat surfaces, water moves – a motion that is seldom 'uncomplicated, or unidirectional.'[83] In sum, the properties and behaviours of water – perhaps even more than Deleuze and Guattari's concepts rhizome and the refrain – offer practical guides for thinking through the materiality of place.

Notes

1.   Tim Edensor, 'Building Stone in Manchester: Networks of Materiality, Circulating Matter and the Ongoing Constitution of the City,' in *Re-shaping Cities: How Global Mobility Transforms Architecture and Urban Form*, by Michael Guggenheim and Ola Söderström eds. (Abingdon, Oxon: Routledge, 2010), p. 218.

2.   Luci Attala, *How Water Makes Us Human* (Cardiff: University of Wales Press, 2019), pp. 18–19, 33–38. On water's messy 'in-between' states: Stuart McLean, 'Black Goo: Forceful Encounters with Matter in Europe's Muddy Margins,' *Cultural Anthropology* 26:4 (2011), pp. 589–619.

3 .   Felix Driver and Raphael Samuel, 'Rethinking the Idea of Place', *History Workshop Journal* 39 (1995), p. vi.

4.   Tim Ingold, *Being Alive: Essays on Movement, Knowledge and Description* (Abingdon, Oxon: Routledge, 2011), p. 149.

5.   See Ingold, *Being Alive*, pp. 14, 83–84.

6.   Gilles Deleuze and Félix Guattari, *A Thousand Plateaus: Capitalism and Schizophrenia*, translated by Brian Massumi (Minneapolis: University of Minnesota Press, 1987 [1980], p. 12.

7.   Deleuze and Guattari, *Thousand Plateaus*, p. 347. See Timothy S. Murphy and Daniel W. Smith, 'What I Hear is Thinking Too: Deleuze and Guattari Go Pop,' *Echo: A Music-Centred Journal* 3:1 (2001) <http://www.echo.ucla.edu/article-what-i-hear-is-thinking-too-deleuze-and-guattari-go-pop-by-timothy-s-murphy-and-daniel-w-smith/> [accessed 7 March 2023].

8.   Edensor, 'Building Stone in Manchester,' pp. 211–229; Edensor, 'Materiality, Time and the City: The Multiple Temporalities of Building Stone,' in *Spatialities: The Geographies of Art and Architecture* (Bristol: Intellect, 2012), pp. 35–52; Doreen Massey, 'Places and their Pasts,' *History Workshop Journal* 39 (1995), pp. 82–192; Massey, 'A Global Sense of Place,' *Marxism Today* (June 1991), pp. 24–29; Chris Otter, 'Locating Matter: The Place of Materiality in Urban History,' in *Material Powers: Essays Beyond Cultural Materialism*, ed. by Tony Bennett and Patrick Joyce (Abingdon, Oxon: Routledge, 2010), pp. 38–59.

9.   Jacqueline Nassy Brown, *Dropping Anchor, Setting Sail: Geographies of Race in Black Liverpool* (Princeton, New Jersey: Princeton University Press, 2005).

10.   Ingold, *Being Alive*, p. 162.

11.   John A. Agnew, 'Space and Place,' in *The SAGE Handbook of Geographical Knowledge* ed. by Agnew and D. Livingstone (London: SAGE, 2011), pp. 316–330.

12.   David Harvey, *Justice, Nature and the Geography of Difference* (Oxford: Blackwell Publishers, 1996), pp. 293–294.

13.   Ingold, *Being Alive*, pp. 145–146.

14.   Otter, 'Locating Matter,' pp. 41–43.

15. Marc Augé, *Non-Places: Introduction to Anthropology and Supermodernity*, translated by John Howe (London: Verso, 1995).

16. Agnew, 'Space and Place,' p. 319.

17. Driver and Samuel, 'Rethinking Place,' p. vi.

18. Massey, 'Global Sense of Place,' p. 24.

19. Massey, 'Places and their Pasts,' p. 183.

20. Edensor, 'Materiality, Time and the City,' p. 37; Edensor, 'Building Stone in Manchester,' p. 21).

21. Edensor, 'Materiality, Time and the City,' p. 41.

22. Edensor, 'Building Stone in Manchester,' pp. 218–224.

23. Otter, 'Locating Matter,' pp. 48–49.

24. On Liverpool's maritime history, see: *Liverpool 800: Culture, Character & History*, ed. by JOhn Belchem (Liverpool: Liverpool University, 2006); Graeme Milne, *People, Place and Power on the Nineteenth Century Waterfront* (London: Palgrave MacMillan, 2016); Francis Hyde, *Liverpool and the Mersey: An Economic History of a Port, 1700–1970* (Newton Abbot, Devon, 1971).

25. Brown, *Dropping Anchor*, p. 23.

26. Brown, *Dropping Anchor*, pp. 9–10.

27. Brown, *Dropping Anchor*, p. 9

28. Classifying the events of 1981 is contentious. Widely referred to as 'riots,' this term can be seen to downplay the political grievances of those involved, hence the 'uprising' is often preferred by Toxteth residents.

29. Brown, *Dropping Anchor*, pp. 65–69.

30. Brian Hatton, 'Shifted Tideway, Liverpool's Changing Fortunes,' *The Architectural Review* 1331 (2008), p. 41.

31. 'Woolyback' ('wool') implies proximity to sheep, denoting a perception that Wirral is more rural than Liverpool.

32. Walter Dixon Scott, *Liverpool* (London: Adam and Charles Black, 1907,) pp. 2-4

33. Geoffrey Howe, 'Letters to Prime Minister Margaret Thatcher' (National Archives: NA PREM 19/577), August, September 1981.

34. *Liverpool '84: Festival Guide* (Liverpool: Brunswick, 1984), p. 205.

35. Michael Heseltine in *Cleaning Up the Mersey: Contribution to a Mersey Conference Organised by the Secretary of State for the Environment* (1983), p. 1. Via *Mersey Basin* website <http://www.merseybasin.org.uk/archive/assets/9/original/DoE_1983_Letter_from_Michael_Heseltine_and_Govt_Consultation_Paper.pdf>. [accessed 7 March 2023].

36. Will Medd and Simon Marvin, 'Making Water Work: Intermediating between Regional Strategy and Local Practice,' *Environment and Planning D: Society and Space* 26 (2008), pp. 280–299.

37. David Owen, *The Manchester Ship Canal* (Manchester: Manchester University Press, 1983).

38. Sally Sheard, 'Water and Health: The Formation and Exploitation of the Relationship in Liverpool, 1847–1900,' *Transactions of the Historic Society of Lancashire and Cheshire* 143 (1993), pp. 141–163.

39. Ed Atkins, 'Building a Dam, Constructing a Nation: The "Drowning" of Capel Celyn,' *Journal of Historical Sociology* 31:4 (2018), pp. 455–468; Attala, *Water*, pp. 132-145.

40. Ingold, *Being Alive*, p. 148.

41. Brown, *Dropping Anchor*, p.133.

42. Brown, Dropping *Anchor*, p.131–133.

43. Herman Melville, *Redburn: His First Voyage* (Harmondsworth, Middlesex: Penguin, 1976 [1849]), pp. 93–94.

44. Melville, *Redburn*, p. 263.

45. Melville, *Redburn*, p. 198.

46. Melville, *Redburn*, p. 238.

47. Stephen D. Winick, '"Sung with Gusto by the Men": A Unique Recording of "The Leaving of Liverpool" in the AFC Archive,' *American Folklife Center News* 30:3–4 (Summer/Fall, 2008), p. 6.

48. William Main Doerflinger, *Songs of the Sailor and Lumberman* (Glenwood, Illinois: Meyerbooks, 1990 [1951]), pp. 104–105.

49. Clinton Heylin, *Revolution in the Air: The Songs of Bob Dylan, Vol. 1: 1957–1973* (London: Constable, 2010), pp. 152–153, 172–174.

50. Frank Kidson, *Traditional Tunes: A Collection of Ballad Airs, Chiefly Obtained in Yorkshire and the South of Scotland together with their Appropriate Words from Broadsides and from Oral Tradition* (Oxford: Chad Taphouse and Son, 1891), pp. 103–104; Greil Marcus, *Invisible Republic: Bob Dylan's Basement Tapes* (London: Picador, 1998), pp. 249–250

51. Kidson, *Traditional Tunes*, pp. 103–104.

52. Robert Strachan, 'From Sea Shanties to Cosmic Scousers: The Sea, Memory and Representation in Liverpool's Popular Music,' in *The Beat Goes On: Liverpool, Popular Music and the Changing City* ed. by Strachan and Marion Leonard (Liverpool: Liverpool Univeristy Press, 2010), pp. 46–50.

53. Stan Hugill, *Shanties from the Seven Seas: Shipboard Work Songs and Songs Used as Work Songs from the Great Days of Sail* (London: Routledge, 1979), pp.404–406.

54. A childhood Kindertransport refugee, Spiegl later gained renown as a documenter of Liverpudlian folklore and dialect. Dennis Barker, 'Spiegl, Fritz (1926–2003), *Oxford Dictionary of National Biography* (Oxford: Oxford University Press, 2011). <http://www.oxforddnb.com/view/article/89835> [accessed 7 March 2023].

55. Strachan, 'Sea Shanties to Cosmic Scousers,' p. 59.

56. Paul Du Noyer, *Liverpool: Wondrous Place: Music from the Cavern to Cream* (London: Virgin Books, 2002), pp. 50–64.

57. Jeremy Price, 'From "Nellie Ray" to "Maggie May": Re-enacting the Past of the Streets of Liverpool,' *Keeping the Lid on: Urban Eruptions and Social Control since the Nineteenth Century*, ed. by Susan Finding, Logie Barrow and François Poirier (Newcastle: Cambridge Scholars, 2016), pp.77–92.

58. Deleuze and Guattari, *Thousand Plateaus*, pp. 137–138.

59. Deleuze and Guattari, *Thousand Plateaus*, pp. 24–25.

60. Oscar Hammerstein II, 'Ol' Man River,' *Lyrics* (Milwaukee: Hal Leonard Books, 1985), pp. 57–60. Given the controversies that the song and its characterisation of African Americans, I have chosen to edit the stylised dialect in Hammerstein's original lyrics here. See: Todd R. Decker, *Who Should Sing 'Ol' Man River'? The Lives of an American Song* (Oxford: Oxford University Press, 2015). Note: Dylan borrowed similar lines for his song 'Watching the River Flow.' Bob Dylan, 'Watching the River Flow' (1971), *Bob Dylan.com* <http://www.bobdylan.com/songs/watching-river-flow/> [accessed 7 March 2023].

61. Decker, *Lives of an American Song*, pp. 176–178.

62. Paul Gilroy, *The Black Atlantic: Modernity and Double Consciousness* (London: Verso, 1993), pp. i, 4.

63. Gilroy, *Black Atlantic*, pp. 4, 13; Peter Linebaugh, 'All the Atlantic Mountains Shook,' *Labour/Le Travail* 10 (Autumn 1982), pp. 87–121.

64. Gilroy, *Black Atlantic*, p. 17. Paul Robeson was attuned to the latter point: his autobiography described how his embrace of pan-African politics was influenced by conversations with black 'seamen in the ports of London, Liverpool and Cardiff.' Paul Robeson with Lloyd L Brown, *Here I Stand* (Boston, Massachusetts: Beacon Books, 1988 [1958]), pp. 32–35.

65. Ed Vulliamy, 'Toxteth Revisited,' *The Observer*, 3 July 2011 <https://www.theguardian.com/uk/2011/jul/03/toxteth-liverpool-riot-30-years> [accessed 7 March 2023].

66. Vulliamy, 'The Real Thing: Soundtrack to the Toxteth Riots,' *The Observer*, 3 July 2011 <https://www.theguardian.com/music/2011/jul/03/children-ghetto-real-thing-toxteth-liverpool> [accessed 7 March 2023].

67. Brett Lashua, 'Mapping the Politics of "Race," Place and Memory in Liverpool's Popular Music Heritage,' in *Sites of Popular Music Heritage: Memories, Histories, Places*, ed. by Sara Cohen, Robert Knifton, Marion Leonard, Les Roberts (Abingdon, Oxon: Routledge, 2015), pp. 45–61.

68. Paul McCartney foreword in Du Noyer, *Wondrous Place*, p. xi. See also: James McGrath '"Where You Once Belonged": Class, Race and the Liverpool Roots of Lennon and McCartney's Songs,' *Popular Music History* 9.1 (2014), pp. 11–31. Another rhizomorphic aside: McCartney's phrase 'melting pot' refers to a metaphor for American multiculturalism popularised by the title of a 1909 play by Zangwill, who also wrote a book about Jewish Londoners entitled *Children of the Ghetto* (1892). Meri-Jane Rochelson, 'Israel Zangwill,' *The Oxford Encyclopaedia of British Literature*, ed. by David Scott Kastan (Oxford: Oxford University Press, 2006) <https://www-oxfordreference-com.ezproxy.uwtsd.ac.uk/view/10.1093/acref/9780195169218.001.0001/acref-9780195169218-e-0506> [accessed 7 March 2023].

69. Ian Inglis, 'Synergies and Reciprocities: The Dynamics of Musical and Professional Interaction between the Beatles and Bob Dylan, *Popular Music and Society* 20:4 (1996), pp. 53–79.

70. Walter Everett, *The Beatles as Musicians: The Quarry Men through Rubber Soul* (Oxford: Oxford University Press, 2001), pp. 254–256, 287–288.

71. Everett, *Beatles as Musicians*, p. 405.

72. David Kinney, *The Dylanologists: Adventures in the Land of Bob* (New York: Schuster and Schuster, 2014), pp. 29–31.

73. Dylan, 'Roll On John' (2013), *Bob Dylan.com* <https://www.bobdylan.com/songs/roll-john/> [accessed 7 March 2023].

74. Price, '"Nellie Ray" to "Maggie May,"' p. 88.

75. Price, '"Nellie Ray" to "Maggie May,"' pp. 87–89.

76. Michael Gray, *The Bob Dylan Encyclopedia* (London: Continuum, 2006), p. 643.

77. Deleuze and Guattari, *Thousand Plateaus*, p. 24.

78. Deleuze and Guattari may even have met Dylan during a tour of the United States. François Cusset, *French Theory: How Foucault, Derrida, Deleuze and Co. Transformed the Intellectual Life of the United States* translated by Jeff Fort (Minneapolis: University of Minnesota Press, 2008), p. 68; Jason Demers, *The American Politics of French Theory: Derrida, Deleuze, Guattari and Foucault in Translation* (Toronto: University of Toronto Press, 2018), pp. 151–168.

79. Deleuze and Claire Parnet, *Dialogues*, translated by Hugh Tomlinson and Barbara Harbejam (New York: Columbia University Press, 1987 [1977]), pp. 7–10.

80. Richard Elliot, 'The Same Distant Places: Bob Dylan's Poetics of Place and Displacement,' *Popular Music and Society* 32:2 (2009), pp. 259, 265.

81. Dylan, 'Nobel Lecture,' *NobelPrize.org*, 4 June 2017 <https://www.nobelprize.org/prizes/literature/2016/dylan/lecture/> [accessed 7 March 2023].

82. Ingold, *Being Alive*, pp. xii, 149.

83. Attala, *Water*, pp. 33–34.

9

THE EXTRAORDINARY
THROUGH THE PURSUIT OF THE ORDINARY:
THE ACTIVITY OF SWIMMING AS A LIMINAL ACT

Morag Feeney-Beaton

Introduction

We are used to seeing the ordinary and the extraordinary as existing in different realms of experience. Yet the distinction is easily questioned when we examine everyday experiences. For Christopher Tilley and Kate Cameron-Daum, 'everywhere we look, the everyday and the ordinary become extraordinary'.[1] The focus of my investigation is the extraordinary as an activity, or rather as a state of activity, and its subject of enquiry is the everyday pursuit of swimming, investigating to what extent it can be understood as a liminal act. In the course of this enquiry, it will be essential to explore the concept of sacred space in addition to that of the liminal experience to see whether they can indeed be applied to what is ostensibly a physical occupation.

An underlying motif that runs through this study, and in many ways was the trigger for it, is the question of accessibility to locations that are deemed to be sacred space that may have the potential for providing a liminal experience. Such sites themselves may be subject to contested ownership and to management strategies that may in turn elicit restricted access and a tendency towards exclusivity.[2] As a result, one of the beneficial offshoots of seeing the extraordinary in the ordinary is a form of democratization whereby the experience itself is available for anyone who wishes to take part.

Liminality and the liminal experience

The notion of liminality is one developed by Victor Turner from Arnold van Gennep's demarcation of the three stages of the rites of passage used by all societies. The liminal phase, whose name is derived from the word *limen*, Latin for threshold, is the second stage – the phase of transition or margin. Turner set about applying this concept to a modern post-agrarian social structure, arguing that within all ritual there is an element of the concept of passage.[3] The liminal state for Turner is the phase where cognitive logic and social mores no longer apply; he defined it as 'an interval, however brief, of *margin* or *limen*, when the past is momentarily negated, or abrogated, and the future has not yet begun. There is an instant of pure potentiality when everything trembles in the balance'.[4] Time and space therefore have become distilled into a suspended moment, a phase he describes as 'time outside time', whereby the future and the past have no bearing.[5] However, this marginal transitory phase also marks a passage, and that passage leads towards a sense of rejuvenation, a re-birth, the pathway to a new status, hence the appropriateness of the image of the womb given by Turner as indicative of the liminal state.[6]

While Turner draws attention to the fact that the liminal state may be characterized by challenge and ordeal, the quality associated with liminality which is particularly relevant to this study is the conjunction of 'sacredness and lowliness'.[7] In the liminal state the self becomes subjugated. There is a shift away from social time, whereby everyday matters recede in the consciousness. This reduction of the self and the awareness of a greater perspective is an important constituent factor in the kind of liminal experience investigated here, one that corresponds to the kind of suspended knowledge that Thomas Berry describes as the supreme communion of the self and the greater cosmos, a state he equates to being both at the centre and at the circumference, experiencing 'the supreme mystery in which the universe and the self exist'.[8]

In such a moment, there is a perceived fusion of time and place which can give rise to a sense of awe and wonder, and even a palpable sensation of the presence of something sacred. This resonates with what Mircea Eliade terms a 'hierophany', a manifestation of the sacred.[9] Its etymology from the Greek *hierophantēs*, from *hieros* 'sacred' and *phainein*, 'show' or 'reveal', implies a revelation, essentially a moment in which the sacred is revealed, made manifest.[10] This evokes what Turner anticipates when he describes the phenomenon as 'an interval, however brief', thus highlighting the apparent transient and fleeting quality of the liminal experience.[11]

Such encounters may be triggered by settings characterised by great natural beauty, whereby the self and humanity become both re-dimensionalised and re-defined by the context of the entire cosmos; they may also be triggered by geographical locations heightened by previously established spiritual properties, or by constructed edifices such as temples or stone circles.[12] In each case the liminal experience for the participants seems to be largely contingent upon being there actually in location, materially present.

This imperative for being physically at hand is upheld by Christopher Tilley, whose notion of acquiring a phenomenological understanding of location would seem to be contingent upon what he calls 'being *in place*'.[13] As the 'process of observation' involves not only time but a sense of 'feeling for the place', he urges repeat visits for an in-depth and intensified encounter.[14] Consequently, journeying to sacred places can take on the characteristics of a modern pilgrimage, the aspiration being, as Fiona Bowie suggests, to 'make contact with something beyond everyday experience'.[15] One unforeseen consequence of this could be a tendency towards exclusivity. Through pressures of time, budget, responsibilities and modern living, such sought-after experiences may in turn be reduced to unobtainable aspirations, with the result that those without access to such locations and resources could be excluded from similar encounters of spiritual connectivity. However, the hypothesis that swimming is a liminal act could perhaps serve as an alternative conduit towards the liminal state, available to the many rather than the few. This everyday activity can be said to exemplify the afore-mentioned democratization of the liminal experience, proposing an area in daily life which holds the potential for the extraordinary to be attainable whilst held within the confines of the ordinary.

The ordinary and the extraordinary

The binary relationship between the ordinary and the extraordinary modes of existence have extended beyond the dualistic perspective of mutually exclusive domains, the Durkheimian notion of the sacred and the profane.[16] Abraham Maslow's notion that the sacred resides in the ordinary, 'to be found in one's daily life', once viewed as secularist 'folk-science', now resonates with a more holistic view of sacrality, one not controlled by an on/off switch, with space and human activity understood as occupying a position along a scale of relative sacrality.[17] As Lynda Sexson writes, 'there are universal experiences which are common yet set apart, ordinary yet consummately extraordinary'; adding they are 'mundane yet sacred'.[18] Christopher Tilley and Kate Cameron-Daum emphasise the significance of this discourse, of seeing the extraordinary within the everyday and the common place. They warn against regarding the ordinary as 'a superficial manifestation of culture', suggesting that the 'enormous depth and complexity' that are present in the ordinary remain hidden unless taken seriously.[19]

The need for textured thinking and the desire for a more pluralist perspective are advocated by scholars such as Belden Lane. His concern is that in our search for spiritual uplifting, we tend to look unwittingly beyond the ordinary, stating that 'we scoff at the commonplace in the process of reaching for a grandeur we're convinced it lacks - ironically, in doing so, we miss both'.[20] Indeed, one of Lane's axioms for the understanding of the sacred is that 'sacred place is ordinary place, ritually made extraordinary'.[21] For him, it is a notion of valuing the ordinary for its own sake, its true essence, and in so doing, recognizing its capacity to act as, to what he calls, an 'entrée to something more'.[22]

In this discussion, the entrée to the extraordinary is activity-led, through the physical pursuit of swimming. Turner himself explored the idea of accessing liminality through performance, where the performer 'disengages what is mundanely connected', adopting the term *liminoid* for lesser experiences, including those in the sports arena.[23] However, scholars such as Sharon Rowe have since made the case that sports are 'genuine liminal phenomena' acting as 'powerful modern ritual'.[24] Perhaps, then, it is possible to consider that the physical expertise and mental sublimation of repetitive movement, characteristic of many sports, could function as an entry point to liminality.[25] I myself have come across this idea of the access to a liminal space through repetitive movement in my work with handspinners, where the constancy and the uniformity of circular rhythm can lead to the practitioner entering what Roy Rappaport calls extraordinary time, a trance-like mesmeric state.[26]

The sacrality of water

Having examined aspects of the theoretical debate that underpin the notions of sacred space and liminality, I will turn my attention towards the material entity without which swimming cannot happen, namely water. In many contemporary societies swimming is primarily regarded as a means of the pursuit of physical well-being. The act of swimming itself requires the human body to be submerged, floating being an activity executed on a horizontal plane, freed from the confines of the usual grounded vertical mode of operation. For the swimmer, then, the watery environment is a suspended environment. Veronica Strang points out that water's critical significance to the organic processes of living combined with its effervescent 'numinous quality has encouraged human societies to draw associations between water and spiritual being'.[27]

Bodies of water, especially moving water such as springs and rivers, in mythology and in folklore can be considered divine. The rivers Shannon and Boyne in Ireland, for example, still bear the name of their associated water deity. Indeed, Strang suggests that 'there was a time when almost all societies worshipped water beings'.[28] Likewise, water can also be seen acting as a passageway to the gods, as a threshold to the divine. At the Ise Grand Shrine in Japan, which is dedicated to the Shinto sun goddess Amaterasu-Omikami, it is the waters of the River Isuzugawa that delineate the sacred area, traditionally separating the sacred forest from the outside world.

Cleansing and purification

Much of the sacrality associated with water can be derived from its ritual cleansing properties, less concerned with cleaning the physical body, rather more serving as a spiritual purification. For many religions and cultures, an act of total immersion into water is considered a sacred ritual, cleansing the body to purify the mind. For example, in Judaism the act of purification known as Tevilah entails ritual immersion where there is an emphasis placed on running water, so-called 'living water'.[29] Indeed one of its applications is for initiation into the Jewish faith. Christian baptism, rebirth through water, for the most part no longer involves total immersion, but the symbolic ritual lives on in the font, in holy water, and the healing powers of holy wells.

Likewise, the Shinto practice of purification that requires devotees to be fully immersed, has evolved, through an act of symbolic transference, into the purification rituals undertaken by believers at the entrance to a shrine. This transference should not be considered reductive or as a form of secularization that serves to diminish ritual procedure. The purification rite as a ritual is still observed. Within Hindu practice, for example, one of the most elevating sacramental ceremonies is ritual bathing in the sacred River Ganges, seen as the body of the Goddess Ganga herself, and representing, according to Nathaniel Altman, 'feminine energy of the universe that is connected to both life and death'.[30] For those to whom the River Ganges is inaccessible, waters closer to home can be considered an appropriate alternative. From this we can infer that, while the spiritual act of purification and rebirth is centred on specific holy waters such as the Ganges or the River Jordan, by-proxy ceremonies occur in other waters, fonts, and mikvehs all over the world, indicating the importance of the ritual and its capacity for symbolic translocation.

I can record two observations of just such ritual transference. The first involved a Hindu water ceremony, taking place on the sands at Clevedon on the Bristol Channel, negotiating with ease the flat sands and the fast running tide. From an observer's stance, there was no real sense that the authority of the ritual was in any way compromised by its location. The second instance, highly relevant to this study, occurred in a Central London swimming pool, where a young man could be observed by the other bathers involved in his own personal ritual activity. Seemingly, the ritual events were effectively performed in shared water with no apparent need for isolation, with the other swimmers in the pool being entirely respectful. For him, it would appear, the ritual was sufficiently important that, although his only access to water may have been this inner-city basement pool, he was able to perform his ritualised sequence in a space that was sufficiently neutral (adaptable) to provide the location.

Wild swimming

In searching for the potential for liminality within swimming, one of the first places to explore is wild swimming, where the swimmer's chief imperative is to be at one with the natural cycle of their surroundings. Accordingly, they are likely to avoid the sanitized banality of the swimming pool to seek wild water, untamed by chlorine or life-guards, whereby they become part of, and contribute to, the rhythm of the environment. This sense of concord, this at one-ness, concerns the balance of the self and the ecosystem, the human within the cosmos, mirroring Berry's notion of being simultaneously at the centre and circumference that this paper referred to earlier.[31] This congruence of self and cosmos is also one of Belden Lane's axioms for the conditions for sacred space, as well as resonating with Turner's fusion of 'sacredness and lowliness' that he saw as a hallmark of liminality.[32]

Here again, the afore-mentioned issue of exclusivity arises, provoking echoes of the debate regarding pilgrimages and a democratized access to liminality. There are naturally occurring wild swimming hotspots that prove to be a *must* for the devotee, for whom the experience is the focal point of the activity. A location such as the Fairy Pools on the Isle of Skye, where crystal clear icy waters descending from the Cuillan mountains have created magical natural pools of running water, attracts swimmers intent upon a spiritually enhancing experience. They are advised, however, by the local tourist board, to get there early to 'avoid random tourists roaming along Glen Brittle'.[33]

In order to sample the physical nature of the experience, I found myself in the cold waters of the Ladies' pond, reserved for female swimmers, on London's Hampstead Heath. Here, it did not matter that I was not alone; the communal nature of the experience did not ruin it – to the contrary, it contributed to it. The overall sensation was one where all my senses were heightened: the coldness of the water intensified sensitivity and an immediate awareness of the water moving around the body. There was therefore a physical-ness of being active in the water, a connection, one that led to a true sense of belonging to the natural environment, corresponding directly to Tilley's notion of 'being *in place*'.[34] The physical phenomenological response that it evoked was a form of heightened muscular knowledge, a knowledge that is communicated both by surface sensation and by a vivid awareness of one's internal structure. Moreover, the murky pond water was more opaque than the clear chlorine 'blue' of leisure pools, rendering my limbs strangely, but almost mythologically, golden.

Urban leisure facilities

If it is possible to say that wild swimming has the potential for a transformative experience by extension it now becomes appropriate to explore the possibility that this awareness of belonging to, and defining one's immediate surroundings, can be felt within the context of urban leisure facilities. The architect Eva Cantwell takes a contrary viewpoint.[35] She says that in contrast to natural swimming – that is swimming in the sea, in a river or anywhere within a natural environment – swimming in an indoor pool is a sterile non-sensory experience. Certainly, with the appearance of municipal swimming pools in the nineteenth century, there was a certain sense of taming the dangerous freedom of a natural swim, together with not a little sense of societal control. The urban swimming pool began to operate as an instrument of social constraint and the maintenance of class order.[36] Swimming became an indoor pursuit, thus imposing a filter or barrier to the natural activity, and thereby prioritizing a culture of physical health and cleanliness. Enormous swimming palaces arose, cathedrals to the new phenomenon of leisure. The Sutro Baths in the Golden Gate National Park in San Francisco, for example, contained seven swimming pools and could house up to 25,000 spectators and swimmers. It was next to the ocean, but swimming had been given a communal locale and an institutional infrastructure, with its own rituals and etiquette, a micro-society, prompting scholars, such as Susie Scott, to view the swimming pool as 'negotiated order'.[37]

Eva Cantwell's assessment of urban leisure swimming is possibly a little harsh. It can be argued that it is feasible to make an alternative analysis, one seen within a ritualised context, the ordinary viewed as extraordinary. The locale of the municipal swimming pool can be the forum for not only physical well-being, but for, as Lane says, 'something more', and it is the human dynamic that changes and qualifies the space.[38] This can be seen by comparing an active pool to a quiet one. The act of swimming provides the pool itself with physical agency, alive with activity it generates a conspicuous and almost abrasive energy. Taking on the rhythm of the swimmers' movement, reflected light across the water stays constantly in flux; indeed, both sound and light are delineated by human endeavour. Once the pool is emptied of swimmers it falls silent and still. However, a memory of physical activity can linger in the water, which, while remaining motionless, may also be transmorphic, pregnant with potential.

Liminality, ritual and activity

In his book, *Waterlog*, Roger Deakin talks about entering the water in elemental terms. The experience of floating and of being submerged in a watery universe with its intimations towards the origins of human life, for him, is equivalent to the 'terror and bliss of being born'.[39] This brings to mind Turner's notion of liminality as a re-birth, and his use of the image of the womb.[40] On entering the water, immediately the swimmer's perception of sound is altered, there is a strong awareness of internal breathing, and a heightened sense of volume as the water envelops the body, especially when that water is cold.

While the swimming experience could be said to be predominantly sensory, the swimmer's sensation of self develops its own contrasting duality involving the synthesis of internal pulse and external rhythm. This is defined by the outward trajectory of the swimmer's stroke harmonically co-ordinated with the controlled regularity of internal breathing. These simultaneous realities of existing inside and outside oneself trigger a sense of being on the outside looking in and very much being *inside* one's own body, echoing Thomas Berry's notion of occupying a position at the centre and on the circumference, a fusion of self and the greater universe.[41]

Regular swimmers themselves engage in a certain degree of preparatory activity, of ritual preparation, beginning with the behavioural patterns of getting themselves to the swimming pool, amounting to a daily pilgrimage, perhaps. The changing room, then, offers the locale for not only the removal of daily apparel, but for a redefinition of the day-to-day-persona, in an act of metamorphosis, into a swimming-person, a change of elements from an earth-being into a water-being. Swimming goggles, functional in themselves, act as a mask, and alongside the wearing of a swimming cap providing a form of ritual headwear, together they are instrumental in altering identity, completing the transformation, thereby contributing to the ceremony of swimming, swimming as a performative act.

Lane-swimmers enter the pool with their own specific imperatives. Each swimmer's swimming regime is self-regulated and individual, amounting to an oft repeated and identifiable practice. Over and above the afore-mentioned sensory responses experienced by the swimmer, it is how they occupy their mind while swimming up and down that has the potential for liminality. This could be counting pool lengths perhaps, perfecting technique, or allowing a free-stream-of-consciousness to pour out; Peter Selgin says that he 'drowns' in his thoughts.[42] It is the combination of repeated behaviour and the mind-cleansing circular rhythmic patterns of the swimming stroke, augmented by regular controlled deep breathing – something that swimmers have in common with endurance athletes and dancers – that transports them to a neutral and unique space, opening up the landscape of liminality.

A further significant contributory factor towards the ritual behaviour of swimming is time, and how it is perceived. A dedicated swimmer's ritual control of time may include: designated-time, me-time, not-to-be-wasted-

Figure 1: Fresco from the Greek *Tomb of the Diver*.
Museo Archeologico Nazionale, Paestum,
image: Heinz-Josef Lücking, Wikimedia Commons.

Figure 2: David Park, *Two Bathers*. 1958, oil on canvas.
De Young Fine Arts Museum of San Francisco. Courtesy of
Hackett Mill, representative of the Estate of David Park.

time, chosen-activity and allotted-time, even personal-best-time. In a very real sense, co-ordinated timing is vital for swimmers in order to propel themselves through the water, and to breathe above it. Consequently, through the activity of swimming, the swimmer's perception of time becomes defined by a form of rhythmic time, controlled by the harmonised rhythms of internal breath and external movement. This co-ordination of submerged breath and movement may lead towards a transference away from strictly chronological time to 'time-outside-time', Turner's definition of liminal space.[43] Through agency, therefore, the swimmer has the potential to journey through ordinary time to gain access to Rappaport's notion of extraordinary time.[44]

In making the case for the activity of swimming to possess the capacity for liminality, this enquiry has explored the notion of access to the kind of liminal state that Thomas Berry describes, as well as touching on the question of democratization of that access. The enquiry also involves activity. This form of liminal experience is less to do with contemplation and self-revelation; it is rather more about *doing*, about quasi-ritualised action, where the liminal state can be achieved as the result, the culmination of a series of harmonised repetitive physical patterns. It is perhaps the pursuit of the transcendent, whereby the pursuit is a genuine physical one rather than metaphorical.

This study is concerned with the relationship, indeed the balance, between the ordinary and the extraordinary. I have made no attempt to isolate or identify the moment when the one is transfigured into the other; almost by definition that moment should be regarded as unquantifiable. As Christopher Tilley and Kate Cameron-Daum write: 'Depth does not reside deep down... It resides within the surface and is everywhere around us. So the project of analysis becomes the recognition and the bringing forth to consciousness of the extraordinary character of the ordinary'.[45]

Notes

1.   Christopher Tilley and Kate Cameron-Daum, *An Anthology of Landscape: The Extraordinary in the Ordinary* (London: UCL Press 2017), p. 296.

2.   Myra Shackley, *Managing Sacred Sites: Service Provision and Visitor Experience* (Holborn: Continuum, 2001), p. 154.

3.   Victor Turner, *Process, Performance, and Pilgrimage: a Study in Comparative Symbology* (New Delhi, India: Concept Publishing Company, 1979), p. 16.

4.   Turner, *Process, Performance, and Pilgrimage*, p. 41.

5.   Victor Turner, 'Images of Anti-Temporality: An Essay in the Anthropology of Experience', *The Harvard Theological Review* 75, no. 2 (April 1982): pp. 243–265.

6. Victor Turner, *The Ritual Process: Structure and Anti-Structure* (Chicago: Aldine Publishing, 1969), p. 95.

7. Victor Turner, 'Variations on a Theme of Liminality', in Sally F. Moore and Barbara G. Myerhoff, eds, *Secular Ritual* (Assen/Amsterdam: Van Gorcum, 1977), p. 37; Turner , 'Liminality and Communitas', p. 96.

8. Thomas Berry, *The Sacred Universe: Earth, Spirituality, and Religion in the Twenty-first Century* (New York: Columbia University Press, 2009 Kindle Edition), Kindle Locations 1099–1101.

9. Mircea Eliade, *The Sacred and the Profane: The Nature of Religion,* trans. Willard R. Trask (San Diego, CA, New York, London: Harcourt, Inc., 1959), p. 20.

10. Oxford English Dictionary.

11. Turner, *Process, Performance, and Pilgrimage,* p. 41.

12. Belden Lane, *Landscapes of the Sacred* (Baltimore, MD: John Hopkins University Press, 2001).

13. Christopher Tilley, *A Phenomenology of Landscape* (Oxford: Berg, 1994), p. 75.

14. Tilley, *A Phenomenology of Landscape,* p. 75.

15. Fiona Bowie, *The Anthropology of Religion,* 2nd edn (Malden, MA, and Oxford: Blackwell, 2006), p. 259.

16. Émile Durkheim, *The Elementary Forms of Religious Life,* trans. Carol Cosman (Oxford: Oxford University Press, 2001), p. 36.

17. Abraham H. Maslow, *Religions, Values and Peak-Experiences* (New York: Penguin Books, 1970), pp. 67–8; Lucy Bregman, 'Maslow as Theorist of Religion: Reflections on his Popularity and Plausibility', *Soundings: an Interdisciplinary Journal* 59, no. 2 (Summer 1976): pp. 139–163.

18. Lynda Sexson, *Ordinarily Sacred,* (Charlottesville, VA, and London: University Press of Virginia, 1992), p. 3.

19. Tilley and Cameron-Daum, *An Anthropology of Landscape,* p. 297.

20. Lane, *Landscapes of the Sacred,* p. 70.

21. Lane, *Landscapes of the Sacred,* p. 65.

22. Lane, *Landscapes of the Sacred,* p. 65.

23. Victor Turner, *From Ritual to Theatre: the Human Seriousness of Play* (New York: Performing Arts Journal Publications, 1982).

24. Sharon Rowe, 'Liminal Ritual or Liminoid Leisure', *Journal of Ritual Studies* 12, no. 1 (Summer 1998): pp. 47–60.

25. Rowe, 'Liminal Ritual or Liminoid Leisure', pp. 47–60.

26. Roy A. Rappaport, *Ritual and Religion in the Making of Humanity* (Cambridge: Cambridge University Press, 1999), p. 225.

27. Veronica Strang, *Water, Nature and Culture* (London: Reaktion Books Ltd., 2015), p. 41, Kindle Location 458.

28. Strang, *Water, Nature and Culture,* p. 49, Kindle Location 539.

29. Rachel Lichtenstein, 'Mikvahs for the 21st Century: Cleaning and cleansing in the life of Jewish women', *Jewish Quarterly* 50, no. 3 (2003): pp. 81–88.

30. Nathaniel Altman, *Sacred Water: The Spiritual Source of Life* (Mahwah, NJ: Hidden Spring/Paulist Press, 2002), p. 136.

31. Berry, *The Sacred Universe,* Kindle Locations 1099-1101.

32. Lane, *Landscapes of the Sacred,* p. 19; Turner, 'Liminality and Communitas', p. 96.

33. walkhighlands, www.walkhighlands.co.uk [accessed date 23 May 2018].

34. Tilley, *A Phenomenology of Landscape,* p. 75.

35. Eva Cantwell, *Swimming and the senses, Building Material* 8 (Spring 2002): pp. 48–51, at http://www.jstor.org/stable/29791455.

36. Susie Parr, *The Story of Swimming, a social history of bathing in Britain* (Stockport: Dewi Lewis Media, 2011), p. 91.

37. Susie Scott, 'Re-clothing the Emperor: The Swimming Pool as a Negotiated Order', *Symbolic Interaction* 32, no. 2 (Spring 2009): pp. 123–145.

38. Lane, *Landscapes of the Sacred*, p. 65.

39. Roger Deakin, *Waterlog: A Swimmer's Journey through Britain* (London: Vintage Books, 2000), p. 3.

40. Turner, *The Ritual Process*, p. 95.

41. Berry, *The Sacred Universe*, Kindle Locations 1099–1101.

42. Peter Selgin, 'The Swimming Pool', *Fourth Genre: Explorations in Nonfiction* 13, no. 1 (Spring 2011): pp. 33–45, at http://www.jstor.org/stable/41939094.

43. Turner, *Images of Anti-Temporality*, pp. 243–265.

44. Rappaport, *Ritual and Religion in the Making of Humanity*, p. 225.

45. Tilley and Cameron-Daum, *An Anthropology of Landscape*, p. 297.

10

WIND, WAVES AND WOODEN WOMBS: AN ETHNOGRAPHY OF AN EAST COAST HOUSEBOAT COMMUNITY

Melanie Long

Introduction

Throughout the 1990s I lived on a decommissioned World War Two Motor Gunboat on the River Deben in Suffolk. Ten years after leaving, I revisited the community to engage in ethnographic research, focussing particularly on the relationships between the community, their floating homes, and the environment around them. The research for this chapter is based predominantly upon the perspectives of the original members of the houseboat community. However, I held interviews with current houseboat owners and local inhabitants of the town: councillors, business owners, tourists, and other visitors from the wider local area. In addition, conversations with other boat owners, across the

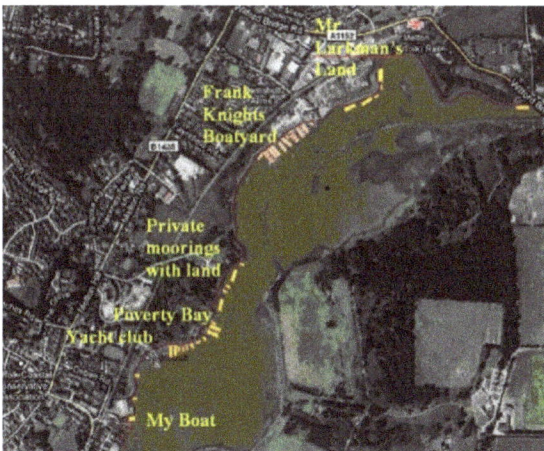

Figure 1. Map of section of Deben River, Suffolk, in focus in ethnographic research (2009, source: google maps, with boats and notes added by author)

country, have also been included. As the primary gatekeeper, due to my personal relationships with many of the informants, as well as the fact that I also applied my own auto-ethnography, it was necessary to apply reflexive principles; I considered my own position in relation to both the formation of questions, in order to avoid leading the flow of conversation, and the analysis of the data collected.

There are small houseboat settlements in various places along the westerly, most built-up, side of the Deben River, but my research is limited to the final mile-long section of the estuary, beginning at the northernmost part of Woodbridge and ending where the river turns into fresh water beyond the weir at the village of Melton. Despite this section of the estuary being some distance from the sea, it is nonetheless tidal and therefore exposed to the harsher elemental influences of the winds and lunar pull on the tides. This area has an unusually high number of houseboats, either on private moorings, or on a stretch of 'no-mans-land' known locally as 'Poverty Bay', whereas most other houseboat communities on the river tend to be based in boatyards. Boatyard-living forces boat dwellers to live closer together, in a more protected space defined by the rules of the yard-owner, and have set rents; all of these issues change the dynamics of the experience. Most of the houseboats today are in boatyards, and aside from a handful of privately-owned moorings there are far fewer inhabited boats; this is predominantly due to political reasons, which are not being explored here.

Figure 2. Nordwind, the author's boat (1996, author's image)

This chapter will firstly give an overview of the primary factors which influenced the reasons why this way of life was chosen, before considering how boats, their non-human neighbours and the environment in which they sit, influence the people who inhabit them, because, as Tim Ingold wrote, 'human beings do not dwell on the other side of a boundary between society and nature but in the same world'.[1]

Why choose a boat for a home?

The primary reason for initially choosing boat-living seems to be economic, because it is cheaper than living on land, and a degree of relative poverty was the lived experience of all informants.[2] This was, for many participants, also related to their age, as many of the boat dwellers in my study were between seventeen and twenty-five. In addition, most of the rest of the community were under the age of forty. These individuals were mostly unemployed, self-employed, or doing seasonal work on zero-hours contracts, and were therefore without reliable incomes. It also allowed some of the community to be invisible, working cash-in–hand and surviving without the need for a bank account or any official record.[3] All informants were generally fit and healthy and there were very few children living on boats, with most people leaving to live on land once they had children or if they suffered from any long-term health issues which impacted upon their physical strength.[4]

The second reason for boat-living concerns what the space offers. Informants stated that being close to nature was as important to them as the ability to put distance between the intensity of society and self.[5] Many participants stated that they found people hard to understand, whereas the so-called natural environment made more sense to them.[6] This is a liminal space, a 'threshold';[7] as Robert Preston-Whyte wrote, 'liminal spaces are intangible, elusive and obscure. They lie in a limbo-like space often beyond normal social and cultural constraints'.[8] The boats are placed on the threshold between land and water, sitting on land when the tide is out and on water when it is in, in flux between floating and being static.[9] In addition, there are a series of transitional lines to be crossed after leaving the town and before reaching the river's bank, as it is dissected from the town by a road, railway-line, and tow-path, thus providing separation from all the pressures of 'normal' social expectations and constraints. This physical location therefore supports the space as being one where there are no definite rules as to what to expect from society, just as much as from the unpredictable natural environment, and creates an enhanced sense of distance and difference from the rest of the wider local community; this therefore allows a communitas, as Edith Turner put it, with its own set of norms to develop and maintain itself.[10]

The third reason people stated for living on boats is the boat community itself and the sense of kinship experienced on the river. From the perspective of the passer-by walking on the tow-path, it is clear that this is a supportive community who work together, but for those who have come to really know members of this community there is, in the words of one of the two young female informants who lived alone on a boat, a freedom here to be 'yourself' amongst people who are 'non-judgemental, regardless of personal flaws and mistakes'. This is a place where people who do not feel like they fit into 'normative' society can be party to creating a culture which is tailor-made for them, a place where they can be accepted regardless of any differences.[11] There is a high likelihood for invisible, neuro-diverse differences/disabilities being predominant within this group (as a specialist in this field I was able to do preliminary assessments for this during data collection to validate this theory).[12] It would also be true to say that some liked being there because the communitas was supportive, or at least accepting, of transgressive behaviours, so they felt safe to be crossing the lines of British laws without fear of being reported.[13]

Obviously, a combination of these three main reasons, in varying degrees of importance depending on the individual in question, were factored into the decision-making process, with other personal reasons added into the mix. As time passed, members of the community often changed their focus upon which of these points were primary to their reasons for continuing to live on boats, especially regarding the relationships which developed between the human inhabitants and their boats.

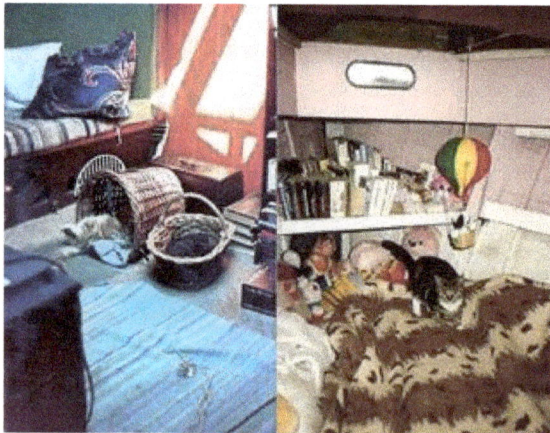

Figure 3. Houseboat interiors (1991, author's images)

Cheap Accommodation

Although some of the owners of larger boats, who had enough accessible funds to have some chance to access a mortgage on a house, could not be considered as poor by the standards of those who were living on the tiny boats with free moorings and no services available, it seems apparent that cost was still the primary reason for choosing this location in which to live.[14] In addition to low or unreliable income, factors such as self-employment causing ineligibility for a mortgage, or being at the bottom of the property ladder only offered the possibility for owning a two-bedroom terrace house in the middle of a built-up area, were mentioned. In contrast, the river gave, in the words of a young male informant, who had been homeless, then lived on a crowded new-age traveller's site for some time before moving onto the river, 'space, solitude and spectacular, ever changing, views' right there on the doorstep, for an affordable price.[15] Owners of the larger boats all either owned the adjacent land or paid rent for secure moorings with some amenities, whereas for the smaller boat owners, most of whom were aged between seventeen and twenty-five, their options were extremely limited. Many of these individuals had nowhere else to go, with family lives stated as being disrupted and dysfunctional, thus providing the necessity to support themselves at a young age. However, with little income, young adults are generally less experienced or qualified, and only limited Income Support (paid by the state) is available to unemployed people in this age-group: the only options available were to live in a room in a shared house, a caravan on the new-age travellers' site, a boat, or to be homeless.[16] 'Poverty Bay' provided a space where they could moor up in any ramshackle floating vessel that they could get their hands on or knock together.

During their time living on boats some informants became more financially secure; however, this does not seem to be the cause of people moving off the river. Similarly, when living on a boat was more difficult and costly, most of those with low incomes did not move elsewhere, unless their boat sank, was unfixable, or the availability of a replacement was limited. Therefore, it is clear that other factors beyond cost are driving decisions to stay on boats.

The choice to live on a boat, within such a community, is never passive. When considering other communities – for instance those within a conventional set-up, such as in a street – it is rare that knowledge of the existing neighbours are a primary consideration or a defining factor, although area or location are often perceived, due to reputation or apparent status or wealth, to be representative of the type of people who are deemed as desirable neighbours.[17] This, however, is a constructed and perhaps misleading image, as boats are cheap homes, so one would initially think that the occupants do not have the option to consider anything more than cost when deciding to live in such a place, but far more factors seem to be prevalent.

Location

In the case of all my boat-dwelling informants, the proximity to open space played some part in the decision to live on the river.[18] Most informants stated that they did not like to be too close to other humans, or to have social 'norms' and rules imposed upon them by such proximity; boats were chosen over house-sharing or caravan-living on an overcrowded site.[19] The boats on this section of river (except in boatyards) are on linear moorings along the riverbank, with space between them; as such there is only a maximum of two other dwellings in close proximity, and only the smallest boats in 'Poverty Bay' were close enough to be immediately affected by the sounds and actions of their neighbours.

It is true, however, that living on a tidal river is immersive, sometimes literally; for those who commit to this way of life, it really is generally an embodied experience, predominantly a sensory one, and this is predominantly down to the environment.[20] The term 'sensory' however, should be considered from the passion of new love, with all its euphoric highs and excruciating lows, plus a great deal of overload. When you live on the river, you embody it, even when moving off boats it takes some time for the sensations to leave you, for just as you can have 'land-legs' and struggle to cope with the movement of a boat, those who have developed their 'sea-legs' do not lose this for some time after moving onto solid ground; for me this offered a floating sensation, one where you are not entirely trusting of the ground beneath you or your physical ability to stay upright. Similarly, the lack of exposure to nature's sounds, such as the rain, wind and birdlife, once inside the walls of a house is hard to cope with, hence I slept with the window open for well over a year after moving off the river, and many of my informants stated similar issues with the nature of houses causing a disconnection with nature's influences.[21]

Being in this space is clearly highly sensory. Taking just the visual aspect alone: there is the beauty of the changing seasons, the reflected patterns on the water, and the myriad of different colours and entertainment provided by the local wildlife. The show never ceases to captivate the audience, from the flight displays of the flocks of dunlins, the aerobatics of terns and kittiwakes, the enigmatic beauty of swans emerging from early morning mist or weaving through the reflected Moonlight, to the treasured rare glimpse of a kingfisher or seal, the phosphorescence of the sea-gooseberries in the wake of a boat, and the sight of a shag or cormorant drying their outstretched wings. One informant said: 'I think many people on the river are lured by the aesthetic'. There is no doubt of the tendency of boat-owners to use names that reflect the sense of how nature, non-human and humans have become merged; with boat names such as Nordwind, Daystar, Waterways, Astra, Bluebell, Orca, Maelstrom, and human nicknames such as Sandy, Bear, Shell, Kingfisher, Bird-dog, or Hawk-eye.

The River Deben has a climate of its own. There is always a breeze, even in the suffocating stillness of a Suffolk summer day. Sometimes the air is filled with dust that gets into your eyes, nose, mouth and hair: it blows in from the sea, so that one side of your boat becomes more weathered as a result. The sun seems hotter here, so your skin darkens quickly, and your bare feet are burnt by the hot deck, whilst inside the boat you are cooked in the enclosed oven-like space. Yet in the biting cold of winter, the harsh and howling wind can feel arctic, cutting into your skin and turning fingers to ice, and whipping the rigging of the sailing boats in a clanking rattle, whilst inside a boat you are cosily warmed by a wood burner, but in the depth of the night, when there is a mere ember left, you are woken by the drip of water melting off the icicles which hang inside your home.

There is always noise; even on the stillest day there is the popping of the mud from worms beneath and the dabbling of beaks from the wading birds, but the loudest noise of all is in the height of summer, when the nights are short and the dusk and dawn choruses almost merge into one all night long party of dunlins and oyster-catchers chattering away in a rhythmic boom. Living within this environment adds a further depth to the sensory experience of this place, for inside the boat there are the sounds of the creaking hull of the boat as the tide lifts or drops it onto the mud, and the lapping of the waves like a heartbeat.[22] The liminal quality of being both within and outside the shell of the home in which you live offers only a marginally muffled interaction with the outside world so that you are not truly separate from the sounds of nature, the passing trains, and the people chatting on the tow-path; in Tim Ingold's words, it 'is as much an exoskeleton for humans as a shell is for a mollusc'.[23] As one of my informants said, it is 'a fragile, unpredictable space, which you rely upon to keep you safe but cannot complacently trust in'.[24] Everyone was in sync with the tides, for lives really could depend on this, and when the neap tides were due, in the middle of a night, where the wind was blowing up-river, not much sleeping could occur, as ropes needed checking regularly to make sure they were set long enough to cope with the swell, then shortened again in time to settle back into its time-worn cradle in the bed of the river.[25] 'To live on a boat in a tidal estuary is, as one informant said, to become part of this environment, living and breathing it, being governed by its cycles and its moods'.

Light has a great deal of significance; it enters the boats in ribbons, through small portholes, whilst the heart-heat is generated by the burner. Sunlight reflects off the water, causing eyes to develop the knack of adjusting quickly to change, and tanning the skin from below, adding to the weathering caused by the salty, sandy, winds and gnarled, calloused, hard-working bodies. A sunny day means less to worry about regarding the impact of the elemental forces against your home and self, an ease of attending to daily tasks, and a little more natural warmth on a winter's day, saving you some precious wood for a colder time.

The Moon impacts too, not just for the light it offers, but also through the things its magnetic pull influences. I was told that the handful of women living on the river menstruated at the same time as each other, when the lunar pull was at its strongest, and many of the boat-dwellers were a little wilder when the Moon and tides were high and full. On a full Moon during fine weather, the community often gathered round a fire to eat, dance, and play music on the riverbank; experiences related to spring tides on full Moons may have influenced inability to sleep at such times, although the Moon's influence alone was enough and the community made the most of this.[26] This all changed when the National River Authority defences against the rising tides piled the bank, bulldozed all the trees, and widened the tow-path, leaving nowhere for these gatherings to occur, whilst simultaneously removing the natural screen from the outside world, causing the line between 'us and them' to become blurred; this was the beginning of the dissipation of the community.[27]

Boat-dwellers are further physically transformed by the environment in which they live. They smell of tar-varnish, sea-salt, mildew and river mud, it is deeply woven into clothes and hair, as well as sitting on the surface of everything they possess, including their skin. My informants proudly embraced their identity, gladly taking on the title of 'river-rat', even when it was spat at them in derogatory form when en-masse they were barred from entering pubs and shops.[28] Being a boat-dweller, as with all types of liminal or transitory communities, presents a conflicting image in the eyes of the outside world, that of the romanticised, 'exotic other', whilst simultaneously being an untrustworthy nonconformist.[29] The 'boatees' sometimes liked being thought of as 'unpredictable', 'dodgy' and 'risky' or 'bohemian', 'exciting', 'colourful' and 'brave' (a collection of words used by different non-houseboat-living informants to describe people who live on houseboats), it added to their sense of status, even if it was sometimes to their own detriment.

It could be argued that the houseboat-dwellers are disillusioned by the broader society in which they live, and thus hark back to what Kate Soper called the 'nature state'.[30] Many of the informants spoke of how they did not want to become shackled by technology for survival or be 'owned' by society by having their presence registered and documented in way which made them feel trapped. Perhaps this is entwined with a flexible interpretation of what is legal or acceptable behaviour when compared to societal perspectives and laws, driven by personal moralities which were predominantly based upon survivalism. However, the community did have its own guidelines on this and policed such issues using its own moral boundaries and 'laws', based upon respect and a different sense of value of things.[31] It was predominantly this difference which was used to destroy the community, because such non-conformist attitudes and choices are often scapegoated at times of austerity and uncertainty for a broader community, and this is certainly a major factor as to why this thriving community dissipated twenty years ago.[32]

Figure 4. A rainbow over Poverty Bay (1989, source: author's image)

Kinship

Bearing in mind the lack of cheap accommodation that can produce homelessness at a young age, and further statements regarding difficulties with blood families and previous relationships, it can be assumed that camaraderie and community spirit would possibly satisfy a deficit within the psyche of an individual with such a background.[33] Only two informants specifically stated that they were aware of their choice being influenced by a desire for community and kinship at the point when they first decided to live on the river. Nevertheless, the kinships formed in the boating community were stated as being important to all informants, not just those from the focus area and, in addition, the supportive community spirit enhanced the reasons for all informants staying on the river as time progressed.[34] One informant's story of his first viewing of the boat he bought:

> It was a spring morning, a beautiful day and as I walked along the towpath the wind was blowing through the rushes and I passed a couple of blokes, messing about with an engine, with smiles on their faces and cheerful banter. I worked in a grim yard at that time with no view and no friendly colleagues, so this camaraderie struck a chord. As I was looking at the boat, the owner of the next boat came and chatted with me and we discovered that we had a mutual friend, so he invited me into his boat for a 'spliff' and a 'cuppa'. I thought to myself 'this is the life'… and so with [the boat] just what I was looking for and the mooring had space on the land for the chickens and goat, I begged and borrowed the money I needed to buy it.[35]

It was this person who introduced me to the river community and was why I went on to live there. He became a central figure in the community and instigated many of the social events which promoted an ongoing supportive community.

Because the community is full of people who do not 'fit' elsewhere, this promoted the need to be certain of the community on the river. It was a vocal group, with an open-door policy, leaving, as Mary Douglas would say, little ambiguity.[36] Soon after moving onto a boat, visits occur from many different members of the community, checking you out for trustworthiness; then the invitations to visit other boats begin. You are not, however, accepted as a proper member of the community until you survive your second winter, as many people move away before they have to endure it: hardiness, resourcefulness, and adaptability must be proven before you are truly embraced by the community, as well as a willingness to support the community when required, as these qualities are necessary for the survival of all.[37]

Interestingly, there is a wider unspoken kinship between all boat dwellers. When interviewing people on the inland waterways, many were suspicious until I explained that I had lived on a boat, they then questioned me about how many winters I had survived. Having told them funny stories to confirm the truth of my many years on a boat – such as going down an icy gang-plank on my bottom carrying a four-foot-long gas bottle – their attitudes altered from suspicion to warmth, inviting me to stay for a meal and introducing me to other 'boatees'; basically I was accepted as kin by my association with boats.

You need to be able to trust in your community to survive in this space, so there is a strong ethos focused upon supporting the community's existence. This includes not just protecting your own home to keep 'face' within the community, but also being actively aware of when you need to help your neighbours in their ability to survive and keep their boats afloat. In addition, the concept of neighbour does not just mean humans, looking after the natural environment and all its inhabitants is just as important for this community, and many indicated that this was underpinned by belief systems which were integrally animist in their origin.[38] Interaction with non-human animals, not just those which are beautiful to perceive, but also some such as rats, who get into the boats, steal food and chew things up, or tube-web spiders and scorpions who can bite and sting you, add to the way that the natural environment is perceived. The close proximity and lack of control over ongoing interactions develop an apparent cross-species kinship, which is not merely guardianship but rather respect for each creature and its own agency; this breaks down the perceived rules on the differences between human and animals.[39] These perspectives may not have been true for all people living within this community, but it was heard as the predominant voice, especially with regards to being guardians of the river, and therefore common moralities were understood in relation to what was acceptable behaviour regarding the environment. _

Within the community the use of non-biodegradable products was frowned upon, as all flushed or drained waste went into the river. Often the boat-dwellers would see unprocessed waste floating past from the nearby sewerage works, inspiring a stronger stand on this issue. By being aware of the impact humans were having on this environment, it effectively raised this community to a position of greater enlightenment and therefore authority in relation to the environment in comparison to the local community of house-dwellers, whose voice was generally louder and more listened to regarding the making of rules about socially acceptable behaviours.[40] Thus, as a result of these perceptions, the boat-dwellers felt justified in expecting a greater respect from the broader local community.

Despite all these types of kinship being present, the most important is the one which is attributed to the boats themselves, as they provide protection from the elemental forces and give warmth and comfort to individuals who are otherwise mistrusting of close human relationships. As such there are many instances where informants described the boats using anthropomorphic perspectives, and it is true that the curved and streamlined shape of most boats is like a body, with ribs of wood or steel supporting the structure around which the hull, or 'skin', is wrapped.[41] The physical experience of living beneath deck, enclosed in this womb, with minimal light sources, of portholes reflecting flickering umbilical light in off the river, or roof lights looking up at the heavens, with the lapping waves sounding like a heartbeat and the rocking motion like the lulling of a parent for a 'babe' in arms, meant that the inhabitants often referred to them as a 'mother'.[42] This embodied experience of the protective and yet aggressive quality of the natural environment makes it easy to see why the community tended to believe in there being a 'Mother Earth', both presiding over them whilst simultaneously protecting them.[43]

Figure 5. A living room with great views and good ventilation (1993, author's image)

It is therefore the kinships developed between the community of humans and other animals, plus the concept of an environment or space as having its own agency, which have remained as being of the most significant influence upon the 'boatees' in the long term.

Conclusion

The findings of this study show that, in many cases, there is as strong a kinship formed in relation to 'nature' and the boats themselves, as to the community and its individuals. Moralities and nature-based animist beliefs grow out of this experience and are enhanced by the dialogues developed by the community with regards to making sense of themselves and the space which they inhabit, both directly (the boats) and indirectly (the environment). These dialogues are driven by a number of factors, from difficult life experiences causing isolation and an anarchistic attitude towards socially imposed rules, to a real desire to show gratitude to an environment which offers them solace and acceptance. There is no doubt that the natural experience specific to this space helped the individuals in this community develop beliefs and perspectives which enhanced their own agency and sense of self and that all the kinships formed will be long-lasting. I would like to end with one of my informants' words:

> It was the most supportive family, full of the craziest people I have ever known, I miss everything about it. I have never felt so alive as I did then. It was the combination of the place, the people and probably the time, which made it what it was, but it is also my boat, plus the sounds, the smells and the sensations.[44]

Notes

1.   Tim Ingold, 'Epilogue: Towards a Politics of Dwelling', *Conservation and Society* 3, no. 2 (2005): pp. 501–508.

2.   A. Dearling, F. Earle, R. Glasse, H. Whittle and P. Gubby, *A Time to Travel* (Berwickshire: Enabler Publications, 1994), p. 50.

3.   Anthony P. Cohen, ed., *Symbolising boundaries: identity and diversity in British cultures* (Manchester: Manchester University Press, 1986), p. 13; Susan Wright, *Anthropology of Organizations* (London: Routledge, 1994), p. 142; P. Cloke, P. Milbourne and R. Widdowfield, 'Homelessness in Rural Areas: An Invisible Issue?', in P. Kennet, and A. Marsh, eds, *Homelessness: Exploring the New Terrain* (Bristol: The Policy Press, 1999), pp, 61–81, p. 66.

4.   Tracey Skelton and Gill Valentine, eds, *Cool Places: Geographies of Youth Cultures* (London: Routledge, 1998).

5.   Yi-Fu Tuan, *Space and Place: The Perspective of Experience* (Minneapolis, MN: University of Minneapolis Press, 2001), p. 50.

6.   Kay Milton, *Loving Nature: Towards an Ecology of Emotion* (London: Routledge, 2002).

7.   Carrie Barron, 'Creativity and the Liminal Space, The Creativity Cure' *Psychology Today* (2013) https://www.psychologytoday.com/us/blog/the-creativity-cure/201306/creativity-and-the-liminal-space.

8.   Robert Preston-Whyte, 'The Beach as a liminal space', in A. A. Lew, C. M. Hall and A. M. Williams, (eds), *A Companion to Tourism* (Oxford: Blackwell Publishing, 2004), p. 350.

9.   Preston-Whyte, 'The Beach as a liminal space', p. 352.

10.   Edith Turner, 'Contrasts: Communitas and False Communitas', in *Communitas: The Anthropology of Collective Joy* (New York: Palgrave Macmillan US, 2012) pp. 13–22; B. Thomassen, 'Revisiting liminality: The danger of empty spaces', in H. Andrews and L. Roberts (eds), *Liminal Landscapes, Travel, Experience and Spaces In-between* (London: Routledge, 2012); Cohen, *Symbolising boundaries*, pp. 11, 13.

11. Alex Marsh, 'Social exclusion and housing: a relationship in need of elaboration', *Radstats, Radical Statistics* 76 (2001); L. F. Berkman, and I. Kawachi, 'Social Ties and Mental Health', *Journal of Urban Health: Bulletin of the New York Academy of Medicine* 79, no. 3 (2001): pp. 459–467.

12. Mark R. Leary, 'Evolutionary origins of stigmatization: The functions of social exclusion', *Journal of Social & Clinical Psychology* 9, no.2 (1990): pp. 221–229.

13. Cohen, *Symbolising boundaries,* p. 13; Wright, *Anthropology of Organizations* (London: Routledge, 1994), p. 142; Cloke, Milbourne and Widdowfield, 'Homelessness in Rural Areas: An Invisible Issue?', p. 66.

14. Patricia Kennet, 'Homelessness, Citizenship and Social Exclusion', in P. Kennet and A. Marsh, eds, *Homelessness: Exploring the New Terrain* (Bristol: The Policy Press, 1999), pp. 37–61, p. 43; Sophie Watson, 'A Home is Where the Heart is: Engendering Thoughts of Homelessness', in Patricia Kennet and Alex Marsh, eds, *Homelessness: Exploring the New Terrain* (Bristol: The Policy Press, 1999), pp. 81–101.

15. Informant's words.

16. Cloke, 'Homelessness in Rural Areas', pp.66, 70; R. E. Sorenson, 'Sensuality and Consciousness VI: A Preconquest Sojourn: The Study of Child Behavior and Human, Development in Cultural Isolates', *Anthropology of Consciousness* 9, nos.2–3 (1998): pp. 34–55, p. 44.

17. Dimitrios Theodossopolous, 'Degrading Others and Honouring Ourselves: Ethnic Stereotypes as Categories and as Explanations', *Journal of Mediterranean Studies* 13, no. 2 (2003): pp.177–188.

18. Dearling et al., *A Time to Travel,* p. 51; Stephen Lyng, ed., *Edgework: the sociology of risk taking* (London: Routledge, 2005).

19. Yi-Fu Tuan, *Space and Place*, pp. 50, 54.

20. D. Seamon, 'Merleau-Ponty, Perception, and Environmental Embodiment: Implications for Architectural and Environmental Studies', in R. McCann and P. M. Locke, eds, *Carnal Echoes: Merleau-Ponty and the Flesh of Architecture*, at https://www.academia.edu/948750/Merleau-Ponty_Perception_and_Environmental_Embodiment_Implications_for_Architectural_and_Environmental_Studies_forthcoming_ (accessed 7 May 2019) .

21. Yi-Fu Tuan, *Space and Place*, p. 53.

22. Allen Carlston, *Aesthetics and the Environment: The Appreciation of Nature, Art and Architecture* (London: Routledge, 2000), pp. xv, 8.

23. Tim Ingold, 'Epilogue: Towards a Politics of Dwelling', *Conservation and Society* 3, no.2 (2005): pp. 501–508.

24. Informant's words.

25. Anne Baring and Jules Cashford, *The Myth of the Goddess: Evolution of an Image* (London: Penguin 1991), pp.154,162–164.

26. C. Cajochen, S. Altanay-Ekici, M. Münch, S. Frey, V. Knoblauch and A. Wirz-Justice, 'Evidence that the Lunar Cycle Influences Human Sleep', *Current Biology* 23, no.15 (2013): pp. 1485–1488.

27. Cohen, *Symbolising Boundaries*, p. 13.

28. Edmund Leach, 'Anthropological Aspects of Language: Animal Categories and Verbal Abuse', in P. Marander, ed., *Mythology* (London: Penguin, 1970).

29. Lasse Hallström (dir.), *Chocolat* (2000); Betsy Whyte, *Yellow on the Broom: The Early Days of a Traveller Woman* (Edinburgh: Birlinn Ltd., 2001); Judith Okely, 'Recycled (mis)representations: Gypsies, Travellers or Roma treated as objects, rarely subjects', *People, Place and Policy* 8, no.1 (2014): pp. 65–85.

30. Kate Soper, *What is Nature?: Culture, Politics and the Non-Human* (Oxford: Blackwell Publishers, 1995).

31. Cohen, *Symbolising boundaries*, pp. 11, 13.

32. René. Girard, and Yvonne Freccero, *The Scapegoat* (Baltimore, MA: Johns Hopkins University Press, 1989).

33. Dearling, *A Time to Travel*, p .44.

34. Morris Freilich, Douglas Raybeck and Joel Savishinsky, eds, *Deviance: Anthropological Perspectives* (NY: Bergin & Garvey, 1991), pp. 66, 115.,

35. Informant's words.

36. Mary Douglas, *Purity and danger: an analysis of concept of pollution and taboo* (London: Routledge, 1966).

37. Channel 4, 'Medway: The Eco Barge', *Grand Designs* (1st broadcast 15 March 2007); Seamon, 'Merleau-Ponty, Perception, and Environmental Embodiment'.

38. John P. Diggins, 'Animism and the Origins of Alienation: The Anthropological Perspective of Thorstein Veblen', in J. C. Wood, ed., *Thornstein Veblen, Critical Assessments* (London: Routledge, 1993).

39. Tim Ingold, *The Perception of the Environment: Essays on Livelihood, Dwelling and Skill* (London: Routledge, 2000), p.164.

40. A. Cohen, 'Boundaries of Consciousness, Consciousness of Boundaries: Critical Questions for Anthropology', in H. Vermeulen and C. Govers, eds, *The Anthropology of Ethnicity: Beyond "Ethnic Groups and Boundaries"* (Amsterdam: Het Spinhuis Publishers, 1994), pp. 59–79.

41. Yi-Fu Tuan, *Space and Place,* pp. 80, 84.

42. Les Brann, Jacky Owens and Ann Williamson (eds), *The Handbook of Contemporary Clinical Hypnosis: Theory and Practice* (Chichester: Wiley and Sons, 2012); Milton, *Loving Nature*, pp. 5, 39; Diggins, 'Animism and the Origins of Alienation', p. 510.

43. Chris Ray, *Soundscapes and the Rural: A Conceptual Review from a British Perspective* (Newcastle Upon Tyne: University of Newcastle upon Tyne, 2006); Milton, *Loving Nature*, p. 17.

44. Informant's words.

MOUNTAINS, WATERS, CALENDAR, AND MAIZE: SOCIAL INTERACTIONS BETWEEN HUMAN AND NON-HUMAN PERSONS

Stanislaw Iwaniszewski

Introduction

Recent debates in anthropology and archaeology have centered upon the notion of 'relational ontologies' as a means to conceptualize the complex relationships between human societies and non-human environments. Under this approach, the ways in which human societies interact with their environments are considered as being modeled upon interactions between human persons, leading to the emergence of different types of sociality that link human societies to their surrounding environments.[1] The patterned ways in which human societies interact with their environments produce functionally and cognitively meaningful lifeworlds containing multiple networks of interacting humans and non-humans.[2] In step with this approach is the idea of specific places in which both human and non-human entities interact with each other. To derive the broadest range of conditions under which such interactions take place, in the present chapter I use the concept of a relational field. In a seminal contribution to the study of human-environment relations, Tim Ingold proposed this concept to analyze fields of social relations involving humans, places, animals, plants, things, and other non-human features of surrounding environments.[3] The relational field is a node that brings together human and non-human beings that occupy different positions within the human lifeworld. 'To exist… is already to be positioned in a certain environment and committed to the relationships this entails'.[4]

Without going into details that I have discussed elsewhere, I will start with the simple observation that ongoing archaeoastronomical and ethnoastronomical research has proved that human modes of engagement with their celestial environments (skyscapes) have usually been embedded in their structural relationships with the world in which they dwelt, the lifeworlds.[5] It means celestial objects and phenomena have often been implicated in such other cultural phenomena such as worldview, myth, ritual, political organization, kinship, gender and ethnic identity, subsistence pursuit, and so on. As well as being historically contingent, these changing modes of human engagements with their (social and natural) environments explain why different societies have different perceptions and interpretations of the motions and patterns in the sky, although they observe the same celestial bodies and phenomena.[6] My point is that this evidence not only documents a great diversity of the existing human modes of engagement with celestial phenomena but also reveals ontological differences in the ways in which they are perceived, represented, and comprehended.

Naturally, such treatment of human-celestial engagements implies that human perceptions of the rotating celestial vault are not immune to the modes of engagements with the environment they have developed through everyday activities. What is important to emphasize here is that not only do different ways of attending to the skies produce variations in how peoples perceive the experience of the connection existing between them and the heavens, but they also incorporate references to socially constructed categories of self and others. As all celestial bodies – the sun, moon, planets, and fixed stars – move, they are considered to be animate beings, because the capacity of movement is an indication that they are animate.[7] Celestial bodies relate to each other, and to humans, as dynamic non-human agents capable of maintaining meaningful interactions. Like the human self and personhood, the celestial self and the personhood of celestial bodies are shaped in part through their social behavior. As a consequence, celestial cycles cannot be treated only as passive expressions of a social order, as some of the epistemological frameworks discussed below tend to interpret.

In this way, a social and ecological understanding of the skyscape proposes that awareness of the lifeworld is gained through engagements with that world rather than through pure cognition.[8] Now, because these relational patterns are both ecological and social, they represent patterns of social engagements with the environmental others. For example, as anthropologists have documented, when noticing the correspondence existing between heavenly and seasonal cycles, people often develop the idea of an existing universal frame of reference in which the spatiotemporal order of cycles mutually synchronizes celestial, climatic, biological, social, ideological and religious processes, providing a sense of a harmonious relationship between human life and the cosmos.[9] The image of the rotating skies seems to bring to light/expose a part of the broader basic structure which regulates, compartmentalizes, and determines any interaction according to the order implied by this structure. Therefore, unsurprisingly, such worldviews often function normatively, showing how 'the world ought to be', and implying that celestial movements are indicative of specific social orders.[10] René Berthelot described this kind of human-celestial relationship as astrobiological.[11]

Using similar arguments, it may said that in Mesoamerica the parallels perceived between the rotating skies and seasonal rhythms of life found its material expression in the orientation of several important public buildings which were often aligned with significant solar positions on the horizon. Cosmological principles also contributed to the development of the quadripartite layout of the urban centers.[12] In addition, in Mesoamerican cosmology, calendrical cycles and numerological computations of time provided a means of revealing a much broader reality in which celestial motions displayed cosmological patterns linking the rulers with their ancestors or non-human persons and legitimizing their right to rule.

Nevertheless, this perspective appears to define the relationship by way of juxtaposing the human world and cosmos in a static and essential mode. This dualist distinction separates a subjective human-made world from that of cosmos which is located 'out there', in the objective world. Possibly, the relationship between people and environments can better be understood from the perspective of the 'ontological turn'. Recognizing that human-environmental relations can be constituted in multiple ways, this approach insists that a human being, in the sense of human self, is shaped through interactions with social and natural environments (lifeworlds). In turn, the relationship between humans and non-human others seems to be substantially affected by how they interact, and is historically contingent. Therefore, activities defined as skywatching, stargazing, sun watching, time-keeping, calendar making, celestial divination and astrology, regular celestial observations, systematic scanning of the sky, etc. should be interpreted as examples of people's active engagements with the celestial environment and ongoing research in archaeoastronomy and ethnoastronomy has long shown there has been significant variation in how people engaged with skyscapes.

Within this approach, people's perceptions of the world, and their modes of engagement with different elements of their environments, establish specific forms of relationship between people, materials, things, seasonal changes, animals, plants and places. Ongoing relationships allow attributing human-like capacities to the items of material culture and natural environment, enabling human societies to interact with them and treat them as human-like agents. The treatment of animals, plants, mountains, meteorological phenomena in ways that are usually typical of the humans alone can produce the sensation of the existing animistic relationships between people and their landscape. However, the kind of human engagement and involvement with the environment is much more nuanced and depends on how both human and nonhuman beings are constituted through the ongoing interactions. These conceptualizations also depend on the types of participation expected from nonhuman beings in everyday activities.

Astronomical alignments: towards a conceptual framework comprising sky-water-mountain-maize-time complex

Archaeoastronomers studying Mesoamerican ceremonial and public buildings have long recognized they were often aligned to specific horizon landmarks where also the daily positions of the Sun throughout the year were perceived.[13] Archaeoastronomical research has shown that one of the probable benefits of skywatching was farming. The appearance of the Sun along architectural alignments could have announced critical moments for important agricultural activities and may have been connected with public ceremonies.

Johanna Broda, who carefully reviewed various ethnohistorical and ethnographic records, proposed that in prehispanic Central Mexico there existed the conceptual unit consisting of several natural elements that should be examined together.[14] Broda – noticing that prehispanic societies carefully positioned and oriented their ceremonial architecture on nearby mountains, cliffs, and caves, that other landscape features where used as ritual places, and that the Sun at critical dates of the agricultural calendar was tracked with special attention – proposed that earthly activities mirrored the unity of the conceptual, cognitive and symbolic system linking together the sky, mountains, waters, and maize. In order to ensure good crops, Mesoamerican indigenous societies, which relied deeply on their physical environment and favorable weather conditions, attached great importance to the mode of interaction with critical landscape features and weather phenomena, endowing them with person-like capacities.

Some years later, in a similar vein, Ivan Šprajc highlighted the presence of yet another very similar symbolic system, which he baptized as Venus, rain, and maize.[15] Another analysis of the orientation patterns encoded in architectural alignments led Aveni and Hartung to suggest that this was a symbolic complex encompassing the sky, water, and the mountain.[16]

Though all these propositions differ in their details, they nevertheless perceive the occurrence of the same or repeating elements: the sky (Venus, Sun), water (rain), mountain, and maize. Following the conclusions offered by all Mesoamerican scholars, especially the recent ones provided by Sánchez Nava and Šprajc, we know now that a significant number of public prehispanic buildings were aligned to sunrises and sunsets on particular dates, apparently to mark either the important dates for agriculture or to determine specific periods.[17] Their orientation data can be explained by the existence of an orientation calendar which fixed the positions of the Sun at specific dates related to the essential climatic-agricultural dates, either directly, through actual observations, or indirectly, through the count of intervals of days counted from the solstices on to horizon features. From the written record, we know that various calendrical intervals were of extreme importance for Mesoamerican scribes and diviners and that the nature of Mesoamerican numerology is derived from the properties of their 260-day calendar. In many cases, those calendar intervals were initiated by the sunrise or sunset position at solstices.

The ritual, symbolic and cognitive framework described as a sky-water-mountain-maize complex was inscribed onto public architecture. Apart from their astronomical properties, most public religious, administrative, and political buildings (altars, monuments, temples, palaces, plazas, etc.) were erected to form part of a public space, thus providing opportunities to conduct collective actions in specific locations on the landscape, as well as to imprint shared memories and social and cultural identities in the landscape. With this in mind, it is possible to hypothesize that many astronomically oriented structures functioned as places where political and religious authorities interacted with places, things, landscapes, weather conditions, ritual practices, and the commoners. They emphasized the role of political and religious authorities as mediators relating human populations to their surroundings.

This symbolic and cognitive complex can explain one of the circumstances in which the Mesoamericans engaged themselves with skywatching, always in connection with water, mountain, calendar interval, and maize. According to Broda, the Aztec ritual specialists negotiated with the gods and goddesses of rain and mountains, of sweet and salt water, and of the maize and earth, to receive sufficient 'water, rain, and agricultural growth'.[18] It can be hypothesized that the moment of time adequate to initiate those negotiations was derived from the positions of the Sun on the horizon. Rain and agricultural almanacs found in prehispanic Central Mexican codices focus on the gods of water or rain, the maize plant, and calendar cycles, while the skybands may depict sun-rays, clouds, rains, or darkness.[19] Examining the orientations of ceremonial enclosures located on the slopes of Central Mexican volcanoes enables us to determine those temporal instances with higher precision.

To conclude this section, the Mesoamericans inhabited a world in which they perceived celestial bodies, landscape features, places, things, animals and plants, ancestors and spiritual entities, as beings potentially alive and acting as persons either momentarily or more lastingly. Though the variations in the relationships between human and non-human persons can be discussed from the point of view of the typology of identifications which contains animism, totemism, analogism, and naturalism, in this chapter, I intend to explore this topic from the viewpoint of the Central Mexican notion of a person.[20]

The natural environment and agriculture

Aztec agricultural relations to nature focused on landscape, climate, rain, and maize, finding their religious and ideological form of engagements in the arrangement of the annual cycle of seasonal rituals. In the Central Mexican uplands, snow-capped volcanoes were considered as sources of water, since thunder and rain clouds appeared above them heralded the arrival of the rainy season and the renewal of nature, and also as sources of sustenance, since the Aztecs shared the Pan-American concept of a sacred mountain, the source of maize. The Aztec cult of maize was closely related to the cult of the Sun and underworld, connecting their rulers to the entities of the sky, earth, and netherworld, defining 'the cosmic harmony between the kings and their subjects'.[21] This network of connections made up the cognitive and symbolic complex advocated by Broda. In order to discuss the kinds of personification of natural and meteorological phenomena, and the Aztec's practical engagement with the landscape, it is fundamental to describe the critical features of the Central Mexican environment briefly.

Climate

As in other tropical locations, periodical climatic changes are produced by trade winds. Between May and October, warm, moist and northeast winds bring high humidity and heavy rainfall, while between November and April the dry west winds bring on drought or very low precipitations. Though the duration, although the start and end points of the seasons may vary across the area, the alternation of dry and wet seasons is the most critical aspect of Mesoamerican climatic seasonality. The yearly weather cycle includes the colder (November to January) and the warmer (February to April) sub-divisions of the dry season.

Agriculture

Mesoamerica is one of the regions where agriculture was invented. Among the earliest domesticated species were squash and maize (corn, *Zea mays*), paving the way toward the agricultural way of life. Farming communities spread over the whole region with the advent of the so-called Early Formative (Preclassic)

Period, which began about 2000 BCE.[22] The regular alternation of dry and wet seasons has, naturally, determined the periodical activities of Mesoamerican farming populations. Maize has distinguishable planting, turning, and reaping seasons. The maize growing season is from May to July; the harvesting may start as early as in September but usually goes through November to January. Despite numerous developments in agro-technology, most farming communities have always depended on climatic conditions and environmental settings. The maize-growing cycle depends on the seasonal rhythms in rainfall; thus, the successful outcome of planting depends on the ability of Mesoamerican farmers to synchronize the maize-growing season with that of the rainfall. Unpredictable rainfall patterns, frequent seasonal drought, heat stress in summer, unexpected early or late frost, maize diseases, adequate soil fertility and cover, and many other factors can affect the crops. To be able to cope with these conditions, the Mesoamericans developed many religious and worldview concepts related to the maize agricultural cycle, fully integrating maize into their intellectual and artistic expressions.[23] All this suggests that maize cultivation has been a major form of human-environmental interaction in indigenous Mesoamerica, indicating significant shifts from hunter-gatherer ontologies.[24]

The rise of archaeoastronomy in Mesoamerica has directed attention to the multiple roles that celestial bodies and phenomena played in its indigenous societies. The behavior of celestial bodies was of primary interest to skywatchers in terms of the significance they carried out for Mesoamerican societies. Though this significance cannot be entirely associated with a single mode of engagement, prehispanic societies have through the centuries revealed their dependence on maize. The activity of farming activated communication between people and their environments in specific ways, involving relationships with the heavens, non-human others, landscape features, and the world of humankind. As outlined above, the principle of reciprocity denoted that people negotiated material exchanges with the entities embodying various elements of their environments. All agricultural production was seen as a joint effort between the essential features of the environment (caves, mountains, springs, agricultural plots, cultivated plants, weather phenomena), which was conceived of as being composed of interacting human and non-human agents.[25]

Naturally, such practical engagements occurring between humans and their environments had a predominantly communicative character. Communication was made possible through collective rituals, and ritual activity was the proper way to interact with the entities that inhabited both the natural and cosmic world. Needless to say, farmers' interactions with particular landmarks adopted the form of interactions taking place between human persons, sometimes leading to the development of family ties. So, the entities found in the environment were not considered as inert, independent objects just being 'out there', but rather as animated or human-like beings equipped with various physical, social and cognitive abilities. Natural phenomena such as rain, wind, rivers, springs, mountains, the Sun, or the Moon were all conceptualized as non-human persons, but hierarchically superior to people and interfering with their lives. All those assumptions (chiming with the Heidegger's notion of 'being-in-the-world', Ingold's notion of 'dwelling with', or the methodological alternative represented through 'relational ontologies') provide new insights into how people engage and understand their physical environments and how they build a meaningful relationship with their surroundings.

This situation refers to the Mesoamerican archaeoastronomy, too. Until now, human-celestial interactions epitomized by the astronomical alignments found in various human-built environments have usually been lifted out of the context in which they functioned and analyzed in terms of the techniques imported from the Western science (i.e., in terms of statistics).[26] Such a position can only contribute to the impression that alignments were passive expressions of the celestial order to which the human societies should have adapted, or that they reflected the cognitive skills of the ancient builders. Rather, astronomical aligning, here understood as a social activity, should be regarded as a part of the long-term relationship between peoples and their surroundings which contributes both to the change and continuity within a society and its concepts of the environment. While it is true that celestial observation was a factor in Mesoamerican city planning, the use of the symbolic and metaphoric complex consisting of the mountains, waters, calendar, maize, and sky offers a better interpretative framework to understand peoples' engagements with the skies in prehispanic Mesoamerica because it allows to treat them as intentionally arranged in patterns enabling their inhabitants to interact with human and non-human persons.

Social agents involved

Dealing with the study of the human-celestial relationships built in the Mesoamerican past, I find a suitable framework in Ingold's concepts of a 'relational field' or 'meshwork'.[27] In its broadest definition, a relational field refers to the situation in which persons, places, and things are identified 'by their positions vis-a-vis one another'.[28] According to Ingold, people shape their understandings of themselves through complex interactions with all components, material and nonmaterial, of their physical settings.[29] In their interactions with diverse environments, people tend to perceive their components as being alive or animated (Latour's 'actants'), that is, possessing some degree of agency, and interactions with them usually take the form of social relationships. Thus, the world inhabited by human societies is conceived of as a 'relational field', or a 'meshwork of entangled lines of life, growth, and movement', a dynamic system of interactions and relationships between people and the material and immaterial components of their worlds.[30]

Such an approach allows one to imagine things, landscape features, meteorological and astronomical phenomena, animals and plants as active members of like-human societies.[31] The idea of interacting objects, subjects, and societies seems to be an excellent point, enabling the application of a relational approach to the human self. Occupying a place in the relational field requires of humans active engagement with their environments. In turn, humans are structured by these relations.[32] Acknowledging that human beings are involved, through ongoing relations, with members of their communities and surroundings, it is important to understand the participation of nonhuman entities in daily human activities. In a manner analogous to the human self (or person), nonhuman others emerge from the ongoing social relations involving humans and nonhuman others. To be a person is thus to be in an ongoing relationship with humans, animals, plants, things, and places that are external to that person.[33] So, the question is how the Mexicas (Aztecs) conceived of a human person and how they related with the critical components of the surrounding world.

The notion of a human person

Among the ancient Mexicas, the concept of a human person, or human being, considered humans to be composed of a material, physical body and three different kinds of nonmaterial forces or entities: *tonalli*, associated with destiny and body warmth; *teoyolia*, related to the vitality and agentivity; and *ihiyotl*, linked to the vital breath.[34] These were believed to reside in the head (*tonalli*), in the heart (*teoyolia*), and the liver (*ihiyotl*). Each human body was believed to be the confluence of these three forces, giving each person his or her unique character. To be able to act as a whole and balanced human person, all three entities should have operated harmoniously with each other. Although individuals possessed the intentionality and capacity to act, they had some constraints imposed by their *tonalli*. While it is true that the quadripartite model of a human person (a material body plus three animated entities or forces) proposed by López Austin for the Postclassic Nahua became applicable to other prehispanic populations in Mesoamerica, it is also important to point out that many scholars have adopted this model for the study of contemporary indigenous societies.[35]

In the Mexica realm, a singular human being was considered to be divisible, comprised of a set of separable and independent animated components that came from outer space, outside of the boundary of the skin and acquired just after the birth. People's bodies were conceived as being permeable (or porous), allowing other entities to move in or move out. In light of the current anthropological discussions about the notions of a human person in non-Western societies, the Aztec notion of a human being could be defined as a composite person and described as both a permeable and partible being. [36]

It is probable that, upon this concept of a permeable and partible person, Mesoamerican societies constituted different conceptualizations of a social person (personhood). [37] The distinction between a person and personhood is critical here and, in my view, allows one to overcome methodological challenges. The social person is also a composite being but in this case she is made up of relationships with other human and nonhuman persons. [38] Using this approach, a person is made up of relationships between humans, features of landscape, animals, plants, and significant objects of social reality. To understand personhood in this manner highlights a person's capacity to relate to and to be related with; people, therefore, are not considered as static in condition but as beings able to change or transform throughout life continuously. [39]

In sum, the Nahua concept of a (human) person refers to a dividual, partible and relational being. [40] As a dividual, partible and permeable person, the Nahua human being is a composite of the animate substances (*tonalli*) received from the distinctive features of the cosmos, and she is, therefore, cosmologically relational. [41] Such a person is a product of the forces emanating from the cosmos. [42] As a dividual and relational social person, she is composed of multiple relationships with animals, plants, things, places, celestial bodies, and various human and non-human beings. Those relationships are connected with the domain of *teyolía*. [43] A properly balanced interaction between all those entities as well as between them and their cosmic counterparts produced a broader sense of harmony, achieved through the cooperative effort of humans and the forces of the Universe.

Having described the Aztec concepts of a human person, I will now describe how agency or intentionality was attributed to different elements and non-human beings in the surroundings, in order to understand the participation of nonhuman entities in interactions with the people.

Gods

As has been shown, according to the Aztec worldview, the universe existed thanks to interactions between humans and the divine. All fundamental processes and forces in the world were personified by gods, but human co-activity was needed to maintain its existence. In being structured by these relations, the Mesoamericans provided natural phenomena and objects with human social attributes. They attributed agency and intentionality to certain animals, plants, astronomical and weather phenomena, objects and places with whom they often socially interacted. Some of those entities were conceptualized as gods. According to López Austin and Velásquez García, the ancient Maya conceived gods as beings superior to humans with a capacity for acting and endowed with intentionality.[44]

The prehispanic deities were composed of both fixed and fluid transformational attributes. Thus, each deity had attributes 'that defined, distinguished, and represented' them, but they also possessed multiple traits shared with other deities, enabling continuous merging or overlapping with them.[45] Eva Hunt described this Mesoamerican phenomenon in the following words: 'The gods were not totally personified as discrete entities, however. Rather, they were clusters of ideas'.[46] Therefore, aside from being permeable entities, the Mexica deities may also be defined as distributed persons.

Such may be the case of Tlaloc, who was unquestionably the primary god of rain in Central Mexico, and the Aztecs performed many rituals associated with his cult at the onset of the rainy season. Sixteenth-century reports inform us that Tlaloc also functioned as a god of the earth.[47] As a rain god, Tlaloc was linked to all the mountains that rise in the Valley of Mexico, because rain clouds usually cluster on mountaintops during the rainy season. One of those mountains, today called Mount Tlaloc, was considered to be the abode of Tlaloc and the earthly representation of Tlalocan, which was imagined as a four-room structure arranged about a patio with four tubes of water assisted by four Tlaloque, assistants to Tlaloc, who scattered rains and stroked their vessels with sticks to produce thunder and lightning.[48] Within this perspective, the personhood of Tlaloc appears to be distributed through the material world in the form of his four assistants embodying different kinds of rain.[49] The dividual perception of Tlaloc shows the god as a composite person incorporating the Tlaloque and their actions (rainfall).[50]

Sixteenth-century texts also shed additional light on the significance of Tlaloc. On the one hand, mountains were conceived as hollow vessels filled with water and with caves leading to the subterranean realm, embodying the place of full food richness and fertility called Tlalocan.[51] On the other hand, the same hills and mountains were believed to be the embodiments of infinite *tlaloque*, the little divine assistants to Tlaloc. Practically, all prominent mountain peaks, especially those around which rainclouds were observed to gather, were believed to be *tlaloque*. High mountains and hills that dominated nearby settlements all played roles in sending rainclouds to the people and were believed to be responsible for the fertility of crops. Sometimes they were identified with local protector deities.[52] In light of the theory of personhood, it is evident that it is the principal deity who distributes its characteristic elements among hundreds of assistants. Again, Tlaloc would represent a concept of a composite, multi-authored person who is distributed throughout the world in the form of little *tlaloque* or mountain gods and, in turn, each such mountain deity would represent a 'distributed person' of Tlaloc. The god's capacity to act, or his agency, is also being distributed among *tlaloque*.

The relationship between Tlaloc and his little *tlaloque* assistants has been explained by Alfredo López Austin, who considered that it reflected the Nahua beliefs in a vertical hierarchy of gods and peoples.[53] This concept was fundamental for the establishment of the order between the human-made architecture, mountains or hills in the surrounding world, and their 'prototypes' in the divine world. Lopez Austin argues that:

> Every superior being shared a substance to create other inferior beings, its replicas (...) At each site inhabited by the people, (certain) mountain was recognized as a replica of the Sacred Mount. At the same time, this earthly copy shared a substance to be projected onto the nearby minor mountains. And the people raised pyramids - artificial substitutions of the mountains – which received a part of the divine substance by imitating forms derived both from the cosmic geometry as well as from the local landscape forms.[54]

In Aztec thought, the elements of the landscape are continuously being composed and re-composed in various ways which imply that it is not possible to identify them with a single bounded and well-defined god. For example, the concepts of the Sacred Mountain and the quadripartition of the world were first regarded as emerging in the divine world and then projected onto the material world inhabited by the humans. The mountain occupying the east direction was considered as being superior to all other mountains and hills, and its deity becomes the patron god of the place. I maintain that each such deity might be conceived of as a kind of a 'distributed person', manifested on certain occasions in particular temples and cult places located in the mountains. From this evidence, it is possible to suggest that, in such ritual sites (conceived as Ingold's 'relational fields'), the essential components of the personhood of those deities were reassessed through the ritual engagements with human persons.

Non-human entities (animals, plants, things, places, celestial bodies, spiritual entities) that emerged as human-like persons through such engagements could have been endowed with more enduring human attributes, enabling the humans to establish social relationships with them.

It can be hypothesized that the inhabitants of Mesoamerica purposely searched for an environment with specific characteristics that covered several symbolic levels, and that they visualized particular landscape prominences as evocations of mythological narratives. Dwelling within such places was extremely meaningful, so the Mesoamerican settlements were often built to reflect the surrounding world that extends around them: temples represented mountains, tombs represented caves that linked humans to the netherworld, and so on.[55] Such places had to recall the mythical moment when the earth was created: an aquatic universe framed by four mountains with a fifth elevation in the middle of the water. According to Garcia Zambrano, the unusual undulating shape of mountains, emphasizing a notch or a split in the top, could have commemorated the split of the mountain of origins (Tonacatepetl, 'Mountain of (our) Sustenance') made by the *tlaloque* to let out the agricultural richness for human sustenance.[56]

Another entity from the Nahua lifeworld that was endowed with animacy was wind.[57] The wind usually embodies the breath, the entity from which the life derives. In Nahua tradition, the wind god Ehecatl blended with the figure of Quetzalcoatl, who created the world, humans, and maize. Like Tlaloc, the rain god who was aided by four *Tlaloque* assistants, each embodying rains originating from one of the world directions, Ehecatl, the wind god, also had four assistants, called *ehecatotontin*, who embodied the winds associated with the four cardinal directions. In turn, the countless small winds could bring disease. Again, like Tlaloc with his *tlaloque*, Ehecatl himself represents a concept of a distributed person through his associations with the *ehecatotontin*.

The Aztecs had numerous other-than-human personifications of maize, both female and male. In many cases, they represented different stages of the plant's growth cycle: Xilonen (tender corn), Chicomecoatl (ripened corn), and Centeotl (dried corn). Agricultural ritual activities connected the life processes of germination, growth, maturation, reproduction, and death with the social rhythms of farming communities. Those other-than-human maize-related persons participated in the social life of farming communities through the variety of rituals performed at specific times in the year. Some of these rituals performed at high-mountain sites were probably based on reciprocal exchanges with the local mountains, caves and springs which were generally associated with the *tlaloque*. Rituals involved debt payments (*nextlahualtin*) in the form of substances required by Tlaloc and the *tlaloque* to recover energy, and the sacrifices of *teteo imixiptlahuan,* child representations of the little *tlaloque* beings believed to be reborn after the death of their human representations. Those sites, usually built in the form of rectangular precincts, were carefully positioned concerning the nearby horizon features.

The flow of time and skywatching

Every year, from February to late April or early May, during the dry season, Aztec ritual specialists and rulers climbed the slopes of the surrounding mountains to produce rain-bringing and fertility rites in mountain shrines. Those ritual enclosures located on the forested slopes or even above the timberline, and far from the cultivated agricultural lands, are supposed to display significant spatial relationships between the shrines and landscape features – mostly hills, cliffs, mountains, caves, and water – drawing attention to their specific location and making them special places. The sites are considered to be deliberately located and aligned, both to command views to specific landscape features, as well as to provide the directions of the rising/setting Sun on specific dates. It is plausible to suggest that the orientation of ritual precincts was chosen so that it would provide the dates either coinciding with the critical moments of the agricultural year or with the intervals of days separated from the solstices by 13-day or 20-day multiples.

The ancient Nahua, as well as all other Mesoamerican peoples, divided the flow of time into sets and subsets through distinct ritual activities. The 260-day divinatory cycle, a combination of twenty-day signs with thirteen numbers representing a cycle of thirteen days, was often composed of more complex sequences of days, the multiples of thirteen or twenty-day units. Among the most used were the cycles or sets of 52 and 65 days which were multiplied by five or four, respectively, to sum up to 260 days. On the other hand, the annual cycle of 365 days, composed of eighteen subsets of twenty days each, to which a minor subset of five additional days was added, produced twenty-day units in the vigesimal counting system so typical for Mesoamerica.[58]

Conclusions

As Johanna Broda put it, the cognitive-symbolic complex comprising the sky, mountain, water, and maize expressed the Aztec concept of 'cosmic harmony'.[59] Therefore, it also means that such a complex relational system provided a meaningful context in which the Aztecs experienced and understood the surrounding world. The identification of this complex gives us some indication of a Mexica understanding of their relationship to their environment.

This perspective constitutes an ontological framework for approaching the concept of skyscape as proposed by Fabio Silva.[60] The cognitive-symbolic complex, which was variously formulated by Broda, Aveni, Hartung, and Šprajc, breaks with Kantian tradition. It is a good starting point to account for the fact that many non-human landscape entities (mountains, cliffs, caves, watercourses), the beings associated with various weather and astronomical phenomena (thunders, rains, winds, the Sun), or with the life processes and the living (maize plant) participated in the organization of the social life among the Aztecs. In the examples provided in this paper, I intended to situate an Aztec skyscape within a broader framework of relationships in order to be able to determine how nonmaterial components of diverse material bodies were distributed among various human and nonhuman agents. As a provisional hypothesis, it can initially be proposed that the rising Sun, embodied by the Aztec Sun-god called Tonatiuh, provided *tonalli* (vital energy) to each daily sign as well as to each living entity. Through the sensation of the warmth, the rays of the rising Sun were regarded as touching all features on the earth, distributing the animating energy of *tonalli* among them. It appears that mountain ritual shrines, the places where weather and nature phenomena were invoked, were endowed with animacy brought by the Sun. In order to understand all cosmic forces, the Nahua diviners utilized a 260-day divinatory cycle, a kind of an interpretative framework or matrix which not only attributed sense and meaning to all environmental and social phenomena but also contributed to the emergence of the sizeable symbolic complex comprising maize, water, mountain, and sky. This is why the mountain shrines usually display vistas to the places on the mountain skyline where the Sun appears on specific dates.

On the other hand, and in a line of what García Zambrano proposed, it may be suggested that essential landscape features, like hills and mountains, manifested the *teyolía* animate entity through direct relationships with human settlements, generating the sense of community identity. Each human settlement, be it a small village or a town, had its own patron-mountain. By establishing a conceptual or symbolic link between peoples and landscape features, the ritual specialists incorporated them into the life process of a community. The symbolical and metaphorical complex consisting of the sky, mountain, water, and maize, together with the idea of the time flow (symbolized by temporal cycles), should be viewed therefore as a Mesoamerican conceptual framework ('Mesoamerican relational field') that shaped and created a society's understanding of their lifeworld. Celestial observations played a very particular role in this form of human engagement with the heavens.

Notes

1.   For example, T. Ingold, *The Perception of the Environment. Essays in livelihood, dwelling and skill* (London: Routledge, 2000), pp. 51–52; M. N. Zedeño, 'Animating by association: index objects and relational taxonomies', *Cambridge Archaeological Journal* 19, no. 3 (2009): p. 409.

2.   I'm following here the concept of a Lifeworld (Lebenswelt) defined as 'the familiar worlds of everyday life', see A. Schutz, and T. Luckmann, *Las estructuras del mundo de la vida* (1977; repr. Buenos Aires: Amorrortu editors, 2003), pp. 25–29, 41.

3.   Ingold, *The Perception*, pp. 144–49.

4.   Ingold, *The Perception*, p. 149.

5.   Consult S. Iwaniszewski, 'Por una astronomía cultural renovada', *Complutum* 20, no. 2 (2009): pp. 23–37; S. Iwaniszewski, 'Alternative archaeoastronomies - an overview', *Archaeologia Baltica* 10 (2008): pp. 253–257; S. Iwaniszewski, 'The sky as a social field', in C.L.N. Ruggles, ed., Archaeoastronomy and ethnoastronomy: building bridges between cultures, International Astronomical Union Symposium 278 (Cambridge: Cambridge University Press, 2011), pp. 30–37.

6.   For example, R. T. Zuidema, 'Anthropology and Archaeoastronomy', in R. A. Williamson, ed., *Archaeoastronomy in the Americas* (College Park, MD: Ballena Press/ Center for Archaeoastronomy, 1981), pp. 29–31.

7.   M. H. Bassett, *The fate of earthly things: Aztec gods and god–bodies* (Austin, TX: University of Texas Press, 2015), p. 13.

8.   T. Ingold, *The Perception*, pp. 40–60.

9.   See J. Broda, 'Astronomy, *cosmovisión*, calendrics, and sacred geography in ancient Mesoamerica', in A. F. Aveni and G. Urton, eds, 'Ethnoastronomy and archaeoastronomy in the American tropics', in *Annals of the New York Academy of Sciences* 385 (1982): pp. 100–3.

10.   On the dual function (a descriptive and a normative one) of a worldview, consult C. Geertz, *The Interpretation of cultures* (New York: Basic Books, Inc., 1973), pp. 93–4.

11.   R. Berthelot, *La pensée de l'Asie et l'astrobiologie* (Paris: Payot, 1949).

12.   Examples include: W. Ashmore, 'Site-planning principles and concepts of directionality among the ancient Maya', *Latin American Antiquity* 2, no. 3 (1991): pp. 199–226; J. Broda, 'Astronomy, cosmovisión, calendrics'; G. Brotherston, 'Mesoamerican description of space, II: signs for direction', *Ibero–amerikanisches Archiv* 2 (1976): pp. 39–62; C. C. Coggins, 'The shape of time: some political implications of a four-part figure', *American Antiquity* 45, no .4 (1980): pp. 727–39; M. E. Smith, 'Can we read cosmology in ancient Maya city plans? Comment on Ashmore and Sabloff', *Latin American Antiquity* 14, no. 2 (2003): pp. 221–8; M.E. Smith, 'Did the Maya build architectural cosmogram?', *Latin American Antiquity* 16, no. 2 (2005): pp. 217–24; I. Šprajc, 'More on Mesoamerican cosmology and city plans', *Latin American Antiquity* 16, no. 2 (2205): pp. 209–16; I. Šprajc, 'Astronomical and cosmological aspects of Maya architecture and urbanism', in J. A. Rubiño-Martín, J. A. Belmonte, F. Prada, and A. Alberdi, eds, 'Cosmology Across Cultures', in *ASP Conference Series* (Astronomical Society of the Pacific) 409 (2009): pp. 303–14; I. Šprajc, 'Astronomical correlates of architecture and landscape in Mesoamerica', in C. L.N. Ruggles, ed., *Handbook of Archaeoastronomy and Ethnoastronomy* (New York: Springer, 2015), pp. 715–28; F. Tichy, *Die geordnete Welt indianischer Völker: Ein Beispiel von Raumordnung und Zeitordnung im vorkolumbischen Mexiko,* Das Mexiko–Projekt der Deutschen Forschungsgemeinschaft 21 (Stuttgart: Franz Steiner Verlag, 1991).

13.   Recent interpretations include I. Šprajc, 'Astronomy, Architecture, and Landscape in Prehispanic Mesoamerica', *Journal of Archaeological Research* 26, no. 2 (2018): pp.

197–251; A. C. Gonzalez–Garcia and I. Šprajc, Astronomical significance of architectural orientations in the Maya Lowlands: a statistical approach, *Journal of Archaeological Science: Reports* 9, no. (2016): pp. 191–202.

14. J. Broda, 'The sacred landscape of Aztec calendar festivals: Myth, nature and society', in D. Carrasco, ed., *To change place: Aztec ceremonial landscapes* (Niwot, CO: University Press of Colorado, 1991), pp. 74–120; J. Broda, 'Astronomical knowledge, calendrics, and sacred geography in ancient Mesoamerica', in C. L. N. Ruggles and N. J. Saunders, eds, *Astronomies and Cultures* (Niwot, CO: University Press of Colorado, 1993), pp. 253–95; J. Broda, 'La etnografía de la fiesta de la Santa Cruz: una perspectiva histórica', in J. Broda and F. Báez–Jorge, eds, *Cosmovisión, ritual e identidad de los pueblos indígenas de México* (México: Consejo Nacional para la Cultura y las Artes and Fondo de Cultura Económica, 2001), pp. 165–238.

15. I. Šprajc, 'Venus, lluvia y maíz'.

16. A. F. Aveni and H. Hartung, 'Water, mountain, sky: the evolution of site orientations in Southeastern Mesoamerica', in E. Quiñones Keber, ed., *In Chalchihuitl in Quetzalli: Mesoamerican Studies in Honor of Doris Heyden* (Lancaster: Labyrinthos, 2000), pp. 55–65.

17. P. F. Sánchez Nava and I. Šprajc, *Orientaciones arquitectónicas en la arquitectura maya de las tierras bajas* (México: Instituto Nacional de Antropología e Historia, 2015); I. Šprajc, 'Astronomy, Architecture, and Landscape in Prehispanic Mesoamerica', *Journal of Archaeological Research* 26, no. 2 (2018): pp. 197–251.

18. J. Broda, 'The Sacred Landscape', pp. 83–4.

19. E. Boone, *Cycles of Time and Meaning in the Mexican Books of Fate* (Austin, TX: University of Texas Press, 2007), pp. 142–51.

20. P. Descola, *Beyond Nature and Culture*, trans. J. Lloyd (Chicago, IL: University of Chicago Press, 2013).

21. J. Broda, 'The Sacred Landscape', p. 82.

22. For example, R.J. Sharer with L. P. Traxler, *The Ancient Maya* (1946 6th edn (Stanford, CA: Stanford University Press, 2006): pp. 154–155; M. A. Masson and M. E. Smith, ' Introduction: Mesoamerican Civilizations', in M. E. Smith and M. A. Masson, eds, *The Ancient Civilizations of Mesoamerica: A Reader* (Malden, MA, and Oxford: Blackwell, 2000): pp. 1–14 (pp. 8–9).

23. Compare B. Stross, 'Maize in Word and Image in Southeastern Mesoamerica', in K. Taube, 'The classic Maya maize god: A reappraisal', in V. M. Fields, ed., *Fifth Palenque Round Table* (San Francisco, CA: Pre–Columbian Art Research Institute, 1985), pp. 171–181; K. Taube, 'The Olmec maize god: The face of corn in Formative Mesoamerica', *Res: Anthropology and Aesthetics* 29/30 (1996): pp. 39–81.

24. This characteristic of agriculture has been recently questioned by D. Dehouve, 'El venado, el maiz y el sacrificio', *Diario de Campo. Cuadernos de Etnologia* 4 (2008): pp. 1–39.

25. M. H. Bassett, '*The fate of earthly things*', pp. 11–15; P. Pitrou, 'Life as a process of making in the Mixe Highlands (Oaxaca, Mexico): towards a 'general pragmatics' of life', *Journal of the Royal Anthropological Institute* 21, no. 1 (2014): pp. 86–105; D. Lorente Fernández, 'Tempestades de vida y de muerte entre los nahuas', in P. Pitrou, M. Valverde Valdés and J. Neurath, eds, *La nocion de vida en Mesoamérica* (México: Universidad Nacional Autónoma de México and Centro de Estudios Mexicanos y Centroamericanos, 2011), pp. 247–274.

26. See for example, A.C. González-García and I. Šprajc, 'Astronomical significance', pp. 191–202.

27. T. Ingold, *Being Alive. Essays on movement, knowledge and description* (London: Routledge, 2011), pp. 84–84, 91–93.

194   Stanislaw Iwaniszewski

28. Ingold, *The Perception*, p. 149
29. Ingold, *The Perception*, pp. 132–151.
30. Ingold, *The Perception*, p. 63.
31. Consult A. L. Brown and W. H. Walker, 'Prologue: archaeology, animism and non–human agents', *Journal of Archaeological Method and Theory* 15, no. 4 (2008): pp. 297–299; B. J. Mills and T. J. Ferguson, 'Animate objects: shell trumpets and ritual networks in the Greater Southwest', *Journal of Archaeological Method and Theory* 15, no. 4 (2008): pp. 338–361.
32. T. Ingold, *The Perception*, pp. 353–354.
33. C. Fowler, *The archaeology of personhood: an anthropological approach* (London and New York: Routledge, 2004): pp. 6–7.
34. On the description of the Nahua concept of a human person, see A. López Austin, *Cuerpo humano e ideología. Las concepciones de los antiguos nahuas* (México: Instituto de Investigaciones Antropológicas, Universidad Nacional Autónoma de México, 1980; R. Martínez González, *El nahualismo* (México: Instituto de Investigaciones Históricas, Universidad Nacional Autónoma de México, 2011); R. Martínez González and C. Barona, 'La noción de persona en Mesoamérica: un diálogo de perspectivas', *Anales de Antropología* 49, no. 2 (2015): pp. 13–72.
35. See Martínez González and Barona, 'La noción de persona', pp. 35–38.
36. For example, M. Strathern, *The gender of the gift* (Berkeley and Los Angeles, CA: University of California Press, 1988); C. Busby, 'Permeable and partible persons. A comparative analysis of gender and body in South India and Melanesia', *Journal of the Royal Anthropological Institute* 3, no. 2 (1997): pp. 261–278; C. Fowler, *The Archaeology of Personhood: an anthropological approach* (London: Routledge, 2004). In reference to the ancient Maya society, consult P. L. Geller, 'Parting (with) the dead: body partibility as evidence of commoner ancestor veneration', *Ancient Mesoamerica* 23, no. 1 (2012): pp. 115–130.
37. I am in no way following Bartolomé's proposal of introducing the concepts of physical, social, and spiritual persons, see M. A. Bartolomé, 'La construcción de la persona en las etnias mesoamericanas' in L. I. Méndez y Mercado, ed., *Identidad: análisis y teoría, simbolismo, sociedades complejas, nacionalismo y etnicidad. IIIer Coloquio Paul Kirchhoff* (México: Instituto de Investigaciones Antropológicas, Universidad Nacional Autónoma de México, 1996).
38. S. Gillespie, 'Personhood, Agency, and Mortuary Ritual: A Case Study from the Ancient Maya', *Journal of Anthropological Archaeology* 20 no. 1 (2001): pp. 73–112; S. Gillespie, 'Body and Soul among the Maya: Keeping the Spirits in Place', in H. Silverman and D. B. Small eds, *Past bodies: body–centered research in archaeology* (Oxford: Oxbow Books, 2002), pp. 125–134; S. Gillespie, 'Aspectos corporativos de la persona (personhood) y la encarnación (embodiment) entre los mayas del periodo clásico', *Estudios de Cultura Maya* 31 (2008): pp. 65–89; W. N. Duncan and K. R. Schwarz, 'Partible, permeable, and relational bodies in a Maya mass grave', in A. J. Osterholtz, K. M. Baustian, and D. L. Martin, eds, *Commingled and disarticulated human remains: working toward Improved theory, method and data* (New York: Springer Media, 2014), pp. 149–170.
39. López Austin and López Luján have developed another approach proposing a relationship between *teyolía* and the notion of group (ethnic to familiar) identity. Be that as it may be, it would be premature today to conclude that a human being and animate entities share elements of their interiorities. See López Austin and López Luján, *Monte sagrado–Templo mayor: el cerro y la pirámide en la traducción religiosa mesoamericana* (México: Instituto de Investigaciones Antropológicas, Universidad Nacional Autónoma de México, and Instituto Nacional de Antropología e Historia, 2009), pp. 104–111.

40. M. N. Chamoux, 'Persona, animicidad, fuerza', in P. Pitrou, M. Valverde Valdés and J. Neurath, eds, *La nocion de vida en Mesoamérica* (México: Universidad Nacional Autónoma de México and Centro de Estudios Mexicanos y Centroamericanos, 2011): pp. 155–180. Also see Duncan and Schwarz, 'Partible, Permeable, and Relational Bodies'.

41. Consult López Austin and López Luján, *Monte sagrado*, pp.105–08.

42. For more on this subject, see P. P. Arnold, *Eating Landscape: Aztec and European Occupation of Tlalocan* (Boulder, CO: University Press of Colorado, 2009), pp. 53–64.

43. López Austin and López Luján, *Monte sagrado*, pp. 105–8.

44. A. López Austin and E. Velásquez García, 'Un concepto de dios aplicable a la tradición maya', *Arqueología Mexicana* 152 (July–August 2018): pp. 20–27.

45. E. Hunt, *The Transformation of the Hummingbird. Cultural Roots of a Zinacantan Mythical Poem* (Ithaca, NY, and London: Cornell University Press, 1977), pp. 54.

46. E. Hunt, *The Transformations*, pp. 54–55.

47. B. de Sahagún, *Historia General de las cosas de Nueva España* (1582, 1829, 1975; second repr. México: Editorial Porrúa, 1979), p. 49 (Bk 1 Ch 21.1); M. Camargo, 'Historia de Tlaxcala', in R. Acuña, ed., *Relaciones geográficas del siglo XVI: Puebla* (México: Instituto de Investigaciones Antropológicas, Universidad Nacional Autónoma de México, 1984): p. 203; D. Durán, 'Libro de los ritos y ceremonias en las fiestas de los dioses y celebración de ellas', in D. Durán *Historia de las indias de Nueva España e Islas de la Tierra Firme* (1570; repr. México: Editorial Porrúa, 1984): Vol. 1, p, 82; J. de Torquemada, *Monarquía Indiana* (México: Editorial Porrúa, 1986 [1615]): vol. 2: 46 (Bk 6 Ch 22).

48. *Historia de los mexicanos por sus pinturas*, pp. 23–25, in A. M. Garibay K., *Teogonía e historia de los mexicanos: tres opúsculos del siglo XVI* (1965; 6th repr. Mexico: Editoriali Porrúa, 2005): p. 26.

49. Similar idea has recently been proposed by Molly Bassett, *The fate of earthly things. Aztec gods and god–bodies* (Austin, TX: University of Texas Press, 2015): p. 155.

50. Following J. Broda, 'El culto mexica de los cerros y del agua', *Multidisciplina* (Revista de la Escuela Nacional de Estudios Profesionales Acatlan UNAM) 3, no. 7 (1982): pp. 45–56, p. 53, I reiterate the difference between Tlalocs (Tlaloque) and tlaloque. While four Tlalocs constitute four different embodiments of Tlaloc linked with the four corners of the universe and four kinds of rain, the innumerable and dwarfish tlaloque, associated with particular mountaintops and hills and different kinds of rain, were conceived of as Tlaloc's assistants (also embodiments), responsible for the watering of maize plots. In both instances, it seems that Tlaloc transferred (distributed) his personhood (agentivity, intentionality) to Tlalocs and tlaloque.

51. Fr. B. de Sahagún, *Historia general*, p. 700 (Bk 11, Ch. 12, 3); 'Histoire du Mexique', p. 118, in A. M. Garibay K., *Teogonía e historia de los mexicanos: tres opúsculos del siglo XVI* (1965; 6th repr. Mexico: Editoriali Porrúa, 2005), p. 105

52. See A. López Austin, *Tamoanchan y Tlalocan* (Mexico: Fondo de Cultura Economica, 1994): p. 212; López Austin and López Luján, *Monte sagrado-Templo mayor*, pp. 80–82.

53. A. López Austin, 'Modelos a distancia: antiguas concepciones nahuas', in A. López Austin, ed., *El modelo en la ciencia y la cultura* (México: Siglo Veintiuno Editores, 2005), pp. 68–93.

54. López Austin, 'Modelos a distancia', p. 77.

55. Dwelling is here treated in the existential sense as a mode of existence enabling peoples to become human persons.

56. A. J. García Zambrano, 'Transference of primordial threshold crossing onto the geomorphology of Mesoamerican foundational landscapes', in A. Megged and S. Wood, eds, *Mesoamerican Memory. Enduring systems of remembrance* (Norman, OK: University of Oklahoma Press, 2012), pp. 215–232. For example, *Leyenda de los Soles*, III, 10–11, consult 'Leyenda de los Soles', in *Codice Chimalpopoca* (1945; 2nd edn, Mexico: Universidad Nacional Autónoma de México, 1975), pp. 119–142 (p. 121).

57. Compare T. Ingold, *Making: anthropology, archaeology, art and architecture* (London: Routledge, 2013): pp. 100–102.

58. This can explain why the intervals of 13 and 20 days or their multiples are found so often in the alignments of Mesoamerican ceremonial and civic architecture. Archaeoastronomical research carried out in Mesoamerica has long shown that alignments of ceremonial and civic architecture projected onto horizon features produced intervals of 13 and 20 days, their multiples, or some other meaningful temporal intervals.

59. Broda, 'The Sacred Landscape', p. 82.

60. F. Silva, ' The Role and Importance of the Sky in Archaeology: an introduction', in F. Silva and N. Campion, eds, *Skyscapes: The Role and Importance of the Sky in Archaeology* (Oxford: Oxbow Books, 2015).

12

ENVIRONMENTAL INTEGRATION VERSUS MODERN CULTURAL AND ECONOMIC ETHOS. AN INTERDISCIPLINARY APPROACH TO MODERN RESOURCE CONSUMPTION: LANDSCAPE AND SOCIETY

Selma Faria

Introduction

Much has been written about the role of cosmology in culture, in both politics and society.[1] It is now well documented that the way we see the skies determines greatly how we organise our societies. I go further to suggest that following the natural integration humans have with the environment could in fact be the *sine qua non* condition for the species to transit into what modern physics calls a *type two* civilization.[2] Archaeoastronomy and environmental archaeology will be the primary scientific branches permeating this interdisciplinary exposition, the final aim of which is to establish that the current non-integrating economic and social model – which has permeated human interaction with the environment since the Neolithic – is no longer sustainable and has been hindering human evolutionary process.

> ... living things are chemically complex and highly organized, take energy from their environment and change it from one form to another, are homeostatic, respond to stimuli, reproduce themselves, are adapted to their environment, and contain the information about all of these functions within themselves.[3]

As Martin Gojda explains, the Czech word for landscape, *krajina*, is of old Germanic origin.[4] In the Early Medieval period, this word designated a portion of land that was tended by a single peasant; therefore, the word for the landscape (*krajina*) referred solely to a piece of land which was perceived by the individual who was working it, and not the land beyond that. Gojda goes on to add that "At the beginning of the second millennium CE, [however] the term [landscape] took on a new meaning for the first time, that of a domain, that of an estate," hence gaining an economic dimension based on land acquisition and possession, and established on the hierarchical relationship between landlord and tenant.[5]

I would, however, argue that the economic importance attributed to land, and to landscape, has been around for much longer than suggested by Gojda, since landscape has been a synonym of possession since the first human communities which made the transition to becoming settlers started working the soils, with the Neolithic revolution. Later, in the Copper Age, when some populations stepped into the complexification of societies, the segregation of land and landscape followed. It was also during this transition that we started seeing across Europe, and in Pre-dynastic Egypt, the first social elites, the first princes, the first kings, the first family hierarchies.[6] As these European communities settled, their first instinct was to start delegating tasks to individuals and groups, including conflict resolution, and soon the one of task distribution itself. From then on every other individual in the community became what we today call a commoner, while the family which was in charge of conflict solving, and for pretty much obvious reasons, steadily gained control over the community itself. These were, therefore, the first chiefs, the first monarchs.

The heliopolitanian triadic elite of Osiris, Isis and Horus in ancient Egypt, and the iconography that portrays them through much of the architecture of the Old Kingdom (which we can see in the temple of Philae, for instance), places these gods as having actually walked Egypt during what we call the pre-dynastic era that preceded the pharaohs, when the territory was ruled by the first tribal chiefs and proto-states. We do not know if these ancient Egyptian mythological accounts were based on real human individuals or not, but there is definitely room for speculation, given that the latest part of the pre-dynastic period was indeed a time of first chiefs. There is abundant literature on the concepts of 'chiefdoms' or 'proto-kingdoms', and how these can, and should be, applied to the Egyptian pre-dynastic period.[7]

Thus, for the first time in the history of human kind, all through the Copper Age, we had a small set of individuals, a group minority, who had control over the majority. Now if we add to this another novelty of the Copper Age, currency, brought about by the sophistication of metalwork, we have the first elites. Further down the road, in the Iron Age in the Iberian Peninsula, in the North West of Portugal and Spain, these chiefs would wear splendid, precisely decorated, heavy torcs and bracelets.[8] The latter would sparkle under the sun and make these first elites look like gods, or like the sons of gods, as gold has always been linked to divinity in every civilization because of its similarity to that big life-enabling sphere we call the Sun. But not only did these chiefs have control over the most noble resource, gold, they now had control over all of them. Resource control is equivalent to landscape control, which leads therefore to the segregation of landscape. And, as we have been seeing ever since, land as possession leads to the indiscriminate exploitation of resources, with no concern as to whether the latter respects the homeostatic balance of planetary and cosmological cycles.

Homeostasis

Cosmology/Biology

The idea that homeostatic balance is conditional to the optimisation of life on the planet is not new. One could even say it originates back in the early 1970s with the advent of environmental philosophy, and especially environmental ethics and environmental humanism, the latter also being referred to as humanist ecology.[9] Humanist ecology's main concern, since the very beginning of its academic inception, was whether nature and environment were a part of human identity itself or not. Such a concern would support the homeostatic basis of the Gaia hypothesis, introduced in the 1970s by the chemist James Lovelock and developed in cooperation by Lovelock and the microbiologist Lynn Margulis.[10] This theory proposes that homeostasis is a preferable factor and an important condition to take into account regarding the quality of human life, given that the evolution of the entire biosphere affects habitability on the planet, together with every factor that enables it, in particular the temperature of the planet and the amount of oxygen in the atmosphere.

What I propose, however, goes further by applying that premise to both the biology of the human body and the cosmic elements of which it is composed. 99% of the mass of the human body is made up of six elements: oxygen, carbon, hydrogen, nitrogen, calcium, and phosphorus; and then there's 0.85% which is composed of another five elements – potassium, sulphur, sodium, chlorine, and magnesium. All of these are necessary for life. How does this biological fact link to cosmology? Hydrogen, for instance, is the most abundant chemical element in the universe, found in our Sun, the gas planets in our solar system, and other stars. Nitrogen, according to the latest findings, was brought to Earth as Jupiter wandered in its orbit in the early stages of the solar system, causing meteorites to be flung into the centre of the solar system.[11] The iron in our blood, the oxygen we breathe, the calcium in our bones and all the atoms we are made of were released during the violent final moments of massive stars when they were dying. Regarding calcium, according to Norbert Schartel (an ESA XMM-Newton Project Scientist), 'The universe contains one and a half times more calcium than previously assumed'.[12] Life-enabling phosphorus, which is capable of triggering the chemical reactions necessary to spark the development of organisms, is the first component astronomers look for when determining whether life could exist on other planets.

Why are we not researching how to mimic the biochemical process of phosphorus in how it produces energy and regulates *Ph*, so as to increase fertilization and avoid issues such as soil erosion and degradation? The facts state that, in addition to being carried to Earth via meteorites, phosphorus is also in the planet's crust, asthenosphere, and lower and upper mantles, as well as in its outer and inner cores. It is no surprise, then, that it also holds a place in our bodies. According to the University of Maryland Medical Centre, all body cells contain phosphorus, with 85% found in bones and teeth.[13] Together with calcium it provides structure and strength to our bodies, while also being essential for the growth and repair of body cells and tissues. In addition, the iron in our blood is the very same found in the planet's inner core and in meteorites.

The question is how far such physical realities are reflected in culture. In his essay on human interactions with the landscape, Martin Gojda also speaks of '... the gradually increasing awareness of the deep mutual relationships between the natural and social environments'.[14] It seems, as per the evidence found in both archaeology and medical and cultural anthropology, this awareness did once exist in past societies, in certain groups at least, and seems to have been somehow lost to most modern communities. Sacrifices were made all over Scandinavia up into the late Iron Age, as blood was believed to fertilise and appease the earth, as discussed by Gavin Lucas and Thomas McGovern in their exposition of the rituals taking place in the Viking settlement of Hofstadir in northeastern Iceland.[15] According to the anthropologist Clarissa Pinkola Estées, in what are now the Balkans and in some regions of Eastern Europe, until very recently (the Middle Ages) women would cyclically, before harvest, hunch down on the ground to let the earth soak up their cycles.[16] On the other hand, it is commonly known in modern chemistry that iron interacts with other minerals existing in the crust, thus propitiating an increase in nutrients available in the soil. As evidence to this one can look into all the various iron-based products used in modern gardening as highly compressed fertilisers. It seems, therefore, to be apparent that, in previous periods of the human presence on this planet, an intrinsic or perhaps instinctive knowledge of this homeostatic relationship – this symbiosis between biology, geology and cosmology, between our own bodies, the planet, and the cosmos – was understood. Given our modern post-industrialization resource interaction and its very ill consequences to both the environment itself and ourselves, it becomes also easy to infer that if the balance between the rate at which the planet can produce and the quantities we can consume is not respected, we do not have resource consumption, but resource exploitation.

Biology/Society

However easy it may be to surmise the existence of a biologic and cosmological homeostatic frame of interaction, how does this connect with social structure, organisation and ethos? With water and skies framing the first agricultural societies and the advent of trade, the environment has been the platform upon which humans have built the framework of modern resource consumption. As such, it will always be the case – because of its interconnecting nature – cosmological and biological homeostasis invariably bleeds into the social framework. So far, all evidence points to the idea that had we simply followed that interconnectedness (that natural synchronisation between all these spatial elements of which we are a part) instead of being guided towards the path of exploitation (for example, extracting and burning coal with disregard for what the burning of fossil fuels does to the environment), we would have a very different state of affairs as far as our relationship with the environment, and our own place in this world. If this synergetic dance had been respected, then by consequence we would have developed an equally symbiotic, homeostatic, balanced society, which we will have, perhaps, when the governing elite and elites – which we as a species elected to do task distribution circa 5000 years ago – starts graduating in its understanding of science and technology.

Conclusion

Following the natural integration humans have with the environment could in fact be the *sine qua non* condition for the species to transit into what modern physics calls a *type two* civilization. I would thus suggest that archaeoastronomy, which together with the environmental sciences have permeated much of this interdisciplinary exposition, look further into this phenomenon, one I have chosen to name pan-homeostasis. It therefore becomes imperative to understand this phenomenon as a means of creating better comprehension about the environment. Knowledge creates policy, and better policy can bring about an economic paradigm that allows for a sustainable resource consumption – one which respects this pan-syncretic integrating relationship humans have with landscape.

The final aim of this chapter is to establish that the current non-integrating economic and social model – which has permeated most of human interaction with the environment since the Neolithic – is no longer sustainable. Thus, it has very little chance of propelling the species into its next evolutionary stage, one in which humanity will know that it is one with the environment it has sprung from, and acts in accordance. I leave an appeal to the scientific community to look further into this matter, so we can hopefully together (in a concerted time-limited effort with the technological community) find a feasible way (meaning one which is adjustable to the current evolutionary stage) of returning to landscape, as opposed to detaching from it. Landscape archaeology has confirmed what nineteenth century environmental philosophy had already alerted us to: the fact that humans are not just an external intervenient, for whom the tool is the connective vehicle. Landscape Archaeology has also reminded us that we are very much 'it', meaning, the landscape and environment itself; that even though we can't grow fur to protect ourselves from the elements like other earthly inhabitants do, we have never been misplaced in this planet: we belong.

At some point, we started to see the landscape as detached from our own existence, and this has led us to treat it as something exterior to us, something which we need to acquire, shape, control, and then later possess and exploit. Pan-homeostasis means that we cannot own that which we are, that all we have to do is become reacquainted with that through silence, and then act from that knowing, when managing this planet's resources. Wise resource consumption is not an option – it's our future and it will come to be once we grasp that homeostatic undercurrent to our connection to the rivers, the mountains, the sky and indeed the sea. In other words, our relationship with the environment is indeed a *harmony event*.

Notes

1.   Nicholas Campion, 'The Importance of Cosmology in Culture, Contexts and Consequences', in Abraao Jess Capistrano De Souza, ed., *Trends in Modern Cosmology* (Rijeka, Croatia: InTech, 2017), at http://dx.doi.org/10.5772/67976 [accessed 13 May 2020].

2.   For information on the Kardashev Scale for the possible structures of supercivilisations, see   Nikolai S. Kardashev, 'On the Inevitability and the Possible Structures of Supercivilizations', in *The search for extraterrestrial life: recent developments, Proceedings of the Symposium, Boston, MA, June 18–21, 1984, Symposium-International Astronomical Union* Vol. 112 (Cambridge: Cambridge University Press 1985), pp. 497–504.

3.   Helena Curtis, *Biology*, 2nd edn (New York: Worth, 1975), pp. 27–31; Paula Derry, 'The Place of Biology in Cosmology', *Metanexus*, 27 May 2009, at https://metanexus.net/place-biology-cosmology/ [accessed 13 May 2020].

4.   Martin Gojda, 'Landscape Archaeology', in Donald L. Hardesty, ed., *Encyclopedia of Life and Support Systems (EOLSS)*, Vol. 1 (Oxford: United Nations Educational Scientific and Cultural Organization [UNESCO] EOLSS Publishers, 2010).

5.   Gojda, 'Landscape Archaeology'.

6.   Antonio Gilman et al., 'The Development of Social Stratification in Bronze Age Europe', *Current Anthropology* 22, no. 1 (February 1981): pp. 1–23, at https://doi.org/10.1086/202600 [accessed 13 May 2020].

7.   Alice Stevenson, 'The Egyptian Predynastic and State Formation', *Journal of Archaeological Research* 24 (2016): pp. 421–468, at   https://doi.org/10.1007/s10814-016-9094-7 [accessed 13 May 2020].

8.   Barbara Ambruster et al., *A Idade do Bronze em Portugal: Discursos de Poder* (Exhibition Catalogue) (Lisboa: Museu Nacional de Arqueologia, 1995).

9.   Freya Mathews, 'Environmental Philosophy', in N.N. Trakakis and G. Oppy, eds, *History of Philosophy in Australia and New Zealand* (Dordrecht: Springer, 2014), pp. 543–591.

10.   James Lovelock, *The Vanishing Face of Gaia* (New York :Basic Books, 2009), p. 255.

11.   Evelyn Furi and Bernard Mart, 2015. 'Nitrogen Isotope Variations in the Solar System', *Nature Geoscience* 8, no. 7 (2015): pp. 515–522.

12.   N. Schartel , J. de Plaa, N. Werner, J. A. M. Bleeker, J. S. Kaastra, M. Mendez, and J. Vink, 'Constraining supernova models using the hot gas in clusters of galaxies', *Astronomy & Astrophysics* 465, no. 2 (2007): pp. 345–355, at https://doi.org/10.1051/0004-6361:20066382 [accessed 13 May 2020].

13.   Evelyn Füri and Bernard Marty, p. 532

14.   Gojda, 'Landscape Archaeology'.

15.   Gavin Lucas and Thomas McGovern, 'Bloody Slaughter: Ritual decapitation and display at the Viking settlement of Hofstadir', *European journal of archaeology* 10, no. 1 (2007): pp. 7–30.

16.   Clarissa Pinkola Estées, Women Who Run With the Wolves, Myths and Stories of The Wild Woman (London, Sydney, Auckland, Johannesburg: Rider, 1998), pp. 292–295.

13

THE O2 IN GREENWICH, LONDON AS SACRED SPACE

Fenella Dean

Introduction

On reading Robert Frost's poem *Dust of Snow*, I was reminded of how I felt when I watched the O2 Arena, or what was then called the Millennium Dome, being constructed almost 20 years ago near where I live; how a disused, heavily polluted industrial space was being transformed before my eyes and I was mesmerized. The structure still has this effect on me and is elucidated by Robert Frost who wrote how a dust of snow, ' Has given my heart, A change of mood', thus conveying, I believe, how landscape and therefore space can transform not just materially but also temporally.[1] As Maurice Merleau-Ponty stated, 'perception of landscape is never a purely cognitive process'.[2] Therefore, in this chapter I attempt to demonstrate that the O2 in Greenwich, London, possesses, for me at least, a materiality of spirit and place as sacred space.

In exploring the materiality of spirit and place as sacred space, it is first necessary to define sacred space. David Chidester and Edward Tabor Linenthal, in their book *American Sacred Space*, highlight the difficulty of defining sacred space in a contemporary urban context, due to the definition being dependent on the perspective of the individual or group defining it.[3] Additionally, there is the issue of how the sacred is defined. As R.L. Stirrat stated, '[T]he concept of the sacred is… one of the more problematic categories used in anthropology'.[4] This has led to there being three directions in which the study of sacred space has developed: the phenomenological, the ontological, and the social and cultural. In view of this, the following chapter sets out to explore the validity of these three perspectives of sacred space in terms of the materiality of spirit and place with reference to the O2.

The O2 and the Greenwich Peninsula – History and the Present Day

The O2, originally known as the Millennium Dome, is a dome shaped structure built a few metres from the Meridian Line, the Prime Meridian of the World, on the Greenwich Peninsula on the banks of the River Thames in South East London. It was built to celebrate the official start of the new millennium on the 1st January 2001.

Figure 1. Cropped Image of O2 Arena
© Danesman1 2012. From *Wikimedia Commons* [accessed 13 September 2021].

The Greenwich Peninsula, originally owned by British Gas, was heavily polluted and during World War II the area was extensively bombed. The regeneration of the area began in the 1990s. The original design of the O2 structure was conceived by Mike Davies of the architects Rogers, Stirk, Harbour & Partners and Gary Withers of the branding consultants Imagination. Prior to the finalisation of the structural design, both men 'plotted the projection of the comets and stars, dawns and dusks onto the Dome's surface'.[5] Davies, the architect, being interested in astronomy, had the idea to incorporate time into the design; when interviewed, he said, 'The 12 hours, the 12 months, and the 12 constellations of the sky which measure time are all integral to the original concept', highlighting the role of the Meridian Line in its design.[6] As a result, it has twelve 100 metre high yellow support towers and from above can be seen to be circular, with a diameter of 365 metres representing each day of the year. Its circumference is one kilometre and it is 50 metres high in the centre. There are 24 scallops around the edge of the structure for each hour of the day. The panels of the canopy are based on the celestial lines of longitude and latitude.[7] There is also a hole in the roof to accommodate a ventilation shaft from the nearby Blackwall Tunnel, a Victorian road tunnel under the River Thames.

At present it is the most successful entertainment venue in the world by ticket sales, a position it has held since 2008.[8] The venue, as of November 2018, houses a main concert arena known as the O2 Arena, with a capacity of 21,000, a smaller concert venue, nightclubs, 11 cinema screens, an avenue of restaurants and bars, a 210,000 square foot shopping centre known as 'Icon Outlet', and two large spaces for private hire. There is excellent transport infrastructure composed of underground, bus, road and river links, plus there is the option of being able to book to walk across the roof of the O2 if you so wish.[9]

The Greenwich Peninsula has and continues to be transformed, undergoing additional re-generation on a grand scale, initially with the construction of the Millennium Village and now with further construction of what is being described as an 'Urban Village'.[10]

The Perspectives of Sacred Space

Turning to the three views of sacred space, we begin with the phenomenological perspective or how an individual experiences things (and therefore the meanings that can be ascribed to these things), in this case the O2. Maurice Merleau-Ponty said in his book, *Phenomenology of Perception*, '[I]t is a matter of describing, not explaining or analysing'. Furthermore, when observing, he stated that, '[A]ll my knowledge of the world is gained from my own particular point of view, or from some experience of the world'. In observing people, I realise, just like Merleau-Ponty, that '[N]othing is more difficult than to know precisely *what we see*'.[11]

Additionally, there is the etic/emic or outsider/insider dilemma and the issue of reflexivity to consider. We have to be aware of our reactions and that the same information could be being viewed from two or more points of view. Further, Kim Etherington pointed out that there is a requirement to be conscious 'of the personal, social and cultural contexts in which we live... and to understand how these impact on the ways we interpret our world'.[12]

To bring this issue into the physical realm, my experience of the O2 is as an insider, but my observations of other individuals in the O2 is as an outsider. I am inside the O2 along with all other individuals, however, I am also outside other

individuals' thoughts, beliefs and experiences with regard to the O2. So whilst I
am part of the 'group' inside the O2, assuming all the individuals inside the O2
are a 'group', I am outside each individual's experience of the O2. 'I must be the
exterior that I present to others, and the body of the other must be the other
himself', as Merleau-Ponty stated.[13]

Turning to the second perspective of sacred space, the ontological, put
forward by Mircea Eliade in his book, *The Sacred and the Profane: The Nature
of Religion*. Eliade's view explores the character of sacred space and how the
sacred is opposite to the profane. For Eliade, sacred space is completely set apart
from everything profane and possesses an ethereal quality, a numinosity; the
ordinary has been invaded by supernatural forces.[14]

The manifestation of the sacred is via what Eliade described as hierophany.
According to Eliade, a sacred space exists where there is a break in the
homogeneity of space; it is where earth, heaven and the underworld, described as
the three cosmic levels, 'have been put into communication'.[15] Using these ideas,
there is thought to be a universal pillar or *axis mundi* that connects the three
levels. Around this central pillar is the *imago mundi* or what Eliade described
as a 'system of the world', which can be explained as the reconstruction of the
universe on earth.[16] Eliade went on to say that at the edges of this sacred space
is chaos or a profane space that can be understood as 'absolute non-being',
referred to as 'neutral' or 'homogenous'.[17]

There are many interpretations of space that use a sacred/profane
opposition. As Benjamin Ray stated in his paper ,'Sacred Space and Royal
Shrines in Buganda', this opposition is '… one of the most universal modes of
symbolic classification'; however, Ray went on to say that 'the sacred/profane
distinction is not always explicit'.[18] Ray also stated there is thus another
misapprehension with regard to the sacred/profane dichotomy; specifically, it
is absolute, 'that it is systematically pervasive (without contextual variations),
and that it refers to things totally, not aspectually'.[19] Eliade's model of sacred
space, I think, fails to recognise that this opposition represents '*overlapping
dimensions of human experience*', as Belden Lane wrote in his paper, 'Giving
Voice to Place'.[20] Additionally, this dichotomous issue between the sacred and
the profane is highlighted by Chidester and Linenthal in their research into
sacred space, '[I]n search of the sacred, we immediately had to recognise that
these places were intimately entangled in such "profane" enterprises as tourism,
economic exchange and development, and the intense conflict of contending
nationalisms'.[21]

With this in mind, in viewing the O2, I believe it is possible to apply the
paradigm in such a way so that this opposition is more positively created. There

is the O2 and the surrounding Millennium Village plus the ongoing construction of the Urban Village, all built on a regenerated site, in what Eliade refers to as the slaying of a '... primordial being in order to create the world from it', that is the cleaning of the site.[22] The O2 is the sacred world, the Millennium Village and Urban Village the profane world; the relation is '... between complementary forms of order within a binary structure',[23] that is, a sacred/profane structure, as Ray argued. Moreover, as referenced above, Ray stated that the sacred/profane dichotomy is not about the absolute and the relative or even order and chaos but concerns two different forms of reality that are separated, complementary and part of a wider world.[24] Taking it a step further, a system of the world has been created on the Greenwich Peninsula, or as Eliade said, '[F]or what is involved is *undertaking the creation of the world that one has chosen to inhabit*'.[25] Therefore, I believe there is a mutual relationship between sacred and profane spaces when applied to the O2 and the Greenwich Peninsula.

A further possible application of Eliade's model with regard to the argued mutual relationship between the sacred and profane is from the perspective of the regeneration of the Greenwich Peninsula. As previously stated, the O2 was built on a former gasworks; additionally it contains one of the UK's largest water conservation and recycling systems.[26] Alongside the O2, in the surrounding area, is the original Millennium Village, the design of which, as highlighted by Charles Jennings, is underpinned by innovative environmental sustainability, which was an important part of the original project.[27] There is also the Greenwich Peninsula Ecology Park, a nature reserve for the public.[28] Environmentalism has been described as the most powerful secular religion in the latter part of the 20th century by Denis Cosgrove and Luciana Martin.[29] So, once again applying Eliade's paradigm, the site on the Greenwich Peninsula, prior to the O2 being constructed, could be viewed as 'homogenous' and 'neutral'; being a polluted site, it was 'amorphous' or profane in terms of the so called religion of environmentalism.[30] It has been made sacred by re-generation, and so the O2 could be referred to as 'an "irruption", a "break" in the homogeneity of space' according to Eliade's model.[31] Furthermore, the architects actually refer to the O2 as follows: '[T]he ultimate inspiration for the Dome was a great sky, a cosmos under which all events take place – the radial lines and the circles of the high-tensile roof structure recall the celestial reference grid of astronomical maps throughout the ages'.[32] When approaching the O2, it appears to me that it has irrupted from another world, whatever mode of transport I take – be it car, bus, walking or boat, it appears almost like a spaceship, looming on the horizon. There is the sacred world of the O2 and the profane world of the original Millennium Village, the ecological park and the ongoing construction of the Urban Village. There is a mutually positive relationship between the two, creating a world to inhabit. Again, there is a 'mutual relation between the sacred and the profane'; as Ray argued, it is not only about the sacred.[33]

Let us turn to the third perspective, the notion that the sacred is socially constructed. This is a sociological perspective proposed by Emile Durkheim in his work *Elementary Forms of Religious Life.* Chidester and Linenthal describe this situational perspective as 'Nothing more nor less than a notional supplement to the ongoing cultural work of sacralising space, time, person, and social relations'.[34] According to Durkheim himself, what makes an entity sacred, such as sacred space, is the quality acquired '.... when they are ... "set apart and forbidden"', and '... they are "sacred" – but made so by doing'.[35] By doing, these objects acquire a power that is real via what Durkheim referred to as the *'conscience collective'* which is '... the achievement of the mind that transfigures the real world and makes it a shared world'.[36] Additionally, he stated that entities are able to move from the profane world to the sacred world, from a sacred space to a profane space.

Taking Durkheim's model of sacred space and applying it to the O2, we see a large entertainment venue where large groups gather. The entertainment takes many forms, from pop concerts to sporting events and exhibitions. These large groups of people gather and become part of a shared world which also becomes their real world, as Durkheim argued; for example, for those attending a music concert or sporting event, a 'collective identity' takes hold.[37] One can pass from the profane world, observing, to the sacred world, by joining in with clapping, singing, cheering and becoming part of what Durkheim called the *'conscience collective'.*[38]

This illustrates, as do the previous perspectives, the difficulty in distinguishing between the sacred and profane. It is what Larry Wells writes of in his paper 'Sacred and Profane: A Spatial Archetype', in which he says the notion of a dichotomy '... becomes a question of degree only, and everyone experiences to some degree both a spatial and a temporal dichotomy of the sacred and the profane'.[39] Added to which this dichotomy is not necessarily explicit; individuals may or may not be aware of it and that it involves interpretation. To repeat, Merleau-Ponty says, '[N]othing is more difficult than to know precisely *what we see*'.[40]

Russell W Belk, Melanie Wallendorf and John F. Sherry Jr concisely sum up the above issue as follows: '[C]hanges in contemporary life indicate that the sacred/profane/secular distinction is no longer isomorphic with the religious/secular distinction'.[41] The boundaries between the sacred and the profane have shifted and continue to shift, with the secular being sacralised and religion being secularised, as argued by Belk *et al.*[42] The argument that the secular is being sacralised with respect to consumption can be applied to the O2 as follows. The O2 is a multi-entertainment venue, possibly a cathedral or temple of consumption. The music concerts are performed by what Belk et al. refer to as 'deities – charismatic rock stars', representing the sacralisation of music, while during the sporting events –representing the sacralisation of sports –the audiences' experience is intertwined with reverence for the sports person or team with rituals such as cheering and singing.[43] Therefore the O2 becomes a sacred space, much like a temple. The restaurants also represent sacred experiences where eating and drinking can be viewed as a ritual, as can certain food brands such as Nando's and Five Guys, both present at the O2; while the ritual of shopping is played out at the newly opened Icon Outlet .[44]

The secularization of religion was described by Michael Ducey, who observed a decline in traditional church services and an increase in non-traditional church services during the 1970s in the United States.[45] In these non-traditional church services symbols of the sacred were replaced with the profane; for example classical organ music for contemporary guitar music. Today, there is also the use of the media and the Internet by religious groups which, as Belk *et al.* stated, '… demonstrates secularization through the broadcast of sacred rituals into what may be profane spaces or times'.[46] The blurring of sacred and secular is demonstrated at the O2 by the musical concerts performed by musicians playing specifically religious music: for example Rahat Fateh Ali Khan in July 2018, playing Qawwali, a devotional music of the Sufis.

What these examples of restaurants, music concerts, both religious and otherwise, and the shopping outlet illustrate is what Belk *et al.* argue: the boundaries between the sacred and the profane have shifted and continue to shift. Thus, the distinction between the sacred/profane dichotomy becomes an issue of experience and perspective: as Larry Wells argued, it 'becomes a question of degree only, and everyone experiences to some degree both a spatial and a temporal dichotomy of the sacred and the profane, its specific characteristics depending upon the individual and culture in which it emerges'.[47]

As Chidester and Linenthal wrote: 'Sacred space is inevitably contested space, a site of negotiated contests over the legitimate ownership of sacred symbols'.[48] Barbara Bender also argues that sacred space or landscape is defined according to circumstance and culture.[49] The O2 highlights this issue of contested space. She added, '[P]eoples' understanding of the places they visit are wound around memories, resonances, and unpredictable connections'.[50] Additionally, '[E]ach appropriates Stonehenge' and '… in their own fashion, each creates a particular past'.[51] For Stonehenge we could read the O2.

Bringing the Views on Sacred Space to Life

In order to investigate these academic perspectives I took four journeys using
different modes of transport: I walked from my house; took a riverboat along
the Thames; travelled by public transport, a bus; and finally, by car. The form
of travel varied, as I viewed the journeys as a form of pilgrimage assessing
whether each journey made a difference to my observations. As Paul Devereux
stated, '[W]alking is the rhythm in which the human being best relates to its
environment'.[52] The more technological the mode of transport, he continued, the
'more shut off from the environment' we become.[53] Additionally, the geographer
Jay Appleton highlights the phenomenon whereby the faster we pass through
the landscape the more we change the time-sequences which are fundamental to
the experience of the landscape.[54]

By both walking and taking the riverboat to the O2, I grasped the vastness
of the structure, the elements, the noise and the environment. I was, as Tim
Ingold writes, 'enmeshed within webs of environmental relations'.[55] I found by
taking the bus and car that I was shut off from the environment, cosseted if
you will, and concentrated on the destination rather than the experience. As
Appleton says, my experience of the landscape altered the faster I travelled.

When driving and taking the bus, I observed people parking and getting
out of their cars, travelling and exiting the underground stations, but their
actions appeared to have no conscious connection with their surroundings until
they started to walk towards the O2. Their comments centred on aspects of
themselves: 'Let's get into the arena it's so cold', 'We were lucky to get a parking
space so close to the O2'. If E. Alan Morinis' argument that a pilgrimage can be
viewed as a 'A journey undertaken by a person in a quest of a place or a state
that he or she believes to embody a valued ideal', then visiting the O2 to attend
a concert or sporting event can be seen as a pilgrimage.[56] Morinis' definition
blurs the boundaries of pilgrimage to include secular journeys on condition that
these journeys 'share being an intensified version of some ideal that the pilgrim
values but cannot achieve at home'.[57] A pilgrimage focuses on the realisation
of these intensified ideals and, as Morinis argues, represent 'the collective ideals
of the culture'.[58] Further, Morinis emphasises that these collective ideals can be
viewed as sacred and 'it is the pursuit of the ideal (whether deified or not) that
defines the sacred journey'.[59] So, the people I observed journeying to the O2 can
be viewed possibly as pilgrims, according to Morinis' argument. Furthermore,
their comments could be what Devereux referred to as the liminal act of the
pilgrimage when the pilgrim 'left his or her normal life and headed out for the
sacred place, and while on the pilgrimage was neither here nor there'.[60] I observed
that people seemed to strike up conversations with each other, even though they

appeared not to know each other, when approaching the entrance to the O2. This could equate to what Devereux describes when he says, '[B]ecause they were outside the normal social structure, pilgrims could strike up friendships with one another across social class', there appeared to be a camaraderie.

Another aspect of the sacred/profane dichotomy is sacred time. As Albert Cook, in his paper 'Space & Culture', said, '[S]pace and time are intimately joined'; in terms of perspective, '"[B]efore" and "behind" transpose easily from space and time; the past is behind, the future before', as in the New Year celebration.[61] It is also possible to separate out time into sacred and profane periods, such as birthdays, funerals, Christmas and Ramadan where we are ritualising sacred time. With the O2 having been built to celebrate the start of the millennium, it is only metres away from the Prime Meridian and, taking into account the architects comments that the idea of time was uppermost in their mind when designing the structure, I believe it could be said that the O2 is a manifestation of sacred time.

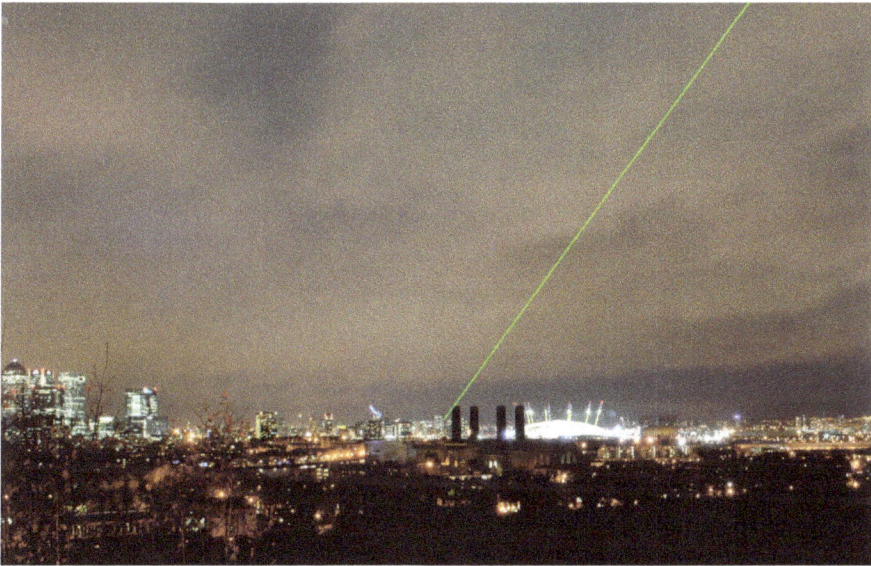

Figure 2: I really love here! The story of Longitude and time.
NMOS332, 'File: Greenwich, Prime Meridian, O2 (6560481201) (2).jpg', *Wikimedia Commons,* 17 December 2011.

However, sacred time also occurs in the context of secular consumption; for example, a person attending a concert, sports event, or going to a restaurant. This implies that sacred time is socially constructed and, as Durkheim stated with regard to the mythologies surrounding sacred objects and sacred spaces, they are not 'encoded from eternity in the mental constitution of man [sic], the rule depends at least in part upon historical, hence social factors'.[62] So the sacred space 'becomes a "blank slate" on which divine or human meanings are arbitrarily inscribed', as Belden Lane argues.[63] Therefore, I believe it is possible that time spent at the O2 by the individual or group is permeated with sacred meaning because of their experience, for example overhearing a little boy talking animatedly to his mother and saying "Mum, that was the best birthday lunch EVER, I will always remember it!". His experience is imbued with sacred meaning and therefore can be viewed as a sacred time. Other examples include attending a concert or an exhibition or the cinema, with these experiences also being viewed as a sacred time.

Conclusion

To conclude, in outlining the nature of sacred space with reference to the O2 and applying various academic perspectives – from the phenomenological where nothing is more difficult than to know precisely what we see, according to Merleau-Ponty;[64] to the ontological with Eliade's system of the world and the earthly reconstruction of the cosmos[65]; and finally to the social and cultural where we can become part of a conscience collective as Durkheim states[66] – I trust I have shown that sacred space in an urban contemporary context, that is the O2, is not an absolute between sacred space and profane space, but rather, overlapping dimensions of human experience imbued with symbolic meaning according to the group or individual's experience.

Figure 3. The Millennium Dome, seen from the jetty near Blackwall Basin.
A author mattbuck, 'File:London MMB »0F0 Millennium Dome.jpg', *Wikimedia Commons*, 21 January 2018, [67]

Notes

1.   Robert Frost, 'Touch of Snow', Poetry Foundation, https://www.poetryfoundation.org/poems/44262/dust-of-snow [accessed 13 September 2021].

2.   Maurice Merleau-Ponti, *Phenomenology of Perception*, trans., Colin Smith, (London: Routledge and Kegan Paul), 1978 [1962], [hereafter, Merleau-Ponti, *Phenomenology of Perception*], p. 58.

3.   David Chidester and Edward T. Linenthal, Introduction, *American Sacred Space*, ed. David Chidester and Edward T. Linenthal, (Bloomington, IN: Indiana University Press, 1995), p. 1.

4.   R. L. Stirrat, 'Sacred Models', *Man* Vol. 19 (1984): p. 199.

5.   Mike Davies's interviews about the Millennium Dome/O2 Arena [hereafter Davies, 'Darkwaters Interviews'] http://darkwaters.org.uk/dark-waters-2008/interviews/mike-davies/ [accessed 13 September 2021].

6.   Davies, 'Darkwaters Interviews'.

7.   Rogers, Stirk, Harbour & Partners, 'The Millennium Dome', https://www.rsh-p.com/projects/the-millennium-dome/ [accessed 13 September 2021].

8.   Pollstar's 2017 Mid-Year Report: World's Best Venues and Tours, 2017, www.mountainproductions.com [accessed 13 September 2021].

9.   O2 Greenwich, http://www.theo2.co.uk [accessed 13 September 2021].

10.   https://www.greenwichpeninsula.co.uk/about/vision/ [accessed date].

11.   Maurice Merleau-Ponty, *Phenomenology of Perception*, trans. Colin Smith (London: Routledge and Kegan Paul) 1978 [1962]), p. viii [hereafter Merleau-Ponty, *Phenomenology of Perception*].

12.   Kim Etherington, *Becoming a Reflexive Researcher* (London and Philadelphia, PA: Jessica Kingsley, 2004), o. 19.

13.   Merleau-Ponty, *Phenomenology of Perception*, p. viii.

14.   Mircea Eliade, 'Sacred Space and Making the World Sacred', *The Sacred and the Profane: The Nature of Religion* (New York: Harcourt, Brace & World Inc., 1959), p. 10.

15.   Eliade, *The Sacred and the Profane*, pp. 36–7.

16.   Eliade, *The Sacred and the Profane*, p. 36.

17.   Eliade, *The Sacred and the Profane*, p. 64.

18.   Benjamin Ray, 'Sacred Space and Royal Shrines in Buganda', *History of Religions* Vol. 16 No. 4 *The Mythic Imagination* (1977): p. 363.

19.   Ray, "Sacred Space and Royal Shrines': p. 364.

20.   Belden C. Lane, 'Giving Voice to Place: Three Models for Understanding American Sacred Space', *Religion and American Culture* Vol. 11 No. 1 (2001): p. 57.

21.   Chidester and Linenthal, *American Sacred Space*, p. 1.

22.   Eliade, *The Sacred and the Profane*, p. 51.

23.   Ray, 'Sacred Space and Royal Shrines', p. 365.

24.   Ray, 'Sacred Space and Royal Shrines', p. 365.

25.   Eliade, *The Sacred and the Profane*, p. 51.

26.   Charles Jennings, *The Place Where Days Begin & End* (London: Abacus ,2001), p. 214.

27.   Davies, 'Darkwaters Interviews'.

28.   Greenwich Peninsula Ecology Park, https://thelandtrust.org.uk/space/greenwich-ecology-park/?doing_wp_cron=1542111266.8106589317321777343750 [accessed 13 September 2021].

29.   Denis Cosgrove and Luciana L. Martins, 'Millennial Geographies', *Annals of the Association of American Geographers* Vol. 90 No. 1 (2000): p. 102.

30.   Eliade, *The Sacred and the Profane*, p. 20.

31. Eliade, *The Sacred and the Profane*, p. 20.

32. RSH-P, 'The Millennium Dome'.

33. Ray, 'Sacred Space and Royal Shrines', pp. 364-5.

34. Chidester and Linenthal, *American Sacred Space*, p. 6.

35. Emile Durkheim, *The Elementary Forms of Religious Life*, trans. Karen E. Fields (New York: The Free Press, 1995 [1912]), p. xlvi.

36. Durkheim, *Elementary Forms*, p. xlvii.

37. Durkheim, *Elementary Forms*, p. xlvii.

38. Durkheim, *Elementary Forms*, p. xlvii.

39. Larry D. Wells, 'Sacred and Profane: A Spatial Archetype in the Early Tales of Ludwig Tieck', *Monatsheft* Vol. 70 No. 1 (1978): p. 31.

40. Merleau-Ponty, *Phenomenology of Perception*, p. viii.

41. Russell W. Belk et al., 'The Sacred and the Profane in Consumer Behaviour: Theodicy on the Odyssey', *The Journal of Consumer Research* Vol. 16 No. 1 (1989), p. 8.

42. Belk et al,, 'Consumer Behaviour', p. 8.

43. Belk et al., 'Consumer Behaviour', pp. 9–12.

44. Belk et al., 'Consumer Behaviour', pp. 9–12.

45. Michael H. Ducey, *Sunday Morning: Aspects of Urban Ritual* (New York: Free Press, 1977).

46. Belk et al., 'Consumer Behaviour', p. 8.

47. Wells, 'A Spatial Archetype', p. 31.

48. Chidester and Linenthal, *American Sacred Space*, p. 15.

49. Barbara Bender, 'Contested Landscapes: Medieval to Present Day', *Stonehenge: Making Space* (Oxford: Berg, 1998).

50. Bender, 'Contested Landscapes', p. 125.

51. Bender, 'Contested Landscapes', p. 112.

52. Paul Devereux, *Re-Visioning the Earth*, (New York: Fireside, 1996), p. 121.

53. Devereux, *Re-Visioning the Earth*, p. 121.

54. Cited by Devereux, *Re-Visioning the Earth*, p. 121.

55. Tim Ingold, 'Culture and the Perception of the Environment', *Bush Base: Forest Farm (Culture, Environment, and Development)*, eds Elisabeth Croll and David Parkin (London: Routledge, 1992), p. 39.

56. E. Alan Morinis, 'Introduction: The Territory of the Anthropology of Pilgrimage', in *Sacred Journeys: The Anthropology of Pilgrimage*, ed. E. Alan Morinis (Westport, CT: Greenwood, 1992): p. 24.

57. Morinis, *Sacred Journeys*, p. 4.

58. Morinis, *Sacred Journeys*, p. 4.

59. Morinis, *Sacred Journeys*, p. 2.

60. Devereux, *Re-Visioning the Earth*, p.128.

61. Albert Cook, 'Space and Culture', *New Literary History* Vol. 29 No. 3 *Theoretical Explorations* (1998): p. 553.

62. Durkheim, *Elementary Forms*, p. 12.

63. Lane, 'Giving Voice to Place', p. 66.

64. Merleau-Ponty, *Phenomenology of Perception*, p. viii.

65. Eliade, *The Sacred and the Profane*, p.10.

66. Durkheim, *Elementary Forms*, p. xlvi.

67. A author mattbuck, 'File:London MMB »oFo Millennium Dome.jpg', *Wikimedia Commons*, 21 January 2018, https://commons.wikimedia.org/w/index.php?title=File:London_MMB_%C2%BBoFo_Millennium_Dome.jpg&oldid=281452670 (accessed 7 November 2018).

INDEX

Word by word alphabetisation

www.ingramcontent.com/pod-product-compliance
Lightning Source LLC
Chambersburg PA
CBHW051245020426

42333CB00025B/3053